INSIDE
F1

INSIDE F1

LEE McKENZIE

BLACK & WHITE PUBLISHING

First published in the UK in 2022 by
Black & White Publishing Ltd
Nautical House, 104 Commercial Street, Edinburgh, EH6 6NF

A division of Bonnier Books UK
4th Floor, Victoria House, Bloomsbury Square, London, WC1B 4DA
Owned by Bonnier Books
Sveavägen 56, Stockholm, Sweden

A CIP catalogue record for this book is available from the British Library.

ISBN (HBK): 978 1 78530 429 3
ISBN (Trade PBK): 978 1 78530 438 5

1 3 5 7 9 10 8 6 4 2

Typeset by Iolaire Typesetting, Newtonmore
Printed and bound in Great Britain by Clays Ltd, Elcograf S.p.A.

www.blackandwhitepublishing.com

You will never know the feeling of a driver when winning a race. The helmet hides feelings that cannot be understood.

AYRTON SENNA

CONTENTS

FOREWORD

by David Coulthard

Let me start by saying that Lee is a brilliant journalist and broadcaster. She is the most versatile presenter in sports television, covering everything from Wimbledon to Formula One.

Within this book are several examples of how she skillfully navigates her way through asking the hard questions of her interviewee, yet doing so in a way that allows them to trust in her journalistic integrity. I can say this without fear of contradiction, as I have been interviewed by Lee in my former career as a Formula One driver and she is now a colleague on Channel 4's coverage of Formula One. The 2021 Saudi Arabian Grand Prix is a perfect example of this: when she interviewed the Sports Minister, Prince Abdulaziz, Lee didn't shy away from asking a range of questions around Saudi Arabia's human rights issues and reasons for investing in sports. When the interview was finished, I spoke with the Prince and he told me that Lee had been "hard but fair". This to me further endorses her professionalism, which is why it's a pleasure to be asked to introduce her book *Inside F1*.

Enjoy the journey through the following pages and, once complete, come and join Lee and me as we travel the race circuits of the world for Channel 4 and see behind the scenes of the fastest sport on earth.

— DC

INTRODUCTION

I N HIS BENETTON OVERALLS, MICHAEL SCHUMACHER walked past me on his way to the garage. That same weekend I met David Coulthard, went to a dinner alongside the legendary Ken Tyrrell who welcomed this "kid" into his motorhome and spent my days walking around in the Formula One paddock thinking, "This is the life I would like to be part of." You see, my first Grand Prix wasn't watching in the grandstands, but it was straight into the heart of the sport. It was in the mid-nineties that I first went to Magny-Cours, home at the time to the French Grand Prix. I appreciate it was an unusual way to enjoy my first race and was an experience that most race fans never get the chance to enjoy, but for me that's just the way it was.

I started watching Formula One in 1991 when my father, Bob, a successful and well-known Fleet Street journalist, was sent to the Mexican Grand Prix to cover for the normal F1 writer who was unwell. Off Dad flew, and I was curious as to where he had gone. I watched the race on the Sunday and was hooked. And as for my father, he covered for that race in 1991 and finally stopped in Abu Dhabi in 2014 – so much for "just one race". In the interim he became close friends with Bernie Ecclestone and most of the paddock and attended Ayrton Senna's funeral. He wrote books on Nigel Mansell and Damon Hill's championship winning seasons and famously, after losing a bet with Mark Webber on BBC Radio 5 Live, ended up running round Silverstone naked on the Sunday of the Formula One Grand Prix whilst body painted in silver like a McLaren F1 car livery with most of the paddock on the grid to watch. Probably enough said about that!

What all of this meant, though, was that I had an in to this exciting world and there was no way that I was going to let it pass me by. Even watching Imola in 1994 on that horrific weekend when Roland Ratzenberger and Ayrton Senna were killed, I wasn't put off; I was just early to understand the potential horrors and dangers of the sport.

I started going to races in my school holidays and spent a lot of time in the paddock, mostly sitting in team hospitalities. I washed the dishes at Ford to help out, chatted to drivers, team bosses and PRs and learned how the paddock "worked". Whilst at Napier University studying journalism, I worked for Formula One Management on the TV side in the gallery as a PA. The rules were very strict then and we weren't allowed to go into F1 hospitality or spend time with the teams, but I used that chance to sneak in and see the people I knew. I interviewed some drivers and engineers and then sold my work to newspapers. I also wasn't a big fan of the food we were given, so some of the teams would shove food out the back of the hospitality for me, as if I were a stray cat!

Working as a PA for FOM wasn't what I wanted to do, but it had given me a chance to get some experience in that world and, after doing some races in 1998 and 1999 when Mika Häkkinen was dominating for McLaren, I left F1 and got my first "proper" job in news.

I was always told that to be a good sports journalist, you have to be a good journalist, and this is something in which I firmly believe. Of course, you can be enthusiastic and a fan, but you have to be so much more than that and ready to ask uncomfortable questions regardless of whether you know or are friendly with the person you are interviewing. I have been to team bosses and drivers' weddings, birthday parties, family funerals, and yet I hope that any friendship or acquaintance would never stop me from asking a difficult question should it be needed. It hasn't yet.

I started young. I used to get a Monday morning off secondary school to go into my local newspaper, *The Ayrshire Post*, where I would write up my rugby report. From the age of fifteen, my Saturday afternoon was spent at Millbrae watching Ayr Rugby Club in the Scottish first division. I would report on the match, interview the players and then on the Monday morning during a free period, I would head into the office and type it all up. I also had an equestrian column called "Horsing around with Lee McKenzie"; I got £15 per week, but it wasn't about the money (which is a good thing, really), it was the experience which was invaluable.

I was lucky in that I knew what I wanted to do, so I dedicated myself in the way that the driver or athlete dedicates their early years to be the best in their chosen field. In motorsport, very few people in the paddock start in Formula One and will have grafted their way up to that level, earned their stripes and started to hone their craft in the junior formula, just like the drivers.

Before Formula One I had worked in DTM, Champ Car and IndyCar. In its final year in 2004, I presented F3000 on ITV. At that time, the team to beat was Arden, owned and managed by Christian Horner. It was a real family business and since then I have been friendly with the whole Horner clan. Christian used to always ask me about the weather, did I think it was going to rain? It's a common question to Scottish people, who spend their time in an amphibious state thanks to the character-building climate! At the start of 2005, Christian was announced as the Team Principal of the new Red Bull Racing team. As a good luck gift, I bought him the *Collins*

Nature Guide to weather and wrote in the front: "I think this is the one that Jean Todt uses." At that time, it had been a period of Ferrari and Michael domination. I like to think my pocket guide to weather and clouds led to Red Bull and Sebastian domination!

Whilst presenting a live motorsport show which, unusually was a chat show with some live motorsport, on ITV1 called *Speed Sunday*, I was given the chance to do some co-driving with Tony Jardine for an MG works team. Before I knew it, I was competing in rallies in the UK and Scandinavia right up to world championship level. In fact, whilst presenting the Goodwood Festival of Speed in 2022 for ITV, I needed to renew my licence for a co-driving feature, so who knows, maybe I will have another go!

Eventually, though, I arrived in F1 (which I describe more fully in the Lewis Hamilton chapter, see page 34). I will always be grateful to the BBC for giving me the chance when they took the rights back at the start of 2009. It was then that I became a regular figure in the paddock and on national television interviewing the drivers.

I did laugh whilst reading Jenson Button's autobiography *Life to the Limit*. I love how he describes the interview pen where I spent much of my F1 career (apparently waving a microphone if you believe him!):

> If you're not one of the top three, you go straight into your interviews, which are held in something we call "the pen". You've probably seen it: it's like an enclosure at a farm park, except with Formula One drivers instead of goats, surrounded by journalists waving microphones at you. Those interviews are always tricky, again because you run the risk of saying silly things you shouldn't (mind you, if that happens you can always use the 'adrenalin excuse' afterwards). You see someone like Max Verstappen doing it, maybe coming out with the odd thing in the heat of the moment that would have been better kept between him and his dad. It

comes with experience, I guess. You learn to calm down, breathe and try to remember that you're not just speaking for yourself, you're speaking on behalf of five hundred other people in the team.

He's not wrong; however, there is an art to that microphone waving, one I hope that I get right more times than wrong! This book will give you an insight into that world and remind you of some of the awkward, hilarious and combative interviews that drivers have done with me over the years – including one of my chosen goats, Jenson Button!

In my time in F1, drivers, people, racetracks have all come and gone. From the colourful and wonderful Indian Grand Prix to the unique love motels of Mokpo and the Korean Grand Prix – I feel I should probably elaborate on this. The drivers all stayed at one hotel near the track, the Hyundai hotel. The rest of us stayed in a variety of "establishments". For some reason, the majority of places to stay were known as "love motels" normally rented by the hour until we came along and booked them for five days. Many of us brought our own bed sheets, sleeping bags, antibacterial wipes – you get the picture. Days in the paddock were passed telling horror stories about what had happened the day and night before. People would return from work and realise their hotel room had been "borrowed". It was a dreadful, yet shared, experience – very F1. As a travelling circus, we were all in it together. Well, all apart from the drivers!

Singapore is another bizarre experience in that we become night owls. We stay on European time, which means we sleep until lunch time, go to work at 3 p.m., leave the track at around 2 or 3 a.m., pop to a hawker market for some food and then go to bed at 5 or 6 a.m. It is totally surreal and the first time you are there, it really throws you, but then you look forward to it and it is, without a doubt, one of my favourite Grand Prix.

I have worked in and covered many sports from rugby to Wimbledon to the Olympic Games but F1 is unique in how we all move around and work. When you cover rugby, you might only see some teams once or twice a season but in F1 we are together over 20 times a year and often we travel on the same chartered flights. There are a few times a year when the Sunday night or Monday is as exciting and as big an occasion as the F1 when some of us let our hair down together. It's this unusual way of living that unites us.

It goes both ways though. Because we are such a tight knit group, crashes and accidents really affect us. Whether it be Jules Bianchi in F1, Anthoine Hubert in F2 or Justin Wilson in Indy Car, we are a small community, and many of us have grown up together, working our way up through the junior formulae. The losses are the moments that never leave you and are a reminder that whilst fun is everywhere, so is danger. Those who have driven in F1 and been around for a while tend to have an attitude of "we all have a limited number of heartbeats, so use them well".

I was actually hoping to write this on my flight to Baku, where I was presenting the Azerbaijan Grand Prix, but it was an F1 charter, which basically meant there were too many people around! Firstly, I like to catch up with everyone and secondly, I wasn't that keen to be writing in case of prying eyes, although I am sure no one really cared. I had Sebastian Vettel, George Russell, Pierre Gasly, Alex Albon and Nicholas Latifi around me and was sitting next to GP Lambiase, Max's race engineer, whom I have known for many years and seen socially at friends' weddings. We did have a good laugh on the flight over and it always becomes like a social event, with everyone moving around and chatting, which was lovely. There were also several engineers on the flight all trying to hide their screens of squiggles, info and prep from each other. It is a constant in-joke of one peering over another's shoulder and saying "thanks", and pretending that they've just spotted something from their rival's screen that will make them two-tenths of a second quicker!

The flight back from Baku was equally amusing. I sat alongside Mark Webber and we were surrounded by pretty exhausted team bosses, all with a story of why their cars and drivers finished where they did – these stories tend to be more honest on a flight back with a G&T in hand than those told in an interview situation. There is a lot of trust – and sometimes a drink or two to relax – on a flight home after a race weekend.

Mark manages the incredible young talent Oscar Piastri, who will be in F1 next year. He lives near me, so rather than Mark have an extra hour on his trip at 2 a.m., I said Oscar could jump in the car with me. On the drive home he was telling me how excited he was to be driving the Alpine F1 car at Silverstone the day after we landed. It was the perfect example of the cycle of F1: no matter how big the names are in the seats on the grid, there is always another group of drivers just waiting for their chance; even hungrier, even younger and maybe even quicker. That's the beauty of F1, it's a constant evolution in every sense.

But to know and appreciate what we have and enjoy now, you need to know where the sport and those involved came from. The history of F1 is as beautiful as the cars we have on track. The drivers all have their own stories of sacrifice, success, drama and, in some cases, devastation.

Hopefully this book lets you discover or reminds you of what these drivers have put themselves through to reach the highs and how they have come back from the lows. I have been lucky enough to share some incredible moments with many drivers, including Michael, Lewis, Sebastian, Max, Fernando, Jenson and Felipe. Writing this and watching back all my old interviews certainly has been a trip down memory lane for me, and I hope it will be for you too.

1

MICHAEL SCHUMACHER

Who would have thought that the man I watched winning week in, week out whilst discovering my love of Formula One would become someone I not only got to know but was able to enjoy some great moments and interviews with. Quite simply, Michael Schumacher *was* Formula One when I was growing up. So in 2010, when he returned to the sport, I couldn't believe my luck to be working in the paddock and have the chance to interview him. During the few years of his "second career", Michael and I enjoyed some big interviews and hilarious times, including when I was asked to take a horse from the UK to Switzerland to compete against him in a western riding competition. It is one of the most memorable weekends I will ever have in my career and probably my life.

The man who helped Schumacher come into F1 (as a relatively unknown F3 driver) was Eddie Jordan, for whom he drove at the Belgian Grand Prix. On Sunday, 25 August 1991, Michael made his debut after being given his opportunity by Jordan F1, who desperately needed a driver. Despite taking pole at the previous race, their regular pilot Bertrand Gachot had been imprisoned for aggravated assault after an altercation with a London taxi driver. Eddie had followed Michael in Formula 3 and had decided to "give youth a chance" and see how Schumacher could develop for the future. Mercedes paid to run Michael in the car – he was part of their young driver academy and thought to be a star of the future. How right they were.

On the Saturday he surpassed all expectations, qualifying seventh, equalling Jordan's season best and outperforming his teammate, F1 veteran Andrea de Cesaris. Looking at the grid, the cars in front of him were a who's who of F1. Ayrton Senna was on pole with Alain Prost alongside. Nigel Mansell and Gerhard Berger were on the second row and in front of Schumacher were Jean Alesi and Nelson Piquet. To get the drive, his manager Willi Weber had promised EJ that Michael knew the circuit. Quite simply, that was not true. Schumacher brought with him a fold-up bike and cycled round and round to learn the track whilst preparing for the weekend ahead.

In the race, he made a good start and, with no regard for reputation, he overtook some of the fabled names in front of him. That was until lap 2, when his clutch went and put an end to any thoughts of a dream ending to his debut weekend. But even in that short time, he had impressed enough to drive at the following race in Italy. Only it wouldn't be for Jordan.

Between Spa and Monza, Schumacher signed for Benetton whilst allegedly still being under contract to Jordan F1. It was a busy week for the legal teams as Eddie Jordan took Benetton to the courts in London, where he subsequently lost the case. Behind the scenes, a deal was done, and Michael Schumacher would see out the rest of the season for his new team alongside Nelson Piquet.

Michael's first championship winning season was in 1994, but it was a year known more for the tragic deaths of Ayrton Senna and Austrian rookie Roland Ratzenberger on the same weekend at Imola. It was also a season which saw Schumacher disqualified from two races and banned for two more.

It is incredibly unusual for a driver to be banned from races and unheard of for them to win the championship in the same year, but it happened. At the British Grand Prix, Schumacher overtook Damon Hill on the formation lap. He received a black flag, which he then ignored. After the race, he was disqualified from the results and handed a two-race ban. Later that year, Schumacher was disqualified again but this time the blame fell on the team. After winning the Belgian Grand Prix, he was thrown out after his car was found to have too much wear on the skid block, breaking regulations. The appeal for his two-race ban was heard around the same time but the decision was not overturned. It meant that after Belgium, Schumacher missed the next two races in Italy and Portugal. With Damon Hill winning every race apart from the European Grand Prix at Jerez, the championship would be fought out in Adelaide, the final race of the season.

One point was all that separated the two drivers as they went wheel to wheel for the title in the finale. The story and outcome are one of sport's most famous. As Hill got alongside the German to overtake for the lead, Schumacher turned into the Williams. The two collided and both cars retired, giving Schumacher his first world title. The controversy ran on about "deliberate intent" and continues to do so, but the black type reads "1994 Michael Schumacher World Champion".

The following year, Schumacher defended his title, becoming the youngest two-time F1 champion in history, a record that was taken from him by Fernando Alonso and that at present belongs to Sebastian Vettel. There was another season of rivalry and crashes in 1995 between Schumacher and Hill, but it was the German driver who dominated, winning nine of the seventeen races and a total of eleven podiums.

In 1996 the Ferrari years began. Schumacher arrived at the Scuderia but, crucially, so did the personnel to build one of the most dominant teams in the history of the sport. Ross Brawn and Rory

Byrne, with Jean Todt at the helm, started to rebuild a team which hadn't won a Drivers' Championship since Jody Scheckter in 1979 and a Constructors' title since 1983.

By the millennium, the foundations were firm and the building had been completed. In came a period of such total dominance that fans were either wowed or switched off completely. Schumacher recorded five consecutive Drivers' titles; each one packed with his trademark brilliance, drama and ruthlessness. He won his final championship in 2004 at his favourite Belgian Grand Prix with four races still to go. In 2005 and 2006 he lost out to Fernando Alonso in the title race, but it was during the final bid for an eighth title that Schumacher announced he would be retiring from Formula One.

I first met Michael in May 2007, whilst hosting the A1GP end of season awards ceremony at the Royal Courts of Justice in London. Nico Hülkenberg had won the championship for Team Germany and the owner of that team was Willi Weber. As well as managing both Michael and Ralf Schumacher, he also managed the seventeen-year-old Hülkenberg, who was tipped for big things. I was told just before the ceremony started that we would have a surprise guest on stage to present Nico with his trophy. Michael Schumacher was in the building. He would come on stage, not speak, just hand over the trophy, shake hands and exit stage right. Preferably, I wasn't to converse with him at all, but that felt very odd and a bit rude, so I did say hello and introduced myself beforehand and he was absolutely fine.

Unusually, we started the night with the main award and as Michael came on stage to hand it over, there was a huge gasp followed by a huge round of applause. His appearance might have been fleeting but it was great for everyone involved that he had come, creating headlines and plenty of coverage for the series the next day.

By 2009, Michael was missing F1 and looking to get back behind the wheel. The arrival of Mercedes as a works team and not just an engine supplier was the perfect time and team for his comeback. Once again, he would be working with Ross Brawn, with whom he had won all seven of his world titles.

To use his words at the Mercedes launch, "It's a nice start for a comeback in many senses. Because I have proven everything there is to be proven in this segment, the nature is that I am just there to have fun ... and the most fun I have is if I win."

With two giants of motorsport coming out of hibernation, it was a joint reawakening that every F1 fan had been craving.

After the drama of 2008 with Hamilton v Massa, followed by the Brawn fairy tale, F1 fans were being treated to a wonderful time in motorsport. Could Mercedes and Schumacher be the next chapter in this rich period? The Silver Arrows had acquired the championship-winning Brawn team but not the drivers. Newly crowned world champion Jenson Button preferred to go to McLaren whilst Rubens Barrichello went to Williams. In came the all-German line-up of Nico Rosberg and the returning Kaiser.

The pressure on Schumacher was huge. What would three years out of the sport mean in terms of on-track performance? The battery might have been recharged over those years but surely even he would be race rusty?

"People ask me, are you still as good as you used to be, I don't really know? All I know is I'm still good enough," said Schumacher in a BBC interview.

The reality, though, was there were times that he struggled, making errors that just weren't present in his "first career". The critics were tough. Whilst everyone willed Schumacher to be back to the level of greatness to which we'd become accustomed, maybe those thoughts were naive.

At Ferrari, Schumacher spent those early years building a team to help him reach the heights that he did. He was the expert at putting everything and everyone in place around him to create the "perfect" car and one which he could extract the best from. He took fitness to a level that hadn't been seen in Formula One before. He was first at the track and last to leave, whether it be on a race weekend or at testing. Would all of that still be the case at the age of forty?

I loved interviewing Michael. You had to be ready, be absolutely on it regarding questions and comebacks, but he was also very fair and you could have fun. Watching back so many interviews, I was surprised by the smiles and laughs as he would give his own interpretation when answering my questions. I would then try to navigate back to the questions I wanted to ask and the answers that he was trying to avoid. It was like dealing with a very clever politician.

At the Monaco Grand Prix in 2010, Schumacher crossed the line in sixth place after a last corner lunge past the Ferrari of Fernando Alonso. Mark Webber had already won the race, but on the last lap the safety car had been deployed. The track lights had gone green, which would normally allow racing to resume.

On this occasion it was different, as according to rule 40.13: "If the race ends whilst the safety car is deployed it will enter the pit lane at the end of the last lap and the cars will take the chequered flag as normal without overtaking."

The FIA got involved and Ferrari were obviously vocal about Schumacher's move. As is normal, the other team responded and in this case Mercedes' Ross Brawn produced evidence as to why Schumacher was correct to overtake and should remain in sixth position.

Whilst this was all going on, I was conducting my post-race interviews with the drivers:

"Michael, no surprise, let's start at the end of the race and work back."

He smiled. "Why start at the end? Let's start at the beginning." He answered for over a minute.

I tried again, "So, seventy-eight laps later and we get to the final corner." This time Michael laughed and did answer the question, adding that he did not expect to get a penalty.

I then reminded him of an interesting fact: "Michael, the fourth steward today is Damon Hill."

"Ah yes, so I hear!" he said with a twinkle in his eye. "He's a good guy and I'm sure he will understand the situation."

Not quite. The FIA gave Schumacher a twenty-second penalty, which dropped him from sixth to twelfth.

I always like to interview drivers away from the track. It is much more personal, and they tend to be more relaxed. I knew Michael was very private, but I also knew his family had a ranch and horses and I thought it would be wonderful to speak to him there. My love, since I was a child, has been all things equestrian and I have ridden all of my life. I had spoken to Michael about this before – the wonderful thing about animals being that they don't care who you are, or what you have or haven't achieved. The idea evolved and one day I got an exciting invite. Michael had invited me and three other F1 TV reporters to his ranch in Switzerland to compete in an "F1 Celebrity" competition at the European Reining Championships that were being held at the family ranch in Switzerland.

Now, I had ridden all my life, but never reining, which is a form of western riding where you learn a test and perform a series of moves. It is a little like less refined dressage at a gallop. It is fast and furious and therefore it was no surprise that Michael was a big fan.

His wife Corinna and daughter Gina are very talented riders, and their CS Ranch in Switzerland has some of the best facilities I have been to anywhere in the world. I needed to learn the ropes pretty quickly and was told to go to West Sussex to the yard of a wonderful woman called Francesca Sternberg, who had represented Great Britain at the World Equestrian Games many times. She was a friend of the Schumachers' and would give me a couple of lessons and whip me into shape.

I went to my BBC bosses to convince them this would be a good idea and, in principle, they loved it. However, I do remember my director, Richard Carr, filling in the Risk Assessment, a crucial document that has to be approved by both insurance and the production manager before any filming can take place.

The conversation was along the lines of:

RC: "Description?"

Me: "Reining."

RC: "What is it, though?"

Me: "It is horse riding, no jumps, a bit like dressage but at a canter or gallop."

RC: "Capabilities?"

Me: "None, but I will learn. I've got a couple of one-hour lessons booked."

Richard was looking increasingly concerned. "You can't do it? Okay, what safety equipment is used?"

Me: "None, no back protector and you can only wear a cowboy hat, not a riding hat, but I will take mine just in case."

By this point I wondered if I would be allowed to go, so I decided to just set everything out quickly to get it over and done with!

"I need to take the horse I am borrowing from the south of England to Switzerland. You don't need to worry about that. Just get me a flight over there. It will be great access, an exclusive interview, and even if we don't film it, I will try and go anyway!"

Richard just looked at me and then we got to the deal breaker. "Do we have to insure Michael Schumacher?"

I smiled. "Definitely not."

That would have brought the BBC to its knees. So off I and my trusty steed went to Switzerland!

Before the competition, Michael had asked me a couple of times at various races how I was getting on with my training. The truth was that I was in a lot of pain and had to borrow one of the Mercedes physios. So whilst Nico Rosberg was away doing something else, I jumped in to get some treatment from his trainer. I'm not sure how much training, if any, Michael did before the event, but eventually it was upon us and we all gathered on a Friday night at his ranch in the Swiss countryside. My producer and great friend Steve Aldous was with me, as well as an excellent cameraman, Andy Parr. Despite both of them having been in F1 for many years (with ITV previously), they were really excited about this opportunity to film and spend the weekend in such revered company – and I am pretty sure they didn't mean me.

My horse, Lexus, was already waiting in the stable for me when I arrived. Whilst he was a veteran of the World Equestrian Games, I certainly was not, although I had competed at a low level in various equestrian pursuits and my family compete at a decent level, so I understood the pattern of what was to come. I was also feeling quite competitive by this stage and was hoping to dazzle the crowds and win. I think since spending time with Michael, his attitude was rubbing off on me!

On the Friday night there would be a warm-up. Michael was there and was unsurprisingly good. Annoying and yet expected. The truth is that he would never have suggested this if he wasn't going to be good at it! I looked to be around the same level as him and then there were a few other people from the F1 paddock. Stella

Bruni from Sky Italia was more fashion over skill, and I was really worried that she might get injured, but she looked good. Allard Kalff from Dutch TV had much, much more enthusiasm than ability and, as a friend, he wouldn't mind me saying that and I am sure he would agree. The crowd loved him but, again, I was nervous for him. Ironically, Allard is the one who has continued to be part of the sport, competes, has his own reining horses, bred his own foal and is so, so passionate about it all. What a lovely bonus from what was just supposed to be one weekend of fun and filming. There were other broadcasters from Austria and Germany too, but we didn't see them until the Saturday of the competition.

At night we had a dinner and were introduced to all the competitors – I mean the real competitors – the ones hoping to become European Champions in their respective classes. We were the sort of half-time entertainment. Slightly higher in the pecking order than a mascot running around to entertain the crowd; more like when school children are allowed to take a penalty kick at goal during half time of a big match.

The Saturday morning came and we headed back to the ranch. There was no more time to practise and we weren't on until mid-afternoon. It gave me a good chance to watch some of the action along with Michael. His wife and daughter were competing too and were very good. We then went out into one of his fields and perched on top of a fence and did a lovely, relaxed interview. But we couldn't delay it anymore, soon it was time to warm-up and head into the main arena for the competition. As everyone knew Michael would be in the ring, we had a packed crowd. Unlike the more silent crowds at dressage and other equestrian events that I'd been involved with, this lot were whooping and cheering throughout. I had never seen or heard anything like it.

Due to the noise of the crowd, my horse was much more excited than it had been in training. My test went well, and the spins and slides and dramatic halts were all over in a matter of minutes. I loved every second of it. We were all doing the same test, and as I came out of the arena, Michael went in with a nod and a smile. He was excellent and quick and brave, as you would imagine, and actually rode with real style. When it came to the scoring, we got exactly the same points and shared the podium. I can now tell people that I stood on the same step of the podium as Michael Schumacher, albeit we were in leather chaps and Stetsons!

We finished off our filming and just when things couldn't get any more surreal, exciting and unbelievable, the afterparty took place. It started in daylight and finished in daylight; it was great. I remember my cameraman Andy doing an excellent solo dance on a small stage to Nena's "99 Luftballons" – a German classic.

By the end of the night there was a small but determined group of partygoers, of which I was one along with Michael and his friends and a few others. The whole weekend was one of the most memorable of my life, despite the alcohol consumption!

At the next race at Silverstone, off camera, I spoke to Michael more about horses than F1. On race day, I was standing on the back of the flatbed truck to go round the track for the Drivers' Parade, and when Michael got on, he came straight up for a chat about it all and to check I had recovered! He was normally with Sebastian Vettel on the parade, and I remember Seb looking surprised as the two of us chatted for ages about the exploits of the weekend before.

Eventually Sebastian said to me, "Lee, are you not going to interview us?" Excellent point, there is always a job to do!

The job must always come first when you are in the paddock. A couple of races later at the Hungarian Grand Prix, a track that Schumacher was so comfortable on that he described it as his living room, the post-race interview was tense, and tough questions had to be asked. Whilst battling against his old teammate, Rubens Barrichello, Schumacher moved across to defend his position on track and Barrichello ran alongside the wall, both travelling at 180mph. The move was lambasted by a host of drivers past and present, saying Schumacher had "stepped far over the line of any sporting code" and Barrichello called it "the most dangerous" in his career.

Schumacher denied responsibility and said to me, "It was tight and tough, but I think I am known not to give presents on track. To pass me, you have to earn it."

Barrichello was incandescent when he learned that his former teammate at Ferrari had not assumed any fault. "It's been my fault for six years. Unbelievable. We will let the stewards say whatever they have to say. His view is that I am always a big crier."

Whilst Schumacher had the backing of Mercedes, he didn't find favour with the stewards, who gave him a ten-place grid penalty for the following race.

It had been a tough comeback year on track, and by the time the season ended in Abu Dhabi, there was a new German world champion in Sebastian Vettel. Schumacher was a friend and mentor but no longer was he the last, indeed the only, German F1 World Champion. The Mercedes driver finished ninth in the championship and with almost exactly half the points of his teammate Nico Rosberg. Whilst Rosberg had been on the podium three times, all in third place, Michael had come close with three fourth positions, but as yet, no champagne.

And 2011 was another mixed bag. Mercedes' best result of the season came courtesy of Schumacher at the Canadian Grand Prix, but he had five non-finishes to his name, which dented any chance of a decent showing in the championship.

The season started with a retirement in Australia, and by the time we had reached the end of the fourth race of the season,

Schumacher's results read: DNF, 9, 8, 12. This was not what he had come back for.

At the end of my interview in Turkey, Michael said to me on camera, "The big joy is not there right now apart from some action, that's about it." Cue headlines around the world: "No joy in F1 for Schumacher."

At the next race in Spain, I was offered a sit-down interview with Michael so he could clarify the comments. In typical Michael style he started off the interview by saying, "I was surprised how famous I made you – or us!" He went on to say that he was talking solely about that race in Turkey and that he was getting joy out of F1 and he was looking at the big picture.

But the fact was, he was being outperformed by his teammate and I needed to ask him about it.

"Why do you think Nico has an edge with it [the car] at the moment?"

"I don't think he has," replied Schumacher.

I was ready, as you had to be when interviewing him, and brought up the stats from qualifying, but Michael was so strong in interviews that nothing fazed him. He answered everything from his point of view and his "fact". It was then for the expert analysts to discuss after it had been aired.

On the week of the British Grand Prix, Mercedes had arranged a feature where Michael would give me a tour of the factory at Brackley. We dropped into the office of Ross Brawn. Sometimes these things are set-up; still, Ross did look reasonably surprised to see us walking in with our cameras as he was working away, but Michael could go where he wanted and I just followed. As we went round the factory you could see what it meant for everyone to have Michael visiting the departments and saying "thank you" as he put it. Some of this was for TV, but Michael really did like to be part of everything going on at a racetrack and behind the scenes and was always very involved. That certainly isn't something that every driver feels the need, or has the interest, to do.

We eventually reached the paint shop. I was told to spray the Mercedes tri-star onto the nose of the car which was getting the final touches before the British Grand Prix. Accuracy isn't my forte and the line was far from perfect – it is a skilled job and a skill I evidently didn't have! I handed the paint gun to Michael, who was meant to paint the car too but for some reason decided that a manicure would be better. He sprayed my nails and the top of my fingers with white/silver car paint. I had actually just had my nails done, but I couldn't really complain and explain that I'd just had a manicure to the most successful driver of all time, so I just grinned and went with it. I do say a little nervously in the interview, "Does this come off?" "Eventually"' should have been his answer!

On the Drivers Parade on the Sunday, where all my Silverstone catch-ups seem to happen, Michael asked to see my hand to see if the paint had come off. The answer was no! In the background was a slightly bemused and eventually amused Vettel, once the unprompted manicure story had been told. Seven days later, after quite a bit of scrubbing, the paint was gone.

At the end of August, en route to Spa for the Belgian Grand Prix, there was a very special trip to Kerpen kart track. Anyone who has karted will have visited the old-school track around twenty kilometres south-west of Cologne. There are so many good circuits in that part of Germany, and it was Kerpen where Schumacher and Vettel both honed their skills. In fact, it is a track that Michael's father used to manage whilst his mother ran the canteen. To mark the fiftieth anniversary, the pair spent the day karting the Wednesday before the Belgian race. A sea of children and a few journalists gathered at the circuit to watch Michael and Sebastian return to where it all began. It was a special day and an excellent reminder that even the greats started somewhere. Their love for driving didn't come in front of packed crowds or watched on TV by millions, but on long, often cold and rainy days at kart tracks as children with parents who gave up their time to drive them around and chase their dreams. A few days later, it was back to normal and they were driving in front of seventy thousand fans in Spa.

For Michael, so much has happened at the Belgian racetrack. His debut in 1991 was followed over the years by some incredible and still talked about overtaking manoeuvres, and he went on to win the race six times.

My first trip to Spa was in 1998 when Damon Hill took the victory. What a Belgian Grand Prix to attend as my first at the track. The rain fell heavily and at the start, David Coulthard's McLaren hit the wall and caused a thirteen-car pile-up. An hour later the race was re-started and, in the mist and rain, Schumacher ran into the back of Coulthard and returned to the pitlane on three wheels. Famously, Schumacher parked his Ferrari and stormed down the pitlane to have it out with DC. The Ferrari mechanics and Jean Todt restrained him from getting into the McLaren garage but volleys of abuse including "Are you trying to f****** kill me" could be made out over the noise of the cars.

The Belgian Grand Prix in 2012 was to be Michael's 300th Grand Prix. The Thursday morning found me and a BBC crew at the town hall in Spa, where he was being given an honorary citizenship. The Belgian town holds Michael in as high a regard as he held the circuit. There is no doubt that the track had more meaning to him than others and he often talked about the "special things" that had happened to him there.

I was meant to travel in Michael's car with him from the event to the circuit and do an interview on the way about his milestone. He was inside the town hall and I was outside with Sabine Kehm, his PR, latterly manager and great friend of the Schumacher family. She was always a joy to work with; firm but fair, and lovely person who was respected by all. She was telling my BBC crew that we could install a GoPro camera to film when, all of a sudden, her phone rang and she had to dash inside to the event. As she left, she threw me the keys to Michael's car and said, "Just sort it yourself and be careful with his things."

I tentatively bleeped the key fob and opened the door of the Mercedes that Michael had driven from his home to Belgium. It was packed full of bags, coats, loads of personal things that I really didn't want to touch. Not only the backseat but the passenger seat was covered too. I showed my producer and cameraman and said I really didn't feel comfortable touching, let alone moving, any of Michael's personal belongings! We agreed to leave it until we could talk to Sabine and highlight the issue. The only problem was that Michael arrived back at the car before Sabine did. The surprise on his face meant he obviously hadn't been told that I had the keys to his car, let alone was standing with the door open.

He did one of his famous eyebrow raises and just said, "Hi Lee, I see you are in my car. Is everything okay?" Even though I got on well with him, I felt so awkward and embarrassed. He did find it funny when I explained, and when Sabine got there she found it hilarious. I was in such a panic at being caught.

I explained about the lack of space in the car, which had been made even trickier with Michael having been presented a large painting at the event by the mayor which now also needed to fit in his Mercedes. I struck a compromise. We would leave the filming in the car if we could have a chat at the racetrack and we all decided that would be the best option – the only option, really. I returned the keys to Michael and headed back to the circuit where

I explained everything to my boss. Thankfully, he found the whole thing hilarious, even though one of our main features for the programme marking Michael's 300th race wouldn't be quite as personal as we had hoped.

If Belgium was a great race for Schumacher, one which bore no luck appeared on the calendar for his second chapter. The night-time street race in Singapore became an F1 favourite from its first running in 2008 but, unlike Spa, it proved difficult for the seven-time world champion to tame. Schumacher took part in three events, and whilst he never failed to qualify in the top ten, when it came to the race, he never failed to reach the end without a fair amount of damage. In fact, in two of three races he didn't finish at all.

In the 2010 renewal, he had a coming together with both Saubers on different laps. The first accident was with Kamui Kobayashi, which saw the Mercedes hit the wall and need a trip to the pits. The next casualty was Nick Heidfeld, who got slammed into the wall, resulting in another trip to the pits for Schumacher in his impressively robust Silver Arrow. By that stage it was silver with a hint of red sparks as the front wing trailed along the ground. Believe it or not, that was his best race under the city lights and, somehow, he finished in thirteenth. Neither Sauber finished the race with their damage.

The next two years, Schumacher was involved in almost identical accidents, the only difference being the where, when and who. The first driver in the wrong place at the wrong time was Sergio Perez driving – yes, you guessed it – a Sauber. In 2012 it was the Toro Rosso of Jean-Éric Vergne, who was rear-ended in an almost identical fashion to Perez the previous year. The critics were scathing.

It was so uncharacteristic to see Schumacher struggling like that. In Singapore the paddock stays on European time, so we go to bed at 6 a.m. and get up around 1 p.m. to head into the track around 3 p.m. On the Sunday morning before the race in 2011, incredibly, Michael had stayed at the track until 5 a.m. I mentioned before that he was known to be first in and last out when he was winning championships, but even when he had achieved all that he had, there was no resting on laurels. He was desperate to find anything that could help him. Throughout everything, his desire to learn, help and be part of a team never left him.

In his final year of racing, we did see flashes of the Schumacher that we all knew. Whilst in his prime and dominating the sport, fans and the paddock might have rolled their eyes at the thought of another pole or podium; in 2012 he was applauded for it.

Schumacher headed into the Monaco GP weekend knowing he was carrying a five-place grid penalty for "causing an avoidable collision" with Bruno Senna at the previous race in Spain. He had already joked in the press conference that he would take pole, start from sixth and then win the race. The first part of the plan certainly worked. Mark Webber was on provisional pole, but Schumacher crossed the line 800ths of a second faster, taking what would have been his final pole position in Formula One. Sadly, the penalty meant that he dropped to the third row of the grid.

In my interview after you could see how much it meant to Michael, who had won the Monaco Grand Prix five times.

"It is simply a wonderful feeling to get pole after such a long time, and particularly here in Monaco. Okay, it has taken a little bit longer than I might have wanted in the second chapter of my career, but that makes it even sweeter. It's just beautiful."

As for the race, that was the one where he passed Alonso and ended up with the twenty-second penalty dished out by the FIA and his old friend Damon Hill.

His final podium came just two races later at the European Grand

Prix in Valencia. After qualifying in twelfth position and on a street circuit with quite limited overtaking opportunities, it wasn't expected to be the one which would see Schumacher's best result since his comeback. It was a race of attrition, safety cars, tyre wear and good strategy which kept Schumacher in the hunt. Alonso won the race from eleventh, Räikkönen finished second and Schumacher was third. It was his 155th podium and the first since the Chinese Grand Prix in 2006. It would also be the last.

Lewis Hamilton signing for Mercedes meant that Schumacher was without a seat for 2013. Other teams including Lotus were very interested but after three years with Mercedes, and at the age of forty-three, Michael announced his retirement from the sport.

The 2012 Brazilian Grand Prix was Michael's last. He had qualified fourteenth, and on race day I saw him jumping over the wall up into the pit lane about twenty minutes before the start of the race. I asked him if I could walk and talk with him to his garage on camera and he said yes. It is one of my favourite memories in F1, not because anything profound was said but because I was able to share that moment just minutes before the race with someone who had made such an impact on the sport and on me. Someone captured a photo of it, and I have it on my office wall.

In typical Schumacher style, even his final race wasn't without drama. An early puncture saw him drop back through the field, but he eventually worked his way back up to sixth. The battle for the championship between Vettel and Alonso was nerve-rackingly close. In the latter stages of the race, Alonso had enough points for the title, but Vettel worked his way back through the field and won the championship by three points. Seventh position would have been enough for Vettel to become champion, although by just one point, but Schumacher made it easy for his fellow German to pass into sixth, giving Seb a three-point buffer. Red Bull boss Christian

Horner said, "It was his gesture to Sebastian, almost like passing the baton on."

The interviews afterwards were reflective but not hugely emotional from Michael. It was actually on the formation lap over team radio on the way to the grid where he said the most.

"Guys, I am on my way to the grid. I would like to use the opportunity to say thank you to the boys, all the mechanics, engineers who I have been working with. I would like to say as well thank you to all the people who have been following us everywhere, around the world, watching us on television. Staying on track, sharing all the emotions and the good times that we have had together . . . I just want to say thank you for being there with us and sharing my particular passion for so long. Thanks for all these wonderful times and good memories. It's going to be . . . thanks again. Now, let's go and get ready to rumble for another race."

Ross Brawn replied, sounding emotional, "Thank you, Michael. From all of us, it has been a real and rare privilege to have worked with you. From all of us, thank you."

Over a minute of warm, thoughtful and considered words on the way to a frenetic start of an always chaotic Grand Prix. Those moments sum up Formula One, the calmness and clarity that drivers need before the lightning-quick reactions and pinpoint accuracy of the battle at dangerously high speeds.

The following year, I went to visit the now retired Schumacher.

"Michael, are you missing F1?"

"It would be wrong to say no, but it is not that I need it, and my life is pretty joyful right now. I wouldn't have had the energy for further years."

The year after Michael's retirement, Mercedes started winning races. I asked him whether he thought he got the credit he deserved for helping to build the team.

"To me it is much more important that inside the team I was credited, and people understood what I was doing and how good I was doing things and I never got the feeling they doubted."

At the time, it was Vettel who was winning championship after championship, so how would Michael feel if his friend and protégé took his records?

"Honestly, I didn't have statistics in my mind when I was racing. It was always a consequence and a nice consequence. I enjoyed that afterwards, but it wasn't the reason I was racing for. I would be pretty happy for Sebastian in achieving this."

Little did we know then that it would be Lewis Hamilton who would be the one breaking Michael's records.

The thing about sport is that there are never any guarantees. Michael Schumacher, Mercedes, Ross Brawn; it all seemed a fail-safe recipe for success, and yet no one would have imagined that it would end the way it did.

You could say the same about life. No matter what you have achieved and endured, there are no guarantees. On Sunday, 29 December 2013, whilst on a family skiing holiday in the French Alps, Michael suffered a life-changing head trauma. He was placed in a medically induced coma and remained at CHU Grenoble until June 2014, when he was transferred to Switzerland, "to continue his long phase of rehabilitation. He is not in a coma anymore," so said a statement from the family, delivered by Sabine Kehm.

The shock surrounding the whole accident and aftermath still affects many people. As the news broke, I was getting the same drip feed as everyone through twenty-four-hour rolling news and social media. My phone was ringing off the hook with broadcasters asking if I could go on radio programmes, news programmes, give interviews about Michael, his life, his condition. I said no to them all. Firstly, I had no idea about Michael's condition and would therefore be speculating, and secondly, I was upset. He was someone I had respected and liked, and it all felt wrong. I certainly didn't want to have any airtime from something so tragic. I appreciate that as a journalist it might not seem very professional, but I didn't care. I have always believed you do what you feel is correct and always reserve the right to say yes or no to something, so long as you can justify it.

Sadly, not everyone took that approach, and some people were just desperate to look like they had news, fastest with fiction across social media. That is probably the difference between social media and news agencies who have a moral obligation to broadcast fact.

I think everyone in motorsport – teams, drivers, journalists and fans – watch Mick Schumacher's fledgling career with a real mix of emotions. He looks like Michael, he has won races and titles as he worked his way up, and reached F1 with Haas and support from Ferrari. But there is no father at the racetrack with him.

Mick has often mentioned Michael in his interviews, and after winning his first F2 race at the Hungaroring in 2019, he was asked about victory at a track where his father had such success (Michael won the Hungarian GP four times).

"It is very special and also thinking back to last year [in Formula 3] when I won for the first time in Spa, where my dad was also very comfortable." It was wonderful to see Corrina there under the podium with her son standing on the top step as the German National anthem played out.

Before the German GP at Hockenheim in 2019, Mick drove his father's championship-winning F2004 Ferrari. The crowds in the packed grandstands were on their feet as Mick parked the car on the start-finish straight and got out to wave to them. You could see the emotion on his face and watching it, even now, gives me goosebumps.

The comparisons between the two are natural and it is something that Mick is already used to, but he is his own man, with his own hopes and dreams.

Few people transcend their sport, but Michael Schumacher is one of them. We miss him but we should also celebrate him and enjoy watching back the moments of brilliance, the moments of drama and even the moments of deviance.

He is responsible for so many of the quality drivers we have on the grid today who grew up watching him. And as the grid gets younger, if they weren't inspired by him, then their parents were.

Michael might have retired from the sport in 2012, but what he brought to Formula One is unequalled. Even in his absence, his light burns brightly.

2
LEWIS HAMILTON

Whether it be sharing a hire car, sharing the flack when interviews make global news or sharing the journey of his record-breaking career, it is fair to say that I have spent a lot of my motorsport career with Lewis Hamilton over the last sixteen years. We met before he started his incredible journey in Formula One and became one of the most recognisable and highest paid athletes on the planet.

Nowadays, it's tricky to remember a time when people, even within motorsport, didn't know who Lewis Hamilton was. His early days as a young karter are well documented and most people will have seen the videos of him as a ten-year-old talking about wanting to drive for McLaren and showing off his skills at kart tracks around Britain. All parents make these films but for the vast majority they stay as "family funnies", destined to cause embarrassment only at future Christmas gatherings. Few turn out to be prophecies. But since Lewis came to fame, the Hamilton home videos have been seen and enjoyed by millions.

In 2004, at nineteen years old, he had his first taste of F1 when he was given the chance to drive a McLaren. The following year saw him claim his first big title, becoming champion in the F3 Euro Series, which he dominated, winning fifteen of the twenty races. Just to put it into context, that season six of those young hopefuls made it to Formula One whilst several others went on to become sports car champions. This was a competitive year in a competitive series, but it was Hamilton who stole the show. Whilst the motorsport world was excited by his potential, the wins so far had all come at racetracks and series away from the eyes of F1. It definitely helps to be on the same billing as motorsport's blue riband series, and in 2006 Hamilton really grabbed the attention of the assembled teams and media. GP2 was the main support race to F1 at ten races and Lewis would be on the grid. It was only then that all the right people were in the same place as he was and could watch him in the flesh. He was accessible to all: they could go to his paddock and speak to him and he could visit teams in the F1 paddock. Crucially, the F1 bosses, journalists and TV channels were there for every race win, every overtake, and lauded him when he won the title.

After twenty-one races and five wins, he finished twelve points ahead of Nelson Piquet Junior in the championship. With the dominance that Hamilton has shown in F1, five wins, less than a quarter of the races, doesn't sound that impressive. But it was where, when and how he won which was crucial. Apart from Monaco, GP2 (now known as F2) had two races every weekend. He won both races in the third round at the Nürburgring in Germany. At the British Grand Prix, he dazzled the crowd with some incredible overtakes and every motorsport fan lucky enough to be in the grandstands watching will definitely remember the second of the two victories which came from eighth on the grid. Winning both those races in the manner in which he did was hugely important. He also dominated in Monaco after taking what was surprisingly his only pole position of the season. Hamilton started 2006 as a rookie in GP2 but finished the year as a signed F1 driver for McLaren. The first part of his dream had been realised.

During 2006, I was working in GP2 doing PR for a Northern Irish driver, Adam Carroll. I had presented the series on ITV the previous year and also when it was known as F3000. Because of Hamilton's much-anticipated arrival, ITV wanted to give the series more coverage and use the existing F1 team to present the programmes. It meant that I was surplus to requirements, which is never nice to hear, but I understood their thinking. None of their presenters or inter-viewers had worked with Hamilton before and they needed to build a relationship, especially if he was going to get to F1 and be as good as everyone thought. I got a call from Adam's management team sometime in the February when I was rethinking my plans for the year ahead. Adam was a driver on the up, having arrived in GP2 in 2005 with no pre-season testing and yet going on to win three races in Imola, Monaco and Spa. He was now linked to BAR Honda, and his management were ramping up the efforts around him. I was asked to suggest someone who could do his PR and travel to races with him that season. I provided a long list of names, and they came back asking me if I would do it! I hadn't put my name on the list as I hadn't done any PR before. We had a couple of meetings and, although I didn't have any formal PR training, I decided that, as Adam was a highly rated driver and a friend, I would give it a go!

The various series in the "lower ranks" of motorsport are always much more intimate than what you see in F1; much more like one big family. One large hospitality unit is shared by all the teams and mealtimes is a free-for-all with everyone grabbing their breakfast, lunch and dinner and mingling. Everyone sits together – mechanics, team owners, drivers, drivers' families, PRs and journalists – and it was a great way for everyone to get to know each other. Many of these people are now in F1, and our relationships and bonds are still there. Regardless of our jobs, we all had the same hopes and dreams and wanted to be successful at what we did.

Most weekends during 2006, I watched the races with Nicolas Hamilton, Lewis's brother. Families didn't really go into the pit lane. Sometimes we would stand at the back of a garage but usually we all just watched from the GP2 hospitality. At that time, Nic was in a wheelchair, so now when I see him walking towards me, I am incredibly proud of the work and effort he put in to get to where he is now. He also achieved his dream of becoming a racing driver and has been competing in the British Touring Car Championship. Back then, I remember running in the sweltering heat from the garage back into hospitality. Nic was sitting eating an ice lolly. I asked him where he got it, since I had never seen or been offered such treats in the teams' hospitality. He gave me one of his big smiles. "Lee, when you are in a wheelchair, you can get anything you want." Then he zoomed off and a few minutes later came back with one for me.

In those days, everyone was very much on a budget and the racing was expensive. To be able to compete, most teams needed money and therefore had to run drivers of differing quality or as close to a similar split in terms of driver ability as they could afford. For many teams, the pattern was that a more skilled driver would sign alongside a less talented driver and the driver with the most talent paid less money. So if a team needed $2 million the talented driver might pay $600,000 whilst the less talented driver paid the $1.4 million, basically subsidising the "better" driver. One of the exceptions was ART, which is owned by Nicolas Todt, son of former Ferrari and FIA boss Jean Todt, and Frédéric Vasseur, the now Alfa Romeo Team Principal. ART always ran two quality drivers, and that was who Hamilton drove for; as did Nico Rosberg, who was GP2 Champion the previous year.

As the drivers and their sponsors were paying so much to be racing on the same bill as Formula One, it meant that for most, everything else was done with the aim of spending as little money as possible, and that included travel. Normally, we all met at a painfully early time at Luton airport for a budget flight to whichever European race we were going to.

At one race, Adam, his trainer Karl and I were going to collect the hire car when a slightly lost-looking Lewis asked for a lift to the track. He either didn't have a hire car or his lift hadn't turned up or maybe he had always planned to blag a lift on landing. You would be surprised how often that happens with motorsport personnel as it is normally a packed flight with everyone heading to the track on arrival! On this occasion, we all squeezed in and off we went, singing LL Cool J and chatting about how hard it was to get into Formula One. That situation didn't last long for Hamilton! Gone are the days of budget flights and scrounging a lift from others – well, at least for Lewis. I can still be found doing both!

Lewis and I recently chatted about those early days and especially about the day that he turned up in the GP2 paddock as an "F1 driver". Lewis has always loved hip hop, and when he first arrived in motorsport he dressed like his hip-hop heroes. From his hair to his clothes, he a was a total reflection of everything he enjoyed and looked so comfortable in himself. But I will always remember the day he arrived as "an F1 driver". One day he turned up in the GP2 paddock looking like he had just signed for McLaren – which he had. The baggy jeans were gone, he was smartly dressed, not a braid in sight, hair shaved close. Everything was smart and neat and "safe".

When we were talking about this during an interview at the British Grand Prix in 2020, Lewis told me, "When I went for my first signing for McLaren, I remember Ron Dennis looking me up and down because I had baggy jeans and didn't necessarily have the smartest of outfits on. My dad always told me you have got to look and be a certain way and speak a certain way to get in. That was hard. I had to feel more uncomfortable because it wasn't necessarily me, but I would do anything to get to my dream, so if it meant dressing a different way for a short time until I got there then that was fine."

And it worked. He got there and, in March 2007, Lewis Hamilton arrived in Australia for his first ever F1 race. Alongside him for the season would be two-time world champion Fernando Alonso, who had just become the youngest back-to-back world champion. The Spaniard was, and over a decade on still is, widely regarded as one of the best drivers around, someone who can outperform a troubled car and compete from just about anywhere on the grid. Alonso was seen as the perfect driver for Hamilton to learn from. He was a natural team leader who knew all about the pressures of the F1 circus: ideal to help a wide-eyed twenty-two-year-old rookie. Well, that was the plan, but it certainly didn't last long! In fact, the master and apprentice concept only lasted until the first corner in Hamilton's first ever F1 race. It was 248 meters of calm before a raging storm.

Alonso was not meant to be outperformed by this "kid", and over the next few months, the relationship between the champion and the team went up in smoke with Hamilton as the touchpaper.

Lewis got his first pole position but also importantly his first F1 victory at the Canadian Grand Prix, a race also famous for a huge accident for Robert Kubica. As the chequered flag fell, James Allan said in his commentary for ITV, "If he can do this after six races, what might he achieve in the future? Surely the first of many for Lewis Hamilton."

How right James was. Just one week later, Hamilton repeated the pole and victory double at the USGP, the race where Sebastian Vettel made his debut replacing the injured Kubica at BMW.

By this point, there was trouble at Woking. Whilst McLaren were ecstatic at leading the Constructors' Championship and having their men at the top of the Drivers' Championship, they were contending with a furious Fernando, who wanted to see his name at the very top. Instead, he was trailing a rookie by ten points and the focus of the world's media was on Hamilton. There was only one number one in Alonso's mind, but McLaren wanted their drivers to race for the title and insisted there would be no favouritism. This is what every racing fan wanted to hear, but was this decision to the detriment of McLaren winning the Drivers' Championship? Without a doubt. Ferrari's Kimi Räikkönen went on to beat both McLaren drivers to become world champion by a single point. Räikkönen 110, Alonso and Hamilton 109.

It was a missed opportunity for Alonso, who was so close to joining the "greats" with a third title. For Hamilton, by finishing joint second in the championship, he had made his mark on the sport. Lewis was seen as the heir apparent. A rookie winning four Grand Prix and beating a multiple world champion meant that it took just twelve months to lose the "apparent" and get a hand on the throne, even if he wasn't quite holding the title.

With every turn of the wheel, every minute spent in the paddock, Hamilton was learning more, not just as a driver but as a person. The crucial mistake that cost him the 2007 title in his debut season was when he beached his car running into the gravel of the pit lane during the Chinese Grand Prix. Mathematically, he could have become champion that weekend, but instead he had his first retirement of the season. It was a huge error, and a costly one, from which he struggled to move on. We spoke about how he had changed over the years and he singled out that moment, saying that after the mistake, he stayed in his hotel room for several days, unable to bring himself to leave. Understanding how to handle the lows is something that Hamilton has worked on over the years. The ability to move on and not to dwell on misfortune is a crucial part of the winning mindset for any athlete and something he has learned through experience.

One year on and we had a more rounded Lewis. The "rookie" tag was gone and so were the errors, so as we neared the end of the 2008 season, he was once again in with a chance of the championship. I am a great believer that when you have been through something once in life, no matter what it is, you are better prepared for the next time. He had endured one full season of F1, visited new countries, discovered different racetracks, been grilled by the media four days every race weekend and come under scrutiny like never before. He had completed a full season, and so when he returned to places like Australia, China and Bahrain the following year, nothing was new and therefore he had more capacity for driving to the best of his abilities.

It had been announced very early that season that, for the first time in thirteen years, the BBC had won the rights to show Formula One from the following season. After several interviews that summer, I was thrilled to learn that I would be part of the team, but my first assignment actually came in 2008 at the Brazilian Grand Prix. What a race to make my BBC and, indeed F1, interviewing debut.

I was to be part of the BBC Radio 5 Live broadcast, standing in for Holly Samos, who was pregnant with her first child. I had never been to Brazil, so to turn up in that paddock, with so many subplots and stories, was both incredible and nerve-racking. Lewis Hamilton versus Felipe Massa for the title. David Coulthard's last race before retiring from the sport and Sebastian Vettel's last race for Toro Rosso before being promoted to Red Bull, taking Coulthard's seat.

First, though, we had to make it to the track – which, as anyone who has been to the Brazilian Grand Prix knows, can be an adventure in itself. There was me, my producer Jason Swales, who went on to mastermind the programmes you see on the F1 web platform, and David Croft, who was the Radio 5 commentator before he joined Sky Sports. Fuelled with coffee and excitement, we set off towards the circuit. The roads are wide, sometimes ten lanes wide with a central reservation, and very often it's total gridlock. It is a complicated journey and a road network comprised of a series of switchbacks and different levels of roads which spiral down from the sky to join each other. Frustratingly for us, we took a wrong turn but rather than add on the indeterminable amount of time it would take us to navigate our way back and possibly visit some less than favourable neighbourhoods, "Crofty" and I encouraged Jason to do a U-turn. Seconds later, we had sirens behind us, around us, on us and a gun in the window!

Was it reassuring that it was a member of the São Paulo Police pointing the gun? Not really, a gun is a gun. Despite Jason enunciating loudly and clearly, as British people abroad so often do, we were told to follow the police car. Jason's loud and slow "Bee Bee Cee" was holding no weight, despite his friendly Scottish accent. We explained to the police that we really needed to get to Interlagos, to the racetrack, and at that stage we certainly felt it was the safest place for us to head – neutral ground, as it were. We were told to drive behind the police; so, in nervous silence, we started to follow. Our concern only grew when the "policeman'" started waving in a sort of royal manner out the window at people on the pavement, who smiled and seemed to recognise him as he drove past – with us in tow. The Paulistas' excitement at seeing the gun-wielder only made us more worried – this didn't strike us as any ordinary copper.

In the car, our mantra had become: "Just get to the circuit. We have passes and will get directly through and be surrounded by people we know." The police, on the other hand would or should be stopped at the gates as they wouldn't have the correct accreditation and it would take a little time for them to explain their actions. The access to F1 is always very strict: a photographic, chipped pass around your neck, a vehicle pass on the windscreen with your name and company printed on it, and only then are you legit! Everyone else, regardless of who they are, will need to explain to security or get a pass into the circuit.

As we drove through the favela in the Interlagos neighbourhood which leads up the hill to the Autódromo José Carlos Pace, we got split up a couple of times by the constant heavy flow of traffic. *Perfect*, I thought in my silent panic. "Perfect!" shouted Crofty, who had started commentating on the journey. But no, the carro de policia waited for us every time the gap got too big, making sure we were still able to rejoin the convoy of doom. We turned off the road to the entrance of the track. This was it – it was time for us to make a break for freedom into the track as the police tried to explain themselves. To our horror, the men on the gates jumped to attention and waved the car and the mystery celebrity police officer straight in. We trailed behind. Forlorn.

We decided to end the misery and indicated right into the media parking and drew the van to a halt. As we parked up, the police circled round us. What on earth was going to happen? This was my first race for the BBC. I was wanting to make a good impression, have a strong debut weekend and ideally avoid prison! The policeman, who we had christened "Colonel Guido" for some unknown reason, pulled up behind us. The window went down, he nodded with a very serious look on his face and then . . . drove off.

We were astonished, relieved, exhausted. If it was a movie, it would be a really disappointing ending, but for us it was just a bizarre and welcome end to a hugely stressful morning. We mulled over what the whole point of it had been. Did he not believe we were accredited media? Was he trying to help us and give us safe passage to the track?

Either way, it was not a good start to the weekend, apart from the fact we remained unscathed. It transpired that everyone knew him because he was one of the highest-ranking men in the São Paulo police force. I had hoped to never again see Colonel Guido in my life, so you can imagine my horror when I met him on the grid before the race on the Sunday. He wasn't there working, he was there as one of the invited dignitaries! Crofty spotted him on camera and even gave Colonel Guido a name check in his pre-race build up. We couldn't explain to the listeners that Colonel Guido was a fictional name or exactly how we came to meet him!

In those days, Red Bull produced a magazine every day of the F1 weekend and in the Friday edition of the *Red Bulletin*, the hold-up and subsequent farce of the BBC Radio 5 Live crew became paddock knowledge!

In the years before I was working in F1, I had been in the paddock a lot and already knew plenty of people, but on that particular weekend it was going to be tricky to keep a low profile, which I was very keen to do. I was the new BBC girl, and working for the BBC brings a real pressure, and of course a level of respect – but there is also the expectation you are good. There would be no easing into the job, particularly not that weekend.

Heading into the final race, Hamilton was leading the Drivers' Championship, seven points ahead of local driver Felipe Massa. When I say local, I'm talking as local as one can get to the track. You will learn more about this story in Felipe's chapter, but in his teens, he once had to deliver food to one of the teams that was working late into the night. Many years later, at the same racetrack where he delivered food, Massa was in a battle to become a world champion.

A maximum of ten points were available for the final race, which meant that Massa could still win the title if Hamilton finished in sixth place or lower – otherwise Hamilton would be champion. If they finished tied on points, it would be Massa who would win the championship, as he had won more races throughout the year.

Sunday afternoon saw Massa line up in pole position while Hamilton was back in fourth, with Jarno Trulli in second and Kimi Räikkönen in third. Starting from fourteenth for his final F1 race was David Coulthard. I knew David but, at that time, it was my father that he was good friends with. The same day as the police incident, having made it safely to the track, I was with my dad in the press room when his phone rang. It was DC who wondered if Dad would wear the Coulthard kilt and stand beside the car on the grid. What an odd day this was turning out to be. And come the Sunday, it was just another random thing for me to contend with on my first ever F1 grid. Firstly, bumping into Colonel Guido, thankfully without his gun, and then trying to get an interview with a retiring thirteen-time race winner whilst my father was standing alongside proudly wearing DC's kilt! Surely the race would seem pretty simple after all of this!

The rain fell and the tension grew. The energy always feels electric at the Brazilian Grand Prix, and it really was palpable up and down the paddock. This was a huge day and I needed to get as good a view of everything as I could. I found an empty garage, sat on top of a freight box and had a great view of the pit lane. Being able to watch a race like that hasn't happened since and certainly doesn't happen now. When I think about it, maybe it shouldn't have happened then, but I wasn't really across the rules then! As soon as the chequered flag fell, I leapt off the box, ran down the pit lane and tried to get into the garages to get the driver interviews, but the story was changing by the second.

The pictures broadcast that day say it all. It was the realisation of a dream for Felipe Massa quickly followed by pain and heartbreak. Felipe had won the race but he was then told that Hamilton had crossed the line . . . in fifth. Felipe Massa was not the world champion, and in fact never would be. Live on television with a camera in his face, the fairy tale had become a nightmare and it was Hamilton who made history. The thought of it still gives me goosebumps to this day, even as I am sitting here writing this. For me, it is the ultimate sporting moment; elation, despair, every dream, every turn of a wheel, every bead of sweat since childhood and all directed at one thing. On that day, it came down to a winner and a loser but it was so, so much more than that.

The BBC team assembled in 2009, ready for the season ahead. Jake Humphrey was the main presenter, with David Coulthard, Eddie Jordan and Martin Brundle as pundits, Jonathan Legard would commentate with Ted Kravitz and myself reporting and interviewing.

It felt a very good time to be starting this new venture; F1 on the BBC with a British world champion in Lewis Hamilton.

All the F1 teams had been very supportive of the BBC's arrival, and whilst very respectful of everything that ITV had done for the sport, we felt ready to try and take things to a new level. Without being arrogant, that's just what happens when any new channel arrives in a sport. I arrived in Australia and didn't feel too much like the new girl. I knew a lot more people and drivers than some on the team and that was a huge help. The Australian race build-up went well. In what would become an incredible season, it was Jenson Button in his brand-new Brawn car who stole the show. Hamilton had been involved in a "mix-up" on track with Jarno Trulli.

That innocent sounding "mix-up" became known as "lie-gate" and cost some of the best F1 brains their jobs. It was discovered they had misled the stewards after allowing Jarno Trulli to re-pass the McLaren behind the safety car. The initial incident wasn't the problem, but the "lying" was. The World Motorsport Council found McLaren guilty on five counts of breaching the International Sporting Code. One of the most respected figures at McLaren, Sporting Director Dave Ryan, was sacked and Lewis Hamilton disqualified from the race.

As a driver seen to be at the start of great things, Hamilton instead found himself in a press conference at only the second race of the 2009 season, glassy-eyed, holding back tears and defending his integrity to TV cameras and journalists.

"I am not a liar or a dishonest person, I am a team player. If the team ask me to do something, I generally do it. But I felt awkward and uncomfortable.

"When I went into the meeting, I had no intention of lying. I just wanted to tell my story and see what happened. I was misled and that's just how it went.

"I sincerely apologise to the race stewards for wasting their time and making them look silly," said Hamilton.

What a start to the season. Add in that the McLaren was not as competitive as it had been and the fact that there was another Brit about to become the darling of world motorsport, Hamilton was having his own version of a fairy tale becoming a nightmare. We hadn't seen Lewis tested like this before. Until 2009, he had always seemed in control, basking in the love and attention that performances good enough to wow a sport brings. There was no doubt, the honeymoon was over.

After winning his title, Hamilton had four more long and lean years at McLaren in comparison to the first two. Teammates came and went in the shape of Heikki Kovalainen, who was replaced in 2010 by the then world champion Jenson Button. McLaren had become an all-British team, with two world champions behind the wheel, but sadly for them it was a car which couldn't stop the Sebastian Vettel and Adrian Newey dream team from winning four titles in a row for Red Bull Racing.

Heading into the final round of 2010, there were four drivers all with a shot at winning the championship. Ferrari's Fernando Alonso was leading with 246 points. Red Bull's Mark Webber and Sebastian Vettel were second and third on 238 points and 231 points respectively, and Hamilton was fourth. Mathematically, it was possible, but twenty-four points behind Alonso with a maximum of twenty-five on offer would be a big ask.

Despite finishing second in the Abu Dhabi finale, the cards didn't fall right, and Hamilton finished fourth in the championship. Sebastian Vettel became the youngest World Champion in Formula One history and led the championship for the first time after the chequered flag fell on the final race of the season.

For Hamilton, these felt like troubled times. In interviews he was emotional, sometimes sulky and it felt like he was struggling, treading water. To start his F1 career with such promise and to suddenly have a car not capable of competing for titles was tough. But he wasn't the first driver to be in that situation and he certainly wouldn't be the last.

Everything he knew, loved and had become accustomed to seemed to be changing. At the races, we were used to seeing Anthony Hamilton, his father, almost as often as Lewis, such was his part in his son's success story. Then came a very public split. It seemed being a father and manager was a difficult line to tread. Anthony had managed and moulded Lewis from being a childhood karter into an F1 champion. He had sacrificed a lot to help Lewis, holding down several jobs whilst still managing to be at every one of his son's kart races. Knowing Anthony, you see where Lewis gets his determination from. The pressure of the business relationship and family one must have been stifling. The fame of being a "Hamilton" wasn't just surrounding Lewis, but the whole family too. By the end of 2010 Lewis and Anthony had parted ways and were barely on speaking terms for several years.

Thankfully, that relationship has been repaired, and at the start of 2020 Lewis wrote on social media:

> Our journey hasn't been an easy one. Over time, we lost that father-son bond, and it has been something we have both wanted back for so long. The past couple years we've been growing closer, and this winter break I asked my dad to come visit me so we could spend some time together, just us. We haven't done this before, so to finally get to spend quality time with him has brought me so much happiness. Family is the most important thing in the world. You can't choose your family, but you can make it work with them no matter what your differences. They are the ones that will be there when you have nothing.

The healing of that relationship has been ten years in the making, but it is heart-warming to see that father and son, Anthony and Lewis, have their place once again.

Also in 2010, Lewis split (for the first time) with his pop star girlfriend Nicole Scherzinger, who was also a regular in the F1 paddock. It did become somewhat of an on-off relationship and there were times it visibly took its toll on the driver. At that point you felt that Lewis was not just wearing his heart on his sleeve but living out every emotion in public, something which he is certainly more guarded about now. I recall a tearful interview with him in the drivers' pen after qualifying in Korea. There were plenty of others around whilst this was happening, so much so that Jenson Button came over and asked me what on earth I'd done to reduce Lewis to tears. "Not guilty!" was my response. His emotions were not about my interview, less about his driving and more about what was happening in his life at the time.

On track, things weren't much better, and 2011 was the first time that Lewis was beaten by a teammate in the championship standings. Both he and Button scored three victories, but whilst Vettel claimed his second title, Button finished second in the championship with Hamilton in a lowly fifth place.

As a journalist, it is always good when your stories make the headlines, but you should never want to *be* in the headlines. I found myself exactly in that position after my interview for the BBC with Lewis at the end of the Monaco GP in 2011.

It was a forgettable race for Hamilton. He started from ninth but during the race he was penalised for causing two avoidable accidents. First, he received a drive-through after an incident saw Felipe Massa crash in the tunnel, and for the next one, involving Pastor Maldonado, he received a post-race twenty-second penalty. It didn't affect his sixth place at the chequered flag, but it certainly hadn't been a good race, to put it mildly.

Punchy interviews with Lewis were becoming the norm, and when he came into the post-race interview pen and walked directly towards me, he was still running on adrenaline and there had been no time to decompress.

Me: "Lewis, two penalties today . . ."

LH: "It's a frickin' joke, I've been to see the stewards five times out of six this season."

Me: "Why do you think you are such a magnet for the stewards just now?"

LH, laughing: "I don't know, maybe it's 'cause I'm Black. That's what Ali G says."

It was a joke. A joke with an edge. These were the days when you sometimes wanted to save Lewis from himself as you could see how it would play out in the newspapers. I kept the interview going for another few minutes and he spoke well about the race, a mistake in the pit stop, his championship chances but there was only one sentence that anybody would care about.

After talking to me, Lewis then had to go back into the stewards to explain his comments to me. They didn't charge him with disrepute, but there was a decent discussion between both parties.

Ten seconds in a really strong and emotionally charged three-minute interview and yet it was the five words "maybe it's 'cause I'm Black" which made headlines around the world. I was staying in Monaco after the race for a few days' holiday and, for maybe the only time in my life, I decided not to look at my phone or social media. On the Wednesday after the race, I switched on my phone and received a huge shock. I was met with a barrage of messages and emails including death threats from Hamilton fans for "being calculated"; for "making Lewis say it"; for "making Lewis get bad press"; and everything else you could imagine. It all seemed very serious, and I called the BBC straight away. This needed to be dealt with.

I already knew that things were tricky by the Sunday night after the race. The race steward who had given the two penalties was my good friend and fellow Scot, Allan McNish. Not only is he a great guy but an ex-F1 driver, sports car world champion and three-time Le Mans winner, so he is more qualified than most to be a steward. I was actually waiting to hear from Paul and Laura Di Resta as the Sunday night after the Monaco GP normally involves a pretty reasonable night out. I messaged them both but got no response, which was unusual. I went to the hotel bar to see if there was anyone I knew. There, sitting alone, was Allan. I joined him and we both had a quite miserable drink together and talked about the race.

Eventually I said that I was looking for the Di Restas. "They are in the restaurant, go and say hi," Allan said. I walked round the corner and there in front of me was a big table of people, including Anthony Hamilton, who was at that time managing Paul. The pieces of the puzzle all started to fit in regarding the lack of comms about the night ahead.

Anthony just looked at me and said, "Did you really need to ask that question, Lee?"

I replied, "I cannot control how someone answers a question Anthony, you know that."

And that was it.

There was frustration but also respect, and the situation had been dealt with. We moved on, had a couple of drinks and all had a good night out – apart from Allan, who I think stayed in the bar himself. A steward's life isn't always a fun one! Allan and I still joke about that weekend now, although I do think he is still relatively trauma-tised by the whole experience.

After the realisation that I had become embroiled in a much bigger story, it started to play on my mind. What happened if Lewis blamed me for the fallout in the media? It was a long season and a difficult career ahead if a world champion took against you. I decided to compose a letter and explain my actions, something which I have only felt the need to do twice in my career, to date.

I certainly didn't apologise for my questioning as I hadn't done anything wrong or asked anything that I thought was incorrect. I did say that I was sorry if the interview had put him in a difficult situa-tion and was causing upset. I also said that whilst many websites and people online were pitching us against each other, it seemed that we were both getting equal abuse from opposing parties. I finished by saying, "No need to reply. See you next week in Canada." I sent it off to Anthony and asked him if he could forward it to his son.

A week a later, I went to a track in Canada to do a filming day with Sebastian Vettel. When we reached the end of filming Seb said, "I heard what happened with Lewis. Don't think for a minute any of it was your fault. You are good at what you do."

It was a lovely and unprompted endorsement from someone whose opinions I respect, and I felt a little less nervous as I headed into the paddock the following day.

Standing at the interview pen on the Thursday and waiting for the FIA press conference to finish, I was nervous. I had never been in a situation like this before and, to be honest, whilst Lewis had always been very fair, you never know who has said what behind the scenes, and it often doesn't take much for a driver or athlete to turn against someone for "getting them in to a difficult situation". There were a lot of people asking me "have you spoken to him since", "do you think he'll be okay with you" or "do you think he will talk to you". I was brushing it all off, but behind the smile I was getting increasingly stressed. The six drivers came out the press conference and down into the interview pen. Lewis looked around and came straight up to me.

He gave me a big hug, something he hasn't done before or since, and just said, "Hey, how are you? Good to see you."

Sigh of relief.

I thought, *Great! We go again!*

By 2012, things between Lewis and McLaren seemed shaky. In both 2010 and 2011 he had finished fourth and fifth in the championship respectively. He'd been beaten by a teammate for the first time in 2011 and by the summer break in 2012, Hamilton had won only two out of eleven races. It had been an incredibly competitive season with seven different winners in the first seven races of the season, the only time that has happened in the history of the sport. But for a driver like Hamilton, watching others enjoying the success which he craved and had previously enjoyed, it was like torture. In 2007 he had arrived as the huge star and the one to beat. By 2012 it was Sebastian Vettel who had become one of the most successful drivers of all time and was heading towards his third world title.

Lewis won the last race heading into the summer break, so when we returned in Spa, which is always a great place to get back to after a few weeks relaxing, we expected a calm and recharged version of him. That was certainly not the case.

In qualifying, the McLaren drivers were using different rear wings. Jenson Button took pole whilst Hamilton ended up in seventh; eight-tenths of a second slower. But it was what happened after qualifying that caused the storm. I was just doing my usual, walking about in the paddock, talking to teams and drivers so I could get some new information to write my "story of qualifying" feature for the race day TV show. I glanced at Twitter on my phone and could not believe what I saw. Without telling the team or his teammate, Hamilton had posted a picture of confidential telemetry from his and Jenson Button's cars. To most of us, it was a page of squiggles. To other teams it was an insight at most, and at the very least a laugh at McLaren's expense. How on earth could a driver think this was an acceptable thing to do and not have repercussions from the team?

McLaren said the tweet had not done much damage, but Button said he was "disappointed" and that it went against the work the team does to improve the car and keep developments private. It was an extraordinary attempt for a world champion to justify himself and prove there was a reason for his lack of pace in comparison to his teammate. It was all about the need for validation.

As Button said to the BBC, "The bit about him losing sixth-tenths on the straights isn't the bit that's important to me, because he should be gaining it back in the corners, he's got more downforce on. And I was eight-tenths of a second quicker in qualifying anyway."

The great thing about coming back to work after the summer break is that we hit two great racetracks, two of my favourite race-tracks, back to back. From the forests of Spa-Francorchamps, we head to Monza in Italy, where the normal story to tell is all things Ferrari, Tifosi, passionata! Not in 2012.

When we arrived in Monza, just outside Milan, my BBC colleague, former team owner, friend and super spy Eddie Jordan was adamant that "McLaren's Lewis Hamilton" was about to become "Mercedes' Lewis Hamilton".

If correct, it was a huge coup for both Mercedes and EJ: the onus being on "if correct". After a lot of discussion between my boss, David Coulthard and others, we decided that Eddie was in the know. He announced it on our BBC coverage and Eddie's "informed" rumour became global news. We led with it on all our programmes, praying and hoping that he was correct. McLaren were furious with not only EJ but also the BBC for running what they claimed, and maybe believed, were untrue rumours.

At that stage, McLaren were still in negotiations with their last world champion and were expecting him to stay. They were, after all, the team who not only brought him to F1, but also paved and *paid* the way for him throughout the junior formulae.

Mercedes were also annoyed with EJ for throwing a massive curve ball their way and disrupting what should have been a straightforward weekend for their drivers, Michael Schumacher and Nico Rosberg.

You see when one driver is rumoured to be joining a team it means someone is going to lose their seat and what it meant for Mercedes was that they too became the focus of every journalist in Monza. Every press conference became, "Is Michael retiring for a second time?" or

"Rosberg has a contract but what about Hamilton joining?" and "Imagine a Schumacher and Hamilton dream team." In short, we had pissed-off teams, pissed-off drivers, an ecstatic EJ and a nervous BBC!

One pebble in the rumour pond always causes plenty of ripples. In this case it was becoming a tsunami. Eddie was adamant – and he needed to be, as he was taking a reasonable amount of abuse from both teams, but especially from McLaren. Ron Dennis and the communications team were incensed. You can understand why: if they truly believed that they were keeping their star then this was a huge blow. There had been plenty of comment and discussion about whether Hamilton would join another team, but it had always been Red Bull or Ferrari who were mentioned. Jordan cited both finances and the opportunity to work with Mercedes, a huge global brand, as the major appeal.

Despite protestations from all sides in Monza, on Friday, 28 September 2012, it was announced that Hamilton would join Mercedes on a three-year deal. Hamilton, now twenty-seven years old, was heading to a team based on future potential. A risk worth taking and, in hindsight, a perfectly timed move.

For McLaren, it was a huge blow to lose the talents of Hamilton, someone they had nurtured and worked with since he was in his early teens. But as the then Vice-President of Mercedes, Norbert Haug, pointed out, "Mercedes-Benz has supported Lewis throughout his career, from karting to Formula 3, to our successful partnership with McLaren." This was being pushed as not a totally new story but simply a new chapter, that Mercedes had always been part of Lewis's career. That is fact.

It also meant that, after a disappointing comeback, the seven-time world champion Michael Schumacher was out. Rosberg was never going anywhere, and it was in 2013 that the now infamous pairing became teammates in F1.

I don't remember a collective sigh of relief from the BBC and a round of applause for Eddie Jordan, but there must have been one. It was an unbelievable scoop from EJ, and one that he still likes talking about now!

Whilst it was being heralded as a deal for big things in the future, Hamilton's first year with Mercedes driving the F1 W04 was not great. During the hard times, he was able to cling on to the fact that his catalyst for changing team was for what might come in 2014 with a revamp in the sporting regulations. Potential was the antidote for the present.

Hamilton got his first win for the team at the Hungarian Grand Prix. It had looked like he might win in front of his home crowd at the previous race, but whilst leading from pole, a tyre blow-out brought an end to those chances. It was his teammate Nico Rosberg who took the win, his second of the season after winning his home race in Monaco. A couple of weeks later, Lewis got his victory, his first for Mercedes, and whilst it wasn't the same as winning a home Grand Prix, getting a much-hyped win for his new team before the summer break was some compensation.

In 2014 one of the biggest set of rules changes in the history of the sport were introduced. Due to development going right down to the wire, many cars were unveiled early morning in the paddock in Jerez at pre-season testing. I, along with an assembled group of journalists, were all wrapped up in winter coats, our breaths hanging in the cold air, as we waited for the big reveals. Oddly, many of the reveals were back-to-back before testing started with the first at around 7.30 a.m. in the paddock. It meant journalists and camera crews congregated outside a team garage in the pit lane, watched a sheet being pulled from the hopeful charger by the drivers before we all sprinted to the next team to see the same again whilst shouting, "Wow, did you see the detail on the front wing on the . . ."

Whilst everyone knew that new regulations would likely bring about opportunity for a reshuffle, no-one could foresee the cataclysmic changes to the overall pecking order in F1. Since 2010, Formula One had been the Red Bull and Vettel show and, although we didn't know it then, those days were over.

The biggest changes were to the engines which moved from naturally aspirated V8's to hybrid V6 turbos with ERS and KERS and a whole load of energy recovery systems that would also lead to much less reliability until teams and engine suppliers could get some mileage into them. The cars would also look very different after a revamp to certain areas, especially to the nose, which had been lowered for safety reasons.

The big question, though, was which team had got to grips with the rule changes quickest? Halfway through the season the answer was clear. It was Mercedes. Incredibly and to the shock of Red Bull, who had won both championships for the last four years, Mercedes won nine of the first ten races, but it hadn't looked quite so clear-cut at the first race in Australia.

On the Saturday, in pouring rain, Hamilton took the first pole position of the new era, and whilst Mercedes were still smiling twenty-four hours later on the Sunday night, it wasn't on Hamilton's side of the garage. His engine lost a cylinder at the start and he only managed two laps before retiring. It was his teammate Nico Rosberg who went on to win the race, finishing twenty-five seconds ahead of Red Bull's Daniel Ricciardo in second (who was subsequently disqualified after the race). It was frustration for Hamilton, but Mercedes had proved they had a winning package – when everything went right!

Hamilton didn't have to wait long for his victory. Just one week later in the tropical heat of Malaysia, he dominated all weekend with pole position, fastest lap and the race win. Two wins in two races, the Silver Arrows were back in business.

Onwards, the F1 power train rolled to Bahrain, but when we arrived in the desert, little did we know that we would be treated to one of the best Formula One races for many, many years.

Bahrain has always been an odd race to go to – never a classic and, despite the nice working conditions, it has never been a favourite destination in terms of a race. Don't get me wrong, I actually have always enjoyed going there and we are always looked after very well. The F1 paddock is picturesque, but the track had become a bit of a snooze-fest. This, though, was to be the first Bahrain Grand Prix held in the evening after the organisers spent over £10 million on floodlights with the hope of turning what was often a dull day race into a night-time spectacle. Oh my, it was certainly that. Rosberg started from pole with Hamilton alongside and the battle that ensued for over fifty laps was breathtaking.

The lead switched back and forth between the two drivers. The Silver Arrows went wheel to wheel as they pierced through what would have been the desert darkness had it not been for the stadium lighting, which gave it an electric, tense atmosphere. Sparks flew, brakes glowed, but ultimately it was Hamilton who saw the chequered flag first. A classic race, with respectful, clean racing which made front-page news and was a shot in the arm for the sport. The fans were in raptures and there was a huge amount of excitement about what was still to come. Whilst it was early days, the championship looked like it would be hard-fought between Hamilton and Rosberg. The last time the two friends battled against each other for a title was in go-karts as teens.

Heading into the summer break, Hamilton trailed Rosberg by eleven points in the championship, but during the Hungarian GP that was eventually won by Daniel Ricciardo, Hamilton ignored team orders to let Rosberg past, saying, "I'm not slowing down for Nico. If he gets close enough to overtake, he can overtake me."

The two were on different strategies, yet Hamilton knew he was racing his teammate not only for the race, but for the title and that, ultimately, every point would matter. In the interview with me afterwards, Lewis was calm and looked assured in his decision. He was keen to get away to relax on holiday, decompress and recharge after a tense few months. Nico, on the other hand, was annoyed. It felt like for both drivers, a line had been drawn. Nico would say the line had been crossed.

The Belgian Grand Prix after the summer break was the game changer between the two teammates. Whilst racing, the two touched. Hamilton's left rear tyre was punctured by Rosberg's front right wing endplate. Hamilton re-joined the race in nineteenth but eventually retired.

After the race I interviewed all parties. Lewis said Nico had crashed into him "to prove a point" whilst Rosberg told me it was just a racing incident and that he would have the backing of the team. I had to break it to him that we had just interviewed a furious Niki Lauda who called it "ridiculous", and Toto Wolff hadn't held back in his criticism of the "absolutely unacceptable situation" either. Rosberg hadn't seen any of the team yet, so I felt at least I had given fair warning before he saw them! These moments are always quite nerve-racking. It's important to get the tone right, be respectful and ask the questions that they most probably won't want to answer.

After the race, I had to go into the hospitality to see someone before I left the track. Only a few friends and family from both sides were there along with some team members, but the atmosphere was awful, and I didn't even wait to see my friend. Sometimes you just know when to leave! The stewards called it a "racing incident" but Mercedes summoned both drivers to a meeting before the next race. Bizarrely, we were told that Rosberg had been given an undisclosed punishment in the "clear the air meeting" and afterwards he publicly took responsibility for the incident, calling it an "error of judgement." The great news for fans was that Mercedes were letting their drivers race on!

Hindsight shows that 2014 was not the year where the relationship between Hamilton and Rosberg was at its worst, but after the Belgian Grand Prix it was hard to believe it could get much more complex. At the Italian Grand Prix just one week later, Rosberg was leading but locked up his brakes and had to dive down the escape road. That led to Hamilton taking the lead. Innocuous enough, you would think, but very quickly on social media and also from respected drivers, world champions like Sir Jackie Stewart, conspiracy theories came to the fore. Was this the undisclosed punishment for Rosberg? Either way, Hamilton was still second in the championship and he needed to close the gap.

Normally that is easier said than done but Hamilton entered a period of total domination winning the next four races: Singapore, Japan, Russia and the US Grand Prix in Austin. It was Singapore where Hamilton regained control of the title race and after that the wins just kept on coming.

Rosberg won the penultimate race of the season in Brazil, keeping his championship hopes alive, but the finale in Abu Dhabi was yet another first for F1. Bernie Ecclestone had come up with the idea of awarding double points for the last race to try and prevent a driver winning the championship so early on in the season, as had been the case on a couple of occasions with Sebastian Vettel. This was unpopular with teams, drivers and F1 fans, who felt it was manipulation.

But as happened so often, like it or not, Bernie's plan worked. It also meant that heading into the final race there was still some jeopardy. Hamilton needed to finish in the top two to guarantee he would be world champion – under the normal points structure he would have only needed to finish sixth to guarantee the title.

In the dusk of Abu Dhabi, Rosberg started from pole with Hamilton alongside him on the front row of the grid in second. Hamilton swept past Rosberg heading into turn 1, but it was on lap 23 when Rosberg's troubles began. He came on the car-to-pit radio reporting a loss of power. Mercedes asked him to retire the car, but Rosberg said pleadingly that he would like to finish the race, which he did in fourteenth place. Nico had never been as close to a championship in F1. His time would come.

Lewis Hamilton was once again world champion, six years after his last. The move to Mercedes had paid off. The risk of joining a team who had not won a title in modern day F1, the chance to help mould and shape a team around him had worked. So much of sport is a balance of risk and reward. The risk had been big, the reward was handsome.

2015 was the most straightforward year that Lewis had experienced in his F1 career, up until that point. By the time we reached the European leg of the championship he had scored ninety-three of a possible one hundred points and was firmly in control. He secured his third title at the US Grand Prix with three races remaining. I was asked to do the official interview with Lewis inside his drivers' room a couple of hours after the end of the race. I will always remember just how calm he was. His first title in 2008 was won in total drama with Massa thinking he had won championship. His second had also gone down the wire with the added complication of double points. This time he had been in control throughout. With eleven pole positions and ten wins, he had retained his crown. Interviews with drivers in their private rooms don't happen that often, maybe after a big race win or a championship victory, and they are always really intimate and slightly surreal. A driver's room at a fly away race like Austin is basically four square metres with a massage bed, a chair, a few race suits hanging up and that is it. Lewis returned to his room, and I was there waiting. There was no chance at that stage that anything had really sunk in and yet, with such domination throughout 2015, he must have seen it coming.

What we didn't see coming was what happened in the rest of the season. For the remaining three races of 2015 it seemed like he had checked out. The title had been won and his work was done. That let Rosberg go on to win the final three races and, in my opinion, gave the German driver the motivation, insight and determination he needed for his title campaign in 2016.

At the end of each year, the BBC produced an end of season review programme. It was always a stressful hour where you sit down with a driver and go through their entire season, highlights and lowlights, and if the driver isn't engaged or says they can't remember, which often happens, then it is not much fun for anyone! Try doing it with twenty drivers and normally only a couple of happy ones. I loved it and loathed it at the same time! The amount of prep it took was hours for each interview and sometimes, depending on the answers, only a couple of minutes might be used.

In 2015 I spoke to Lewis in the hotel in São Paulo where he was staying for the Brazilian GP. It had been a straightforward season, so I was expecting a straightforward chat – and it was, until I mentioned the Hungarian GP. Lewis had qualified on pole but went on to finish sixth. It was a scrappy race littered with uncharacteristic errors, which is exactly how I phrased it to him.

He replied, "This is how the Sunday went. It was a really cool Sunday, actually, until the race started."

This already had me interested because for most drivers, the only thing, the sole reason for Sunday was the race!

"The night before I was invited by Ridley Scott. He said come by the shoot in the morning and I was like 'yes', 'cause he was filming with Matt Damon, the last scene of *The Martian*. So I went to bed, tossing and turning, and I didn't sleep until maybe one o'clock and I woke up at 4 a.m. and then the time came at eight o'clock or whatever it was to leave the hotel. I went to meet Ridley and at the time they were set up for this last scene. He said, 'Matt hasn't come on yet, so why don't you sit where he is and act out his role.' So you know I'm getting nervous . . ."

At this point Lewis is laughing and I could see how excited he still was about the thought of being on set.

"This is Ridley Scott asking me to sit and act, and I don't know what the hell I am supposed to do, and finally Matt came, and I sat with Ridley and he's saying 'action', and just honestly, I couldn't believe it.

"So I left there. Went to the track and I'm on this high for a minute, and then I started doing engineering and I started hitting the wall and I wasn't able to take a nap either. So I got in the car and those first couple of laps to the grid felt terrible and I was like, this is not good, and I knew it!

"I have now told you a story that I should have put in my book one day!"

We both laughed but really it was an incredible story of misspent energy that definitely cost him a race win. Did it matter in the championship? No. Will it give Lewis a great memory? Yes. Only he knows whether it was worth it.

As the world watched him mess up the start of the race, then cut the chicane and drop to tenth, then collide with Daniel Ricciardo at the safety car restart before being given a drive-through penalty, no one would have considered that the bad day at the office was because of *The Martian*!

There are some seasons that stand out as classics; maybe not always for the racing but definitely for the rivalries, and 2016 was one of those.

Rosberg carried that winning momentum from the end of the 2015 season into the start of the following one. He won the first four races: Australia, Bahrain, China and Russia. Since the 2014 Spa incident, the duo managed to keep out of each other's car space, that was until the Spanish Grand Prix.

There was a lot at stake – points, pride, and especially for Hamilton. He claimed pole position three-tenths of a second quicker than Rosberg, but it was the German who was forty-three points ahead in the championship.

We always go to Spain thinking it is going to be one the duller Grand Prix, not because of the track layout, but there is no track in the world that we have all spent more time at, whether it be in junior formulae or pre-season testing. The teams and drivers have literally done thousands of kilometres so there is rarely unexpected drama – unless of course something goes wrong.

In 2016 we watched the start with the normal excitement. Rosberg made an excellent start passing Hamilton for the lead. The world champion tried to get his place back but in doing so went on the grass and came across the track and into the side of Rosberg. The stewards didn't take any action and Mercedes team boss Toto Wolff said it wasn't clear cut, but his Mercedes colleague and three-time world champion Niki Lauda blamed Hamilton for the incident.

That day also marked the arrival of Max Verstappen, who won the race making his debut for Red Bull. But the story of Spain set the tone for the season, the rivalry between the Mercedes drivers became nothing but contemptuous after Barcelona.

In the seven races up until the summer break, Hamilton won six with Rosberg only claiming the European Grand Prix in Azerbaijan. Even those races didn't go without controversy and on the last lap of the Austrian Grand Prix, once again the teammates came together whilst Hamilton was passing Rosberg for the lead. Hamilton went on to win the race with Rosberg going from first to fourth.

After the race, the stewards gave Rosberg a ten-second time penalty, but as he was ahead of Ricciardo by fourteen seconds, it didn't affect his result and he retained his lead in the Drivers' Championship. Hamilton, though, had closed the gap to eleven points.

Unlike Spain, Wolff was uncompromising, calling it "brainless" and saying that after two crashes in five races, he would stop the drivers from racing should it happen again. This wasn't something race fans or indeed interviewers wanted. Those moments after a race or even a crash are the closest we get to seeing the honest emotions in the heat of the battle. Some can hide it well. Others want their opinions to be heard, and in this particular year the fight was as much psychological as it was on the track, and neither driver was holding back.

After his victory at his home race at Silverstone, Hamilton trailed Rosberg by just one point and at the next race in Hungary, he took the lead in the championship for the first time that season. But it wouldn't last long. After the summer break, Rosberg won an incredible four of five races with Daniel Ricciardo winning the other. By that point, the relationship between the two Mercedes drivers was in pieces. Unlike the start of the season where they would happily sledge or blame each other, as the climax of the season got closer, they took the opposite approach in interviews and simply refused to discuss each other. Rosberg went round the houses to avoid saying Lewis or Hamilton, calling him "my team-mate" or "him." Hamilton also went down the "he" or "him" route, often with an accompanying shoulder shrug. The friendship they had enjoyed since childhood had been put aside in the name of world domination.

The Malaysian Grand Prix was a defining moment in the championship. It looked like it was Rosberg who would be most compromised as he was spun around at the start by Sebastian Vettel's Ferrari. He worked his way back up to third whilst Hamilton pulled away at the front. But sixteen laps from the end Hamilton's car was burning. Who can forget the images of the flames coming out the back of his car, Hamilton with his head in hands and the despair on team radio as he begged, "No, no, no." Engine gone, points gone and the championship a little more distant.

In his interview with me after the race, Hamilton alluded to the fact that, out of all the teams on the grid using Mercedes engines, he was the only one who had experienced engine failures that year, saying, "It doesn't sit right for me." I was surprised at the time that he would say such a thing; it alluded to conspiracy. That's exactly what exploded not only on social media, but in the paddock too. What was clear in interviews with Hamilton during 2016 was that he did not think he was getting equal treatment to Rosberg.

Rosberg won in Japan and after that it was a Mercedes 1–2 for the next three races. In the USA, Mexico and Brazil, Hamilton beat Rosberg to the line, which meant we were heading into another Abu Dhabi showdown.

There is no better feeling working in sport and knowing you are going to be there for a historic moment. Whatever happened, it was going to be the culmination of a classic season and a rivalry for the ages. Rosberg started the weekend with a twelve-point lead over Hamilton. Thankfully, there were no double points – that was a one-season wonder – but the permutations for the championship seemed endless depending on who finished where. However, there was one clear headline: Rosberg would become champion if he finished on the podium. With Mercedes domination throughout the season, it would need some amount of bad luck or a reliability issue for that not to happen, but as we had seen, there were weaknesses. You only need to speak to Lewis to confirm that.

Hamilton started from pole and Rosberg was understandably cautious, not wanting to go for a big move at the start. During the race, Hamilton, in control at the front, started to reduce his pace whilst keeping a big enough distance so that his teammate couldn't overtake him. It meant that Rosberg was being backed up into the clutches of a hard-pushing Vettel and Verstappen. The team asked Hamilton to increase his speed and therefore take Rosberg "out of danger" but he rebuffed those suggestions.

After the first request on lap 47 he said, "I suggest you guys let us race", but the then Technical Director Paddy Lowe came on team radio: "Lewis, we need you to pick up the pace to let us race, that is an instruction."

The reply came: "Paddy, I am actually in the lead right now and quite comfortable."

For any fan these are goosebump moments: live insights into the minds of champions. These situations and discussions whilst under vast amounts of pressure and driving at outrageous speeds could and would define the careers of people, both on and off the pit wall.

Mercedes are packed out with incredibly smart people, but it did seem naive that a driver battling for the title would not use tactics to prevent his teammate from winning. For Lewis, though, it wasn't to be enough and, whilst he won the race, Rosberg was second and, with it, world champion.

In my interview for Channel 4 after the race, Hamilton said to me, "What am I supposed to do, just sit there and let the dude win the championship? I had to try and help myself because no one else was going to. Providing in the following years we are given equal cars then there are more championships to win."

I then said, "Do you feel at the end of it all you were given equal opportunity and, on this occasion, Nico Rosberg, the better man won?"

Lewis laughed. "Erm, I don't agree with that necessarily, but I guess I will leave that to your imagination."

A couple of weeks later Nico Rosberg announced he would be retiring from the sport with immediate effect. For him, it was dream realised. Job done.

After that, it all seemed plain sailing. Hamilton won the next three championships with ease. In 2017 and 2018 he won at the Mexican Grand Prix as Sebastian Vettel couldn't finish high enough in his Ferrari to take the fight further.

In 2019 the only driver he was in a battle with was his teammate Valtteri Bottas and even then, you felt the only man that could stop Hamilton was himself. Mercedes picked up their sixth consecutive Constructors' title at the Japanese Grand Prix and just two races later at the US Grand Prix, Hamilton became a six-time world champion with only Michael Schumacher ahead of him in terms of most championships won.

That changed in 2020, when he broke record after record and claimed his seventh title. The start of season, like everything at the start of 2020 had been ravaged by coronavirus. The teams and drivers had made it to Melbourne despite the world around them shutting down. On the Thursday in the drivers' press conferences, both he and Sebastian Vettel were outspoken about the event taking place whilst people, including the McLaren F1 team were falling ill and worse. By the Friday the event was cancelled and a day after spending twenty-four hours in the air, the teams and drivers were heading back to Europe. It wasn't a good look for a sport that should have been ahead of the curve.

The season got underway again in July with the first eight rounds empty of fans but the fact that F1 became the first global sport to return was a huge feat. Events were still being cancelled around the world, the Olympics and Paralympics were postponed to 2021 and football was struggling to get back on the same scale. F1 announced a flexible yet ambitious plan to run twenty-two Grand Prix, a record number of races in half the normal amount of time! Ultimately and incredibly, seventeen races took place in five months.

Throughout the season, Hamilton was sublime, with no real challenge from anyone else. The lack of fans gave a strange privacy at races. There was certainly more time for drivers to chat and spend working on other projects and ideas if they desired. Events in the outside world, from the death of George Floyd to a bigger focus on race and the Black Lives Matter movement meant that Lewis was able to shift some of his focus on to that. He became the figurehead, the spokesman, the galvaniser of other drivers to use their voice.

It was at the fourteenth race of the season in Turkey, where Hamilton equalled Michael Schumacher's record of seven world championships. The writing was on the wall early on and a few weeks before that, he had beaten Schumacher's previous record of ninety-one career wins at the Portuguese Grand Prix, which returned to the calendar at Portimão. It was a season with drama, but for Hamilton, the only thing he had to contend with was covid, which resulted in him missing the Bahrain Grand Prix.

For Hamilton, 2020 was as much about his legacy off track as on track. Black Lives Matter, fair representation and opportunity for all has become his mission, but the story is not a new one for him. Bullied at school and on the kart track, the Hamilton family learned to cope and used success as the best way to silence the bullies and critics. The only difference is that the more famous you get, the more people judge. A good reminder of that is from the American novelist Erica Jong, who says, "Fame means millions of people have the wrong idea of who you are." For Hamilton, equality and anti-racism is not a new "crusade" but something he has dealt with in various ways throughout his life.

The Hamilton Commission has been set up in partnership with the Royal Academy of Engineering to explore how motorsport can be used to engage more young people from Black backgrounds in the school subjects of science, technology, engineering and mathematics. The ultimate aim is to help them reach F1, increasing diversity in the sport.

At the British Grand Prix in Silverstone, I was fortunate to do a long interview with Hamilton, where I shared one of my concerns with Lewis about when he retires. At the moment he is front and centre in a global sport, but when he stops, which will be sooner rather than later, where is that representation of diversity coming from?

"For me, personally, I thought that me being here would be enough. I was hopeful in the years of me doing this there would be young kids looking in and thinking 'if he can do it maybe I can' and that I would inspire people from different backgrounds. But I realise that is not enough. When I stop there is not another me coming at the moment and I don't know for how long that is going to be."

Formula One has given Lewis Hamilton the platform to make a difference, the money, not only to enjoy his life but also to better the lives of others. But Lewis Hamilton has given Formula One the chance to be better and it is important that both continue to work together to make sure it is better in the future.

I've spoken a few times to Lewis about when we started together in GP2 and not imagining the life path that both of us, albeit very different, would go on. Gone are the days of overly emotional and controversial interviews and here are those of an elder statesman who is more comfortable with his place in the world, in his own skin. The thought of him tweeting in anger a picture of his and his teammate's telemetry is unimaginable today.

Hamilton's lifestyle and opinions have made him a divisive character for people, and I do always smile when critics say he should stick to the driving. There lies the difference between him and other drivers. He drives at a level good enough to win championship after championship, at a level that most others can't reach or sustain, and yet he still has the capacity for so much more. He doesn't have to sacrifice everything to be the best F1 driver. It is the responsibility of everyone, teams and drivers, to raise their game.

And that is exactly what happened in 2021. It had the feeling of the inevitable; surely only a matter of time before someone came to challenge Lewis Hamilton. That challenger was Max Verstappen and Red Bull.

Whilst Lewis had dominated the 2020 season, it was Verstappen who finished it with a win, taking the victory in Abu Dhabi.

The timing was odd, as there had been no major rule changes, although a key change did affect Mercedes more than Red Bull. There was no doubt that, from the off, Red Bull meant business and it was obvious from early on that Lewis was in the biggest battle since Nico Rosberg in 2016, but this one was more dangerous. This one involved a different team, therefore more uncontrolled variables and a driver who had a ruthless edge and a huge desire to win. Remind you of anyone?

The first pole position of the year went to Verstappen, but Hamilton took the win. These mini inter-weekend battles continued. It seemed that one would be quick on a Saturday and the other take the win on the Sunday. Ultimately, heading into the British Grand Prix, Verstappen had a thirty-two-point advantage, having won double the number of races of the seven-time world champion.

There is no doubt that what happened in the race at Silverstone set the tone for the rest of the season. That weekend was also the first ever Sprint Race in F1, which was won by the Dutch driver after he overtook Hamilton, who was on pole at the start. That meant that, come Sunday, Verstappen had pole with Hamilton in second.

It didn't take long for the wheels to come off – literally! A terrifying 290kph (180mph) crash at Copse between the two saw Verstappen head to the barriers and then the medical centre whilst Hamilton headed to the chequered flag and another race win despite being served a ten-second penalty for causing the crash.

The fallout was huge, with Verstappen criticising Hamilton for causing the collision and then celebrating in a manner that he felt was not fitting whilst a driver was still undergoing medical checks.

Things started to get public and messy from the teams too. Bosses Christian Horner and Toto Wolff understandably took the sides of their drivers, but the rhetoric was not what we were used to. It was like being on a reality TV show – maybe that's the Netflix and *Drive to Survive* effect!

Fast forward several races to Monza, and another lightning quick circuit where crashes happen just as fast. Hamilton and Verstappen were on different strategies and should have been nowhere near each other on the track, but a slow pitstop by Red Bull meant that Max ended up alongside Lewis after Mercedes made their stop. They were getting closer and closer and eventually the two collided in dramatic fashion. The halo saved Lewis that day, there is no doubt. The front left of the Red Bull rode over the top of the Silver Arrow and rested on the halo, touching Hamilton's helmet. It was very scary and created much debate between former drivers about where the fault, if any, lay. The stewards deemed it lay with Max and he was given a three-place grid penalty for the following race and two points on his licence. It was no longer a one-race incident and there would be no going back. Hamilton at Silverstone and Verstappen in Italy – it was obvious that, to win the championship, it would be a race of not only the fastest but the fiercest.

In Brazil and Qatar both drivers traded penalties and again at Interlagos their elbows were out. This time the multi-million-pound dodgems survived and the championship battle got closer and closer.

F1 headed to the terrifyingly fast Saudi Arabian Grand Prix for the first time. It's a street track with incredibly high speeds. Accidents were inevitable and continuous. Not for the last time, it was a race blighted by FIA controversy, but ultimately it was Hamilton who won from Verstappen, which meant they headed to final round in Abu Dhabi on equal points.

Many felt that Mercedes and Hamilton would have the edge heading into the race. The seven-time world champion's experience of these situations should mean he was equipped for the challenge ahead. And it would be a challenge. It's just that no one expected it to go as it did. Raceday in Abu Dhabi 2021 became one of the most controversial days in the history of any sport.

It was a day, a lap, a decision that has made headlines around the world and sat uneasily with fans, teams and drivers, no matter which side one supported. What made it so wrong for me is that it felt like a whim and a decision that could have gone either way with no theory applied. I think that is what the teams and drivers disliked too. We saw in Saudi Arabia that whether you benefitted from an FIA or Michael Masi decision was like the flip of a coin.

For Lewis, after leading for most of the race, with three laps to go he came out on the wrong side and the championship which he looked set to win was snatched on the last lap by Verstappen. The controversy, which led to the departure of Masi, was around the timing of the safety car, which cars were allowed through to un-lap themselves and whether the race should have been restarted to allow the one lap shoot-out for the title.

The paddock and motorsport were stunned. Not because Max won. He and Red Bull had been excellent all year and had won more races than Lewis, but it was the manner in which it happened.

After the event, Hamilton was dignified. The pictures of his father congratulating Max and Jos – another powerful father-son combination – were beautiful.

Lewis left Abu Dhabi with time to reflect about how he, arguably the greatest of them all, had been treated. His decision not to attend the FIA Awards Ceremony was, in my opinion, absolutely justified. The FIA saying he could be fined was tone deaf and embarrassing.

Hamilton's subsequent silence on the matter was apparently due to him being in deep thought about whether he wanted to continue in the sport that he loves and has transcended in recent years. Lewis might not "need" F1, but F1 certainly needs Lewis.

Off track, Hamilton has long had other interests and it is only in the last few years that he felt comfortable talking about them. Music has always been a passion and for many years he has been recording his own tracks. Recently he admitted to being XDNA, an artist listed on the Christina Aguilera record "Pipe". He had his fashion line, which he designed himself for Tommy Hilfiger. One of the collections of which he is most proud is the 2020 vegan collection, which used all sustainable materials, recycled cotton and denim, organic cotton and plant-based fabrics. Lewis would say that turning to a plant-based diet has been the biggest change to his lifestyle in recent years. He also campaigns for animal charities around the world and is an ambassador for UNICEF, often visiting projects between races.

Whilst his social circle and social calendar is A-list, you get a feeling that, as Hamilton has gotten older, he has grown out of the need to attend everything and be seen at "all the right places". That is surely a sign that he is more comfortable in himself and with the people he has around him. His friends are a core group from school and others from before he got into F1, with a few trustworthy, fun and loyal additions along the way. During the extended times away from the paddock, such as the off-season and August break, Hamilton along with friends and family head to his happy place in Colorado. A beautiful home, on top of a mountain, peaceful and private. You couldn't get a better antidote to the rest of Hamilton's life.

Until 2021, the later you delve into Lewis Hamilton's Formula One career, the more simple, straightforward and successful it has become. It seems glib to just skim over another title and yet another title, but the simple fact is that, for so long, he has been in a different league. Yes, he has had an incredible car underneath him and a relentless team around him but he has delivered when it mattered and his mistakes are few and far between.

A tricky 2022 for Lewis created speculation about whether he would continue. He replied by posting a picture of him in the Mercedes garage on his social media with the words, "Working on my masterpiece. I'll be the one to decide when it's finished."

Lewis Hamilton, the shy kid from Stevenage, has become a global star. A sportsman with a social conscience and a box-office celebrity. But, ultimately, Lewis Hamilton will always be a racer.

3
SEBASTIAN VETTEL

THERE IS NO ONE I HAVE INTERVIEWED more in Formula One than four-time world champion Sebastian Vettel. Such is the volume and popularity of these interviews, if you type Vettel into a search engine, "McKenzie interview" would come up in the list of suggestions. I am not really sure how the idea of funny and often chaotic conversations came to pass, as we have done some big, powerful features together, but it is the ones about red dresses, giving out my phone number, "everyone is a Ferrari fan" that live long in people's memories.

I have always got on with Sebastian. Even whilst race fans and some drivers found him and his celebratory finger-pointing irritating, I have always found him an engaging and intelligent interviewee and a thoroughly decent person. In interviews I would and can push him hard, especially on controversial moments, and he answers thoughtfully, rarely flinching from subjects and that comes from respect, on both sides, which certainly helps.

As the years have passed, and his on-track success diminished, it seems that actually what F1 fans didn't like was "winning Sebastian". As soon as he left Red Bull and went to Ferrari and Aston Martin, he gained a whole new legion of followers. Who knew that to be popular you just need to struggle for victories? Also not always having the best car, the constant pressure to win every race and take every pole position has given him more capacity to relax and reveal more of himself.

What I have always found interesting about Sebastian is that, even with his smiley, respectful, often humorous approach, there is a steely yet slightly volatile undertone which sometimes manifests on track but mostly appears on team radio. Naturally, things change over the years with life experience, circumstance and as people mature, but even at a young age, mostly because of what he has achieved, Vettel was seen as a spokesman. He has always assumed the unofficial role of statesman of F1. If you want a strong and yet sensible answer about the future of the sport, he would be the go-to. With his appearance on the BBC's foremost political programme *Question Time*, he showed he is as comfortable talking about global issues such as climate change and social injustice. He is a father of three and much of his social awareness comes from wanting the world to be better for his children. He will always be a four-time world champion, but now he can show that he is so much more.

Sebastian started karting at the age of three, encouraged by his father, Norbert. A little like Lewis or Max, Vettel came with a strong reputation as he worked his way up through the ranks. By the time he reached World Series by Renault in 2006, he was backed by BMW and had tested for the F1 team. Whilst they were keen to have him involved, when it came to the 2007 season, the German constructor already had their drivers in place, so Vettel continued his bid for the World Series title and it was whilst leading the championship that he was called up full-time by the team.

He made his debut at the US Grand Prix in 2007, replacing Robert Kubica, who had suffered a huge crash in Canada the week before. The Pole insisted he was fit to race, but the doctors had other ideas. Vettel only found out on the Thursday that he would be racing. At nineteen years and eleven months he became one of the youngest to drive in F1 and, when he got to the paddock, he was presented with a baby bottle and bib saying "A Star Is Born". When you see the photos and footage from the race, he looks like a young teenager. He was baby-faced and known as Baby Schumi, such were the rumours about his talent.

By the Sunday night he had shown that he was more than mature enough to be in the sport. He had been in the paddock plenty and driven in seven FP1s for BMW-Sauber in the build-up to Indianapolis but, whilst helpful at getting to grips with the car, it would never be a substitute for racing.

Despite having not been to the track, at the end of first practice he was fourth fastest. On Saturday he had made it into Q3 claiming seventh, just two places behind his much more experienced team-mate Nick Heidfeld.

In interviews after he said, "Towards the end I could have been a bit better, but making it into Q3 was already a big step. I shall sleep better tonight because last night I had the unknown ahead about what will happen."

What did happen on the Sunday was that with an impressive eighth in the race, Vettel became the youngest points scorer in history. It all very nearly went horribly wrong at the start, but because he took evasive action to avoid wiping himself and others out, dropped down the order and then worked his way back up, he showed that he could compete with the very best.

He would have to be patient, though. He was only in Kubica's seat for one race, but Indy had been a great advertisement for his skills. The word was out and it was Toro Rosso who bit first and, surprisingly, it wasn't for the following season but for the second half of that year. BMW released Vettel to join the Red Bull camp and the rest, as they say, is history.

The 2007 Hungarian Grand Prix saw Vettel replace the American driver Scott Speed and partner Tonio Liuzzi. There was no doubt that it was going to be tough slotting into a new team halfway through the year. There were seven races to go, and mostly on tracks that Vettel had never seen. Sixteenth, nineteenth and eighteenth place, plus three retirements doesn't make impressive reading, but also sandwiched in there was a remarkable fourth place at the Chinese Grand Prix. That meant that by the end of the season, he finished above Liuzzi in the Drivers' Championship despite having only done seven races for the team.

For Vettel, that year had taken some unexpected turns, but at least for 2008 he could be better prepared and organised. He knew the car, the team and had a winter to get ready knowing that he was an F1 driver; that was already a head start on the previous season.

As he lined up on the grid for the first of eighteen races, Vettel was brimming with excitement ahead of his first full season in Formula One. Frustratingly, it took until race five for him to see the chequered flag. Collisions at the start in Australia, Bahrain and Spain, not all of them his fault, and a hydraulics failure in Malaysia meant that it was Turkey before he reached the end of a race. Coming last of the finishers in seventeenth wouldn't normally be a cause for celebration, but Vettel was relieved to make the full distance. From then on, things would only get better. In a rain-soaked Monaco, having qualified in eighteenth, Vettel brought the Toro Rosso home in fifth. Two weeks later in Canada, he didn't get to qualify after a crash in FP3 meant the car was too damaged to be repaired in time. But on the Sunday, he repaid the team with another points-scoring finish in eighth.

Vettel headed into his first ever home Grand Prix at Hockenheim knowing that he was being promoted to Red Bull for the following season. David Coulthard had announced at the British Grand Prix that after fifteen seasons in F1, he would be retiring at the end of the year. Sebastian had become a point of fascination in Germany by this stage. He hadn't driven at a German Grand Prix before, many fans hadn't set eyes on him and yet he had already raced for two teams in F1 and was being promoted to a third. In qualifying he showed the fans at Hockenheim his worth, being the highest-placed German in ninth, with his fellow countrymen Timo Glock, Nick Heidfeld and Nico Rosberg further back in the midfield. On the Sunday he took another point after finishing eighth. The car wasn't bad and Vettel was even better, but it was in the second half of the season where he really came into his own. Sixth place in Valencia was followed by fifth in Belgium – and then came Monza.

The Italian Grand Prix weekend had been a washout from the start. I was there with GP2 to present the awards on the Sunday night. It rained so much that the hospitality unit flooded. We sat on tables and watched chairs float around. The TV screens showed pictures of a rain-soaked circuit and, on track, activity for any series was very limited. Saturday was again very wet but, in the spray and gloom, Vettel took an incredible pole position, becoming the youngest driver in the history of F1 to do so.

Everyone was hugely impressed but most people thought it would be a different story come Sunday. For those in Monza, the concept of drying out or feeling warm again had long been forgotten. It was as if winter had arrived and the forecast said that race day was to be just as wet, if not worse. It had poured in the morning and the race started behind the safety car. Whilst others struggled in the conditions, Vettel remained out front and in control. I wasn't working that day and it is not often I get the chance to go out and watch a race with the fans, so we went out and stood amongst the Tifosi, who also realised that something special was happening. After a total of fifty-three laps, Sebastian Vettel was a Grand Prix winner. Praise was forthcoming from the whole paddock, including championship leader Lewis Hamilton, who remarked how easy it would have been for F1's latest winner to make mistakes under pressure. It was also the first victory for Toro Rosso and as we recently saw, they had to wait eleven years for their next!

Vettel was in the top ten for all the remaining races and in the points for three of the four. It meant that by the time he left Toro Rosso at the end of the season, he was eighth in the Drivers' Championship and ahead of the Red Bull drivers, Webber and Coulthard. In the constructors, it's incredible to think now that Toro Rosso finished ahead of Red Bull with thirty-five of the thirty-nine points scored coming from Vettel. Nowadays, it is unimaginable to think of the might of Red Bull Racing being headed by its "little brother" across a season.

In 2009 Red Bull and Vettel weren't the force that they went on to become, but by the end of the season, they weren't far off. It was the fairy-tale year of Brawn so all eyes were on them but Vettel kept himself in the story. Everyone had watched the inter-team title battle between Jenson Button and Rubens Barrichello and yet at the end of the season it was Vettel who separated the two and took second in the Drivers' Championship.

The first of his four wins came in China, the third race of the season. It was a relief after a scrappy start to the year not finishing the first two races. Until the Saturday of China, Red Bull had never had a pole position before. It was a great lap from Vettel, who was two-tenths ahead of Alonso in second and three-tenths ahead of his teammate Mark Webber.

On the Sunday, it was another wet race which had been the story of the year so far. For Vettel and Red Bull, everything went smoothly. The German was in command throughout and took the second F1 victory of his career, giving Red Bull Racing their first ever win. Webber got his best career result with second place. There was no doubt, Red Bull were a team on the up.

Button won six of the first seven races of the year, but he never had a great record at his home Grand Prix whilst Vettel, albeit still new, loved Silverstone and seemed to revel in the history of the track.

This was the first time that Vettel managed the hat-trick of pole, fastest lap and race win. He dominated all weekend and won the race by over 15 seconds from Webber, who was a further 25 seconds ahead of Barrichello in second.

Maybe it is hindsight and knowing that Jenson went on to become champion, but it always felt like a Brawn year. At Silverstone, Christian Horner said that Red Bull could mount a series title challenge and, in a way, they did by winning six races to Brawn's eight. Webber got the first win of his career in Germany and won again in Brazil whilst Vettel won at Suzuka, another track that he loved and somewhere he went on to enjoy plenty of success. But it was the win at the final race of the season in Abu Dhabi that was an indication of what was to come in 2010: the start of four years of Vettel and Red Bull domination.

It was domination in that he won the title in four consecutive years, but in two of those seasons, the championship went down to the last race. Four drivers were able to become world champion on that final day in 2010. Famously, it was Vettel who won his first, having only led the championship after the last race of the year. Talk about cutting it fine!

Five drivers split the nineteen race victories between them. The four still in contention at the end were Red Bull Racing's Vettel and Webber both looking for their first, Ferrari's Alonso desperate to secure his third title and McLaren's Hamilton, who was in search of his second.

One thing that stood out in 2010 was how quick the Red Bull was over one lap. Vettel and Webber took pole position at the first seven races and by the end of the season the tally was fifteen of the nineteen. But when it came to the Sunday, they won only nine races, with the other ten split between Button, Alonso and Hamilton. It made for a compelling season. Red Bull were determined to let their drivers race, and that too made for some juicy battles.

Two mechanical issues meant that Vettel didn't finish the first two races of the season despite having led both. Even at that stage he knew that every point would matter if he wanted to win the title. He said that he went into his driver's room at Albert Park, threw his helmet on the floor and was screaming, "Why is it always me?" But the next race in Malaysia would show that it wasn't always him, and he took his first win of the year with a controlled and mature performance. Webber won Spain and Monaco, so when we headed to the next round in Turkey, the two Red Bull drivers were tied on points at the top of the championship.

What happened during the race was not only a turning point for the season but also in terms of the relationship between the drivers and the team.

Webber had started from pole with Hamilton in second and Vettel in third. Had Hamilton not lost a position in the pit stops then the story might have been different, but he dropped back a place, which let Vettel get close enough to Webber to challenge for the lead. Yet in the attempt to overtake, the two touched at high speed, sending Vettel spinning several times. His car was too damaged to continue, whilst Webber was able to carry on, although he had to pit for a new front wing. The Australian finished third behind the McLarens.

It is the images of a furious Vettel signalling "crazy" as he got out the car. He had already screamed on team radio "What the f*** are we doing here? We are working hard to win the championship. What a stupid action."

I interviewed him whilst the race was still on. "Was it a racing incident? Your fault? Mark's fault?" I asked.

He replied, "I am not the kind of guy who pushes the fault on to one guy. We are a team at the end of the day, so we have to respect that fact. Unfortunately my race is over and it was important points for myself and the team."

What didn't help the situation after the crash was the decision or insistence by the team to blame one of the drivers. They could have chosen to remain silent, take their time, say that they needed to watch it back, but what happened was that Horner initially said he thought Vettel was to blame. Helmut Marko blamed Webber and then Horner did a second interview with me saying that, actually, Vettel should have been given more room and that Webber held some responsibility. It was messy and played into the hands of people who felt that Vettel was being favoured. As it happened, Webber was one of those people.

The following weekend, I went to Zandvoort in the Netherlands to the F3 Masters. It is always a great event and that year Sebastian was to be there as well. I interviewed him for the BBC and asked if he was the number-one driver within the team and also about the rumours of favouritism.

"Neither driver, Mark nor myself are being favoured in any way. We go out and try to find who is the better one, as it should be and you should never forget that you are a team."

The two continued to trade blows. Vettel won in Valencia and Webber the next race at Silverstone. Even though nothing had happened on track during the British Grand Prix, it was still a controversial one. At the end of FP3, a front-wing failure for Vettel meant he needed a new one for qualifying. What happened next was all the proof of favouritism that Webber needed. The remaining new wing which had been destined for Webber's car, should it be better, was given to Vettel. Webber was given no choice but to stick with the older front wing. Vettel took pole from Webber by just over a tenth of a second. In the FIA press conference after qualifying, the two drivers were asked about the wings. Sebastian gestured for Mark to speak first.

"I think the team are pretty happy with the result today."

Sebastian, sitting alongside him, smiled nervously. Whilst answering, Mark slammed his glass down, water escaping out the top.

It set the tone for the Sunday. Webber was determined to show he didn't need the wing and was quick enough with simply his own talents. And he was. He got his elbows out with Vettel on lap 1, which sent the German wide and into contact with Hamilton. Eventually, Mark crossed the line first, with Vettel back in seventh. As Webber took the chequered flag, he said over team radio, knowing the whole world would hear it, "Fantastic guys, not bad for a number two driver."

In the press conference afterwards, Mark said he would be having conversations to ensure that he was never put in a position again where he was considered second best and joked that lots of other drivers offered him a front wing, but not Seb! In these situations, Mark was one of the best at creating a smiling, joking, passive-aggressive energy. He revelled in the chaos. In Vettel, though, he seemingly had someone who could shut everything out.

After the race I asked Sebastian what the atmosphere was like within the team. "I have my opinion, sometimes good and bad, you get to know people a bit better and see their true faces, but I think I learned my lesson and I will focus on myself."

As the championship battle continued, another win in Hungary for Webber meant that, as we headed into the summer break, it was the Australian who was leading the championship; four points ahead of Hamilton and ten in front of Vettel in third.

Formula One returned from its holiday with everyone recharged and up for the fight. In recent years it has been the wonderful Spa circuit and the Belgian Grand Prix which has opened the second half of the season, and this was the case in 2010.

It was a costly weekend for Vettel. He qualified fourth after being caught out by rain showers, which affected only some parts of the track. In the race, things got awkward when rain started to fall just as he tried to pass Jenson Button for second. He lost control, damaging Button's car and requiring his own pit stop for a new front wing. That dropped him back – but it got worse. Halfway through the race, Vettel got a puncture after contact with Tonio Liuzzi but was unable to go straight into the pits and had to do a full lap before he could get repaired and back up to racing speed. It dropped him to twentieth before he eventually worked his way back to fifteenth. Hamilton won the race from Webber, and so the Brit took control of the championship.

What was so exciting and nerve-racking about that season, for both fans and drivers, was the knowledge that every result had a consequence and that the championship lead could change after every race.

That was the case after the Italian Grand Prix a week later. The top three in qualifying were the top three on the podium and in the same order. It was a great day for Ferrari with Alonso winning and Massa in third, with Button sandwiched between in second. Vettel was fourth and Webber sixth. A retirement for Hamilton after a collision meant the championship had been flipped again.

Webber was back in control, but there were other big movers too. Vettel had dropped two places to fifth whilst Alonso was now in third and getting closer to his rivals. History tells us that Vettel wasn't out of the title race, but 24 points behind Webber with four drivers ahead of him didn't make him a likely champion.

Formula One left Europe and headed east. Another win for Alonso in Singapore saw him move up to second, but Suzuka was a circuit that Vettel loved and had won at the previous year.

On the Thursday of the race weekend, Sebastian and I went out on the track for an interview.

"Seb, if you were writing your school report card based on this season, what would it say, very good or could've done better?"

"It is not over yet. In terms of speed and performance, I think we can be very happy and proud. In terms of results, they didn't always match our expectations. It's been pretty much up and down. In the end, with all the downs, and we had quite some, we are still in a good position."

I asked him about his relationship with Webber. "In the garage it is very peaceful – as peaceful as it was at the beginning of the year, but of course we are competitive."

What stood out was how confident he was that he could be champion. There was no "it depends on others" or philosophical answers about what might be. When I asked him if he could still be champion, it was a definite "yes". Sebastian went on to win the Japanese GP that weekend with Webber and Alonso behind him. Webber was 14 points ahead in the title race with Alonso and Vettel now tied in second position.

There are enough unknowns in Formula One to keep drivers and teams on their toes, and in 2010, Yeongam and the Korea International Circuit was one of them. When we arrived, the place was in total disarray. The main bridge to take us from the TV compound to the paddock was sitting on the track. The paddock surface was uneven, so when the teams were trying to push tyre trolleys, they would hit a hole or undulation and the tyres would fly off. The hotels – well, I will say no more than I did at the start of this book! We all just got on with it, and whilst it wasn't exactly a fun weekend for any of us,

Michael celebrates his record seventh F1 World Championship alongside the Ferrari Team after winning the Belgian Grand Prix in 2004.

Me on Lexus competing at Michael's ranch in Switzerland.

Michael gives me an impromptu manicure at the Mercedes factory instead of painting the car! Paint takes a while to come off!

Brazil 2012. Michael in the pitlane before his final ever Grand Prix. I saw him walking alone and ran and asked him for an interview. One of my favourite photos.

Brazil 2008: Lewis celebrates his first world title with McLaren after one of the most incredible season finales.

Lewis interviews from over the years: the pen in Abu Dhabi, inside the Mercedes motorhome and sharing a joke before filming at Silverstone.

© REUTERS / Alamy

Sebastian wins his first F1 world title in Abu Dhabi 2010. The only time he led the championship that season was after the chequered flag!

Abu Dhabi 2014. Seb's last race for Red Bull. Walked to the grid on camera with him.

Hungary 2019. One of our many popular interviews over the years!

Needing directions. Seb drove me round the proposed New Jersey Street circuit in 2011. The race never took place.

Hosting an event for Sebastian. Always entertaining!

One of my favourite interviews. Lewis and Seb together in Bahrain 2015. It is so unusual for teams to allow rival drivers to get together on camera.

Monza 2015. Lewis driving the original Silver Arrow – the W196.

I should be interviewing the drivers on the parade but instead I am having a lovely chat with Michael!

MAX VERSTAPPEN

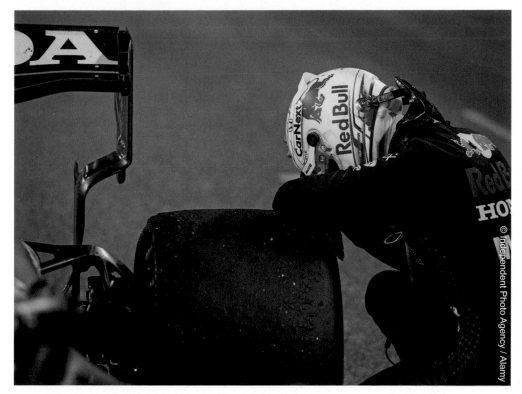

Abu Dhabi 2021. Max overwhelmed after winning the world championship with a last lap overtake on Lewis. A race that will be forever discussed!

Making inappropriate shapes with fruit! Pre-interview fun at the Belgian Grand Prix 2017.

Canada 2015 when Max was at Toro Rosso and about to take part in just his seventh F1 race weekend.

FERNANDO ALONSO

Fernando becomes youngest back to back
world champion in 2006.

So many pre-race
interiews with Fernando
over the years. Always a
pleasure to chat with him.

At the Fernando Alonso
Museum in Spain, July
2015. A wonderful
collection of cars and
trophies.

FELIPE MASSA

Felipe and I at the Interlagos kart track in Brazil where drivers dream of making it "over the wall" to the F1 circuit.

In the Williams motorhome. Always loved chatting with Felipe.

Hungary 2009 and one of the worst days at a race track. Felipe is seriously injured and airlifted to hospital. He still has this helmet in his house in Brazil.

© Tamas Kovacs / EPA / Shutterstock

JENSON BUTTON

Above: Hungary 2006. Jenson was as surprised as anyone to get his first F1 win.

Left: With his father John after winning the World Championship in Brazil 2009.

Not a bad taxi driver for Tokyo – even with a broken hand!

Vallis School, Frome. Going back to school with Jenson after his world title success.

it was worse if you worked for Red Bull. Saturday was a day of celebration for the team as they locked out the front row of the grid in qualifying. Vettel was on pole with Webber in second. Alonso and Hamilton were over their shoulders.

When it came to the race, heavy rain before and during saw cars sliding off, and the race was suspended until conditions improved. After the safety car had gone in, it was tentatively game-on. Vettel kept his lead but Webber was pushing in second until he touched the painted kerbs, which sent him spinning into the wall. I remember waiting in the paddock for him to return. He walked past, helmet on and straight into his driver's room. It proved to be the costliest mistake of his career.

I remember at that stage of the race that the light was very poor and the flag would likely be waved at dusk, at best! The Race Director, Charlie Whiting, announced that the race wouldn't go on the number of laps but the finish would be timed due to the decreasing sunlight.

Vettel continued in the lead, albeit with Alonso closing him down. The gap was as close as one second – and then Vettel's engine let go. Alonso swept past for the victory and the lead of the championship for the very first time that season. It was a tough day for Red Bull and worse for Vettel, who was now 25 points adrift in fourth.

Two races to go and all to play for! In Brazil, bizarrely qualifying went the way of Nico Hülkenberg. I am not being disrespectful when I say that, and Nico is a great friend of mine, plus a very talented driver. It is just that no one imagined it would be a Williams on pole position and it was in fact the only pole of Hülkenberg's F1 career.

At the start of the race both Vettel and Webber swept past the Williams. Vettel was in the lead throughout and went on to take the chequered flag and the victory. The race finished with the four title contenders in the top four positions.

And so it would come down to the last race of the season in Abu Dhabi. The four hopefuls posed for a photoshoot; their smiles belying their nervous energy. Alonso was the man in control of the championship on 246 points. Webber was eight points behind in second, Vettel was fifteen points off the lead in third and Hamilton was a long shot and twenty-four points adrift of Alonso.

Heading into qualifying, Vettel had been fastest in two of the three practice sessions, and when it came to the shoot-out for pole position, it was the German who was just thousandths of a second faster than Hamilton. Alonso was third with Webber back in fifth.

Race day. I remember the emotions of that Sunday morning so clearly. Whilst Sebastian and Mark were in a titanic battle but able to hide away in their driver rooms, the parents and families had to share the Red Bull hospitality. I always remember seeing Mark's mum Diane so stressed on the morning of the race. Both dads were pacing around trying to put on a brave face. This wasn't Alan or Norbert's battle, it was their sons, and maybe it wouldn't even be Mark or Sebastian celebrating. After all, it was Fernando's title to lose.

When the lights went out, Vettel and Hamilton kept it clean whilst behind them cars collided and the safety car was deployed. On the restart, it was the same story with the front two heading off into the distance. Webber and Alonso both brushed the armco but continued unharmed. After pitting, they got caught up in a Vitaly Petrov train whilst at the front Vettel continued to open the gap. In these situations it is not as simple as winning the race, which Vettel did. To become world champion, he was dependent on the finishing position of others.

Team radio lit up with the French voice of race engineer Guillaume Rocquelin, or Rocky as he is known: "Okay, Sebastian, good job. I need to wait until everybody crosses the line."

There was urgency in his voice. "I need to wait but it is looking good. You just wait, sunshine. You just wait . . ."

Such was the gap to the following cars that Vettel had pulled out; he did have to wait and it felt like a painful amount of time. Sebastian remained silent.

"Hamilton P2. Button P3. There are another two cars coming round turn 15 and 16. You wait, we just need the two cars, mate. Just those two cars. I think you'll like it. Rosberg P4. Kubica P5."

And that was it. Sebastian Vettel was Formula One World Champion. The youngest world champion in the history of the sport.

It was then that we heard Seb crying on team radio. "I love you guys, I just need a moment."

It was his moment. For the others, it was a dream that hadn't been realised. Against the odds, Vettel had won and, famously, the only time he led the championship that season was after the chequered flag at the final race.

In the FIA press conference afterwards, despite saying he was speechless, Seb spoke for three minutes, stunned, emotional, overjoyed.

"I don't know what you are supposed to say in this moment. It has been an incredibly tough season for myself, for all of us, physically and mentally especially.

"This morning I got up and tried not to think of anything. Tried to avoid contact with people too much, just tried to do my own thing.

"To be honest I didn't know anything until I crossed the chequered flag. For the last ten laps I was wondering because my race engineer, Rocky, he was trying to give me some advice and try help me carry the car home. I was thinking, 'Why is this guy so nervous? We must be in a good position.'"

He also thanked everyone in karting, some of whom were in Abu

Dhabi and others were watching in Kerpen, the kart track where he honed his skills. In his hometown of Heppenheim, the place was going wild.

Whilst 2010 was Sebastian Vettel's year, little did we know it was the start of an era.

After the drama of the previous season, 2011 was a breeze for Vettel. It was the kind of domination that hadn't been seen since the Schumacher days. By the end of the season the German had won eleven of the nineteen Grand Prix and taken fifteen pole positions. Until that year, the record for the number of pole positions in one season was fourteen and had belonged to Nigel Mansell. It was a record-breaking season in many ways and cemented Vettel as the golden boy of Formula One.

The championship was won in Japan, and by that stage it was a matter of where and when he would win it, not if. After the race, Vettel was very composed and thoughtful in his interviews. Unlike 2010, there was no shock about how the championship was won. He kept his emotions intact until we showed him a video featuring the roll call of back-to-back champions: Ascari, Fangio, Brabham, Prost, Senna, Schumacher, Hakkinen, Alonso and Vettel. By the time we got to the end of that, there were tears in his eyes. "You shouldn't do that to me," he said, smiling. Christian Horner was alongside him, proud of his driver and their achievements together.

The scrum in the pit lane was huge, with hundreds of people, cameramen, journalists and team personnel all trying to get photos and footage of the moment. These media scrums can be quite dangerous, especially if you are concentrating on getting the best shot or interview and are not aware of what everyone else is doing. I had told my cameraman to get in the thick of it and if he had to run backwards or move then I would be there to guide him and watch his back so he wasn't knocked over. It was going very well until a sudden shove from someone meant the camera belonging to my own cameraman crashed into my forehead. In hindsight I should have got it checked, but I just carried on until I had to go and sit down. That evening some of us were heading straight to Kyoto for a few days of sightseeing. Due to the swelling on my forehead, which looked like a ginormous egg, I don't have a single photo of me there. I still have a scar on my head to this day – not quite Harry Potter, sadly – but a memory of that championship nonetheless!

Vettel went on to win another two races that season: Korea and India. It was the first time that F1 had raced in India and the paddock was hugely excited to visit the country. For Vettel, it was another record-breaking weekend and his first Grand Slam, pole, fastest lap and a lights-to-flag victory. He also broke Nigel Mansell's record of most laps led in a season. He told me he was surprised that there was a record left that hadn't been broken by Schumacher!

After the race, Seb spoke so well about how proud he was to win in India and congratulated them on a great track and Grand Prix. Success and the precarious nature of F1 was something that was never lost on Sebastian, but even he realised that his winning was becoming something of the norm.

After the race he said to me, "Having the opportunity to finish high up in Grand Prix is something special. It's funny, yesterday I wrote a message to my friend, and when I look back at my first pole position, I got about a hundred text messages and nowadays I get only four. But the good thing is, for me, it is still something special and it should be, because, who knows, it could be the last one. It could be the last race win, you never know."

I cheekily said to Seb, "If you want to put your phone number on the BBC, we could get all the viewers to text you and congratulate you on pole positions and victories so you don't feel left out."

He replied, "I'll think about it. You've got my number already and I don't get any text messages from you. And anyone asking themselves, if they want Lee McKenzie's number, just let me know!" He smiled addressing the camera. He certainly had the last laugh!

By the end of the season in Brazil, he finished 122 points ahead of Jenson Button in second. His teammate Mark Webber was third.

Thankfully, for F1 fans 2012 was a much closer season and, like the epic 2010 fight, it went down to the last race. At that time, it was also the longest season with the most races in the sport's history.

Seven winners from the first seven races is what the season is known for. After what we had seen the previous year, it was an odd season for Vettel and Red Bull.

In the first half of the year Vettel only managed one win at the Bahrain Grand Prix and stood on the podium two further times, a second in Australia and third at Silverstone.

Despite the pressures he must have been feeling, he was still in good spirits. It was outside the Red Bull energy station after the podium that David Coulthard and I went to interview Sebastian live on BBC 1. We would always have a big audience in the BBC days and for the British GP it would be over five million. For some reason the interview turned to celebrations. Christian Horner was having his usual post-Silverstone party, and DC and I confirmed our attendance to Seb, who then got a mischievous glint in his eye and said to me, "Will you wear that red dress with that really . . ." whilst acting out what the low-cut neckline of the dress looked like.

I cut in, "Okay, it's time to go, ladies and gentlemen." I left Seb laughing and trying to apologise whilst giggling away with David like naughty schoolboys. For anyone who thought it was offensive, I see it as a mark of respect and friendship that we can all joke and trust each other's reactions. Bizarrely, to this day people still love to mention the red dress interview. And I am sorry to ruin the story but I feel that I should point out, there never was a red dress. It was simply Vettel mischief-making at its best.

We did all go to the party and Seb played his usual first few chords of "Smoke on the Water", and DC, Mark Webber, Sebastian and I did a terrible rendition of the Proclaimers' "500 Miles".

The other interview that stands out from the first half of that season was when Sebastian drove me round the New Jersey circuit for the much-anticipated and long-awaited New Jersey Grand Prix. Ten years on it is even more long-awaited! I think David, Seb and I might be the only people who have been round it, and probably ever will!

As we did some laps, Vettel did sound pretty shocked that the piece of tarmac we were on was going to be the racetrack. Watching it back again now, it does seem impossible that the layout they had come up with was ever going to make a circuit. Sebastian took the serene approach, and after a couple of gentle sighter laps with the two-time world champion, I went round with DC at an outrageous speed; doughnuts, the works. Not ideal with a slight hangover, and there certainly was one as we had flown on Red Bull's plane from the Canadian Grand Prix to New York, and the rule was there was to be no alcohol on board when we reached the States. There wasn't. The twenty of us on board had consumed it.

Whilst Vettel had a slow start to 2012, Alonso did all his winning that season before the summer break. Three victories for the Spanish driver meant that, as we headed into August, Alonso was at the top of the championship with a commanding 164 points, forty ahead of Mark Webber in second with Vettel just behind in third.

Incredibly, neither Alonso nor Webber won another race that season whilst Vettel was just getting started. The McLaren came to life too, with Button and Hamilton winning four of the remaining races. Räikkönen won in Abu Dhabi for Lotus-Renault and the remaining four went to Vettel.

A dominant run of back-to-back victories in Singapore, Japan, Korea and India meant that after that quartet of wins, Vettel was back in his favourite place: leading the championship.

Abu Dhabi was a race of damage limitation. On the Saturday, Hamilton had taken pole with Vettel in third, but as he crossed the line, he was instantly told by his engineer to stop the car. The Red Bull was so low on fuel that the FIA were unable to extract the sample required for analysis and the matter was referred to the stewards. We all hung around in the paddock until after midnight waiting for a decision. It was actually quite simple: no fuel sample equalled disqualification. Vettel would need to start from the back of the grid.

I remember getting back to the hotel on Yas Island, the same one that the FIA were staying in. It was a tired and busy bar and we were all too late for food! We blamed the FIA for taking so long, but at least they couldn't eat either. Odd, the things you remember in these moments!

Come the race, Vettel cut his way through the field and finished third. Alonso was second behind Kimi.

There was a new venue on the calendar and for the penultimate race of the year we headed to Austin, Texas and the Circuit of the Americas. Vettel had taken pole but it was Hamilton who won. The Red Bull driver was second; Alonso, third. It meant that heading into the final race in Brazil, just thirteen points separated Vettel and Alonso. But when it came to championship shoot-outs in Interlagos, Fernando had previous experience and success.

As you'll read in the Fernando Alonso chapter (see page 145), just eight drivers had been crowned three-time world champions at that point, and either Alonso or Vettel would join them.

As the cars lined up on the grid for the final race of the season, Vettel was in fourth with Alonso in seventh.

It was a nightmare start for Vettel. He bogged down, which meant he found himself dropping down the field. Then contact from Bruno Senna sent him into a spin. He rejoined in last but with damage to his car. However, he rapidly moved through the field and by lap 7 he was back into the top ten.

On lap 8 whilst he was in P8, Rocky came on team radio: "Good job, Sebastian, but don't take too many risks."

His next radio advice was more of a warning. "Massa ahead. Be careful. He has been blocking for Alonso." Then came a weather warning and concern about possible rain ahead. It felt like a game of Mario Kart with all these things being thrown at him. Vettel kept his head down.

On lap 10 Vettel pitted for inters as the rain had started to fall. He had two further stops for dry tyres, which brought him out even further back, and again and again he needed to work his way through the field. In the meantime, a crash between Hamilton and Hülkenberg on lap 54 meant that Alonso had moved up into a championship-winning position. The points difference would be enough. Vettel was tenth but needed to make some places – and quickly.

One lap later and he was called into the pits for intermediate tyres again but, unusually for Red Bull, there was a delay with the tyres. Sitting there in the box waiting for the team to get the tyres on must have seemed like an eternity for the German. Once again, the charge was on, and once again, he cut his way through the field. He passed Michael Schumacher, who was in his last ever F1 race. Michael made it very easy for his protégé and Sebastian gave him the thumbs up as he screamed past. Those overtakes were enough to get Vettel into a championship-winning position. Towards the end, when Paul di Resta crashed out and the safety car was deployed, the race was effectively neutralised.

Sebastian Vettel was a three-time world champion.

"Yes, we did it. They threw everything at us but we bounced back. Never give up. Be ourselves. Get on with it. Yes!" Vettel boomed over team radio.

The post-race interview was the most emotional I had seen Sebastian after a championship win. Of course, three consecutive championships was very, very special but it was the manner in which he won. Emotionally, he was spent. He had experienced every high and low encased in seventy-one laps.

Vettel's titles had either come from titanic battles or total domination, and if 2011 looked easy, then 2013 was even better. His first win of that year was the most controversial of his career and one of the big moments of the sport in the last decade. It is a race that has become synonymous with one phrase: Multi 21.

Malaysia 2013 was one of the most miserable podiums that I have ever seen. Vettel knew that he was in serious trouble with the team, and Webber was furious that his teammate had disobeyed team orders which resulted in Mark being only second. Hamilton was third, but there had also been radio communication between Rosberg and the pit wall. Rosberg was faster but told to stay in fourth. Hamilton was embarrassed by the situation. All in all, three faces and zero smiles on the podium.

The weather was typically Malaysian; rain showers came and went throughout the race. Vettel and Webber had traded the lead, but after the final pit stop it was the Aussie who was in front. The drivers were given the instruction to hold position to the end of the race – the infamous Multi 21 call. But what does it mean? Basically, the driver in car #2 (Webber) must remain ahead of the other driver in car #1 (Vettel). But with thirteen laps to go and an unnecessary on-track battle, Vettel overtook Webber against team orders.

Christian Horner had been saying to deafening silence from car 1, "Come on now, Seb, this is silly."

Webber sarcastically said, "Yep, this is good teamwork" to the reply from his engineer Simon Rennie, "He was told. He was told."

As Vettel crossed the line and started to slow, Mark swiped across the front of him furiously. Rocky came on team radio: "Good job, Sebastian. Good job. You obviously wanted it bad enough. Still, there'll be some explaining to do."

The first time we got to see the drivers together was in the ironically named cool-down room before the podium. As mentioned before, in these situations, Mark is the master!

"Multi 21 Seb. Multi 21." There was no raised voice. Incredulity, yes. Internal rage, no doubt, and yet, he was cold as ice.

Seb didn't respond. Lewis was minding his own business in the background but I am sure keeping an interested eye on this little moment of inter-team meltdown.

In the podium interview with Martin Brundle, Webber said, "After the last stop the team told me the race was over and we turned the engines down to go to the end. The team made their decision. Seb made his own decision, and he will have protection as usual."

After the race Sebastian said to me, "I put myself above that decision today and I didn't mean to. I can only say sorry. Apologise. I know it might sound dull to Mark and the team but it's the truth."

But if Vettel thought that would be the end of it, he was very wrong. He flew from Malaysia to the factory for talks. Dietrich Mateschitz, the owner of Red Bull, called Mark for a full report after the incident which he felt had damaged his company's reputation. For Mark and Sebastian it was relationship over – for that period of time.

Several drivers won races in the first half of the season but Vettel added Bahrain, Canada and his home Grand Prix in Germany to the list. Heading into the summer break, Vettel was at the top of the championship thirty-eight points ahead of nearest rival, Kimi Räikkönen.

But as in previous years, the damage that Vettel inflicted was in the second half of the season. In fact, he won the remaining nine races. Every race and every point available from August to November was his. It was an incredible feat. Even once he had wrapped up the championship in India, he didn't relax as some other drivers would have. He went on to win the three races after that.

Vettel headed into the Indian Grand Prix knowing he only needed a fifth place to secure his fourth title. I sat down with him on the Thursday and had a very open and deep interview with him. We discussed how important it was for him to keep a little bit of himself private. He lamented how team members working behind the scenes in the factory don't get credit. He also said he hadn't planned any celebrations for the fourth title. He felt he would be tempting fate if he did.

I did say to him, "It was here last year when Fernando said he was racing Adrian Newey and not you, but people might not realise Adrian had been part of the team for three years and not won a race until you came along."

"You have to be happy with who you are and what you are. What I mean is, when you face yourself in the mirror or, even better, when you have done something wrong, generally, inside the car, the cockpit, at the track, generally in life; when you have done something wrong, you are the first one to know. The first person you cheat is yourself, so that's what I mean. If you are happy with that, happy with yourself, then there is no reason to doubt anything."

"Any doubts or regrets about Multi 21, in that case?"

"I think what I regretted most after the race was that I didn't obey the team order. I obviously explained that it wasn't the right thing to do in my point of view but I didn't like that I put myself above the team in that moment. I went to see the factory, that's what I mean, you aren't entirely happy inside yourself with what you have done. Obviously, I had a face-to-face conversation with Mark and explained my point of view to him."

Meanwhile, Mark had announced his retirement from the sport from the end of that season. It meant that in 2014 Vettel would have a new Aussie alongside him – Daniel Ricciardo. It would be a new car designed to a huge raft of new technical regulations and the end of the V8s. With hindsight, it was a new era, in every sense.

Sebastian Vettel had won a Formula One Grand Prix in every full season in which he had competed. He was a record breaker, a history maker and with four titles, had become the highest paid driver on the planet. But in 2014 he didn't win a race and the best he managed was four podiums: three thirds and a second. He couldn't even say it was the car because his new teammate Daniel Ricciardo won three races and stood on the podium a further five times, although subsequently he was disqualified from his home Grand Prix. By the end of the season Ricciardo finished seventy-one points ahead in the championship and third to Vettel's fifth.

It was the start of Mercedes domination. For much of the following years, the rest of the teams and drivers were bit players, waiting to step up when opportunity allowed.

Everyone was fascinated to see how Vettel would cope if he didn't have a car to his liking. He had mechanical and engine failures, made some mistakes and was in a position that he had not been in for many years. He was battling for podiums and points. He wanted more.

As I mention later in the Fernando Alonso chapter (see page 145), Sebastian leaving Red Bull was the grenade that went off in Suzuka, even though the pin had been loosening for a while. No one really expected Vettel to leave the team that had given him all of his success quite so soon. The announcement led to the perception that as soon he wasn't able to win races or the championship, he was off. People questioned his loyalty to a team who had helped make him. Others argued that it was just a question of when, not if, he left Red Bull and that it's that ruthlessness that makes a champion a champion. Either way, when I walked into Red Bull that evening in Japan, I knew something major had happened. They are always one of the most welcoming teams in the paddock, but at that moment I wasn't welcome, and engineers and senior personnel were storming out and slamming doors. Sebastian had told them he would be joining Ferrari. What Vettel maybe didn't count on was Red Bull owning the situation quite as quickly as they did.

They instantly put out a statement. "Sebastian Vettel has advised us that he will be leaving Red Bull at the end of the 2014 season. We want to warmly thank Sebastian for the incredible role he has played at Red Bull for the last six years."

There were press conferences about the announcement on the Saturday morning before qualifying and Red Bull had swiftly appointed Toro Rosso driver Daniil Kvyat.

But the whole weekend was overshadowed by the horrific accident which resulted in the death of Jules Bianchi. Everything was put into perspective. A driver moving teams seemed trivial after that.

In Abu Dhabi, I asked Sebastian if I could interview him on his final walk from the Red Bull garage to the grid. He said yes and, on that day, you could feel the emotion. He went round the garage, shaking hands with every member of the team and hugging them for one final time. They had a pit board reading "Danke Seb, 49 poles, 35 wins, 4 Championships".

When it came to that interview, he could easily have changed his mind, as it had been a difficult weekend for the team. After quali-fying fifth and sixth, the two cars were disqualified by the FIA, who discovered that the front wings on both cars were too flexible. It meant that for his final race for Red Bull, Vettel would be at the back of the pack. He went on to finish eighth. As he walked out the paddock on the Sunday night, the Red Bull chapter was finished.

Despite the obvious lure, Scuderia Ferrari is not always the easiest place to be. The pressure, the focus, the history can weigh heavily on a driver. What would make things easier for the incoming four-time world champion is that his teammate Kimi Räikkönen was his closest friend on the grid. The two knew each other away from the track, lived near each other in Switzerland and played badminton on a regular basis. He arrived at Maranello briefed and with some good inside knowledge.

A bit like Fernando Alonso's time at the Scuderia, it's easy to think of the six years that Sebastian Vettel spent there as unsuc-cessful. It depends really how you measure success. Most drivers would love to win fourteen races for Ferrari, but most drivers aren't multiple world champions; and for the ones who are in that exclu-sive group, all they want are even more titles.

It was a period of Mercedes domination, but even during that time, Vettel managed to finish second in the championship twice, splitting the Mercedes drivers.

It was a good start to 2015 for Vettel and his new team. A podium in the opening race in Australia was followed up by his first win for Ferrari in Malaysia. It was a good strategy which meant staying on track when the safety car was deployed. Whilst both Mercedes came in, Vettel stayed out. From that moment on until the end, he was in control. It was his fortieth win, his first for the Scuderia and their first victory for almost two years. After the race Sebastian said in the press conference, "This year's car seems to suit me very well. Obviously, it's a big change, but the team has been phenomenal, welcoming me the first day. I remember when the gate opened in Maranello, it was like a dream coming true. I remember the last time I was there was as a young kid watching Michael over the fence driving around in the Ferrari, and now I'm driving that very red car. It's incredible."

In Bahrain, after much back and forth with press officers, somehow, we pulled off a real coup and got a long interview with Sebastian and Lewis together. I was really looking forward to it.

I could tell they were excited about it before I had even asked a question. I told the guys that I would try and keep it quick. Seb replied, "I do long answers," and I agreed.

Lewis then chipped in, "Dude, you do the longest answers. When we did press conferences when you used to win, it would be like, okay we are here for another half an hour. It used to be the worst. I was falling asleep always." He was laughing but there was definitely some truth in it.

"Used to win" made me smile at the time. I knew then that it would be interesting! It was so unusual to see the two together that the whole paddock was fascinated and so many people had come over to watch. There were even photographers who had climbed into the bushes outside the team hospitality for photos.

The conversation was great. They discussed what it is like to battle with teammates, how special it is to join and win for a new team, and then I brought up what happened at the previous race in China. The two had nearly collided coming out of the pit lane before the race. Sebastian was doing a practice start but Lewis was coming past on to the track.

Lewis also turned to Seb. "Yeah, what happened there, man?"

Seb patted him on the shoulder and said, "I'll tell you what happened. Me being German, disciplined, very calculative – the stereotype German, I read the notes before going into the race and it said do the start on the right-hand side after pit exit where I did my practice start." Lewis was surprised and asked if Seb got penalised, adding, "If it was me then I would have got penalised."

Sebastian kept making his point, saying he had stopped in the correct place. "I am being a nerd but fine, I enjoy it. Also, it says in the notes you could have crossed the white line."

Lewis just nodded. Point made.

But if you really want to see the difference in people, sometimes fun, quick-fire questions are a good way.

Most expensive thing you have bought? Seb: "A house." Lewis, laughing nervously: "A plane."

How do you spend time away from track? Seb said family, and Lewis joked just partying.

Most influential person met? Lewis said the Queen or Nelson Mandela whilst Sebastian said his parents. Lewis then checked with me that it was meant to be people they had met and added his parents were naturally the most important people in his life. He wasn't letting Sebastian get away with making him look like he wasn't grateful to his parents. Things were getting competitive.

I asked Seb if he knew the names of Lewis's dogs, and with much laughter it transpired that he had bought Roscoe a squeaky ball that the bulldog loved playing with, so much so that it kept Lewis awake all night. "You got the frickin' ball and I got no sleep," said Lewis.

Sebastian replied "Really? I slept very well. Actually I won the race the next day."

"Tactics, definitely tactics," said Lewis.

It was lovely to see the two drivers together. They joked about being teammates in the future at either Ferrari or Mercedes but sadly it never happened. What a pairing that would have been.

As a first season for a new team, both Vettel and Ferrari were getting to know one another. Ferrari say that in Hungary especially,

"Sebastian impressed engineers with his obsessive attention to detail." It must have paid off because that weekend the German won his second race of the season. His final win of the year came in Singapore, where he also got his first pole position for the team.

Vettel finished third in the championship behind Hamilton and Rosberg of Mercedes. It was the first time since 2012 that Ferrari had won three races in a year. You would think that things would only improve, but that is not how Formula One works.

In 2016, Ferrari failed to win a single race. There were plenty of seconds and thirds for Vettel, but no victory. The closest he came was in Austria, when his tyre blew whilst leading the Grand Prix. In Bahrain, he failed to start the race with an engine failure on his way to the grid. In China, he and his teammate crashed on lap 1. It wasn't a season of memorable moments for Vettel fans, but every F1 fan will remember his team radio, which took on a life of its own.

The first and one of the most famous outbursts was in Russia, when he was taken out by Red Bull driver Daniil Kvyat.

"Oh, for f***'s sake!" he screeched. "Who the f***? Oh, I'm out! Crash! Somebody hit me in the f***ing rear! Turn 2! And then somebody hit me in the f***ing rear again in turn 3, for f***'s sake! Honestly! What the f*** are we doing here?"

Spain was another classic outburst, this time about Red Bull's Daniel Ricciardo.

"If I don't avoid that he's just going straight in my car. Honestly, what are we doing, racing or ping pong?"

Ricciardo replied on Twitter, "Honestly, love a good game of ping pong."

Suzuka is always one of Vettel's favourite and most successful circuits but in 2016, the Japanese Grand Prix was one of frustration for the Ferrari driver. "It's ridiculous, ridiculous. I lost a second for nothing. For f*** sake," he ranted about Pascal Wehrlein, and then again ... "For pity's sake, make him go!" Vettel demanded, his advantage over Hamilton reduced. "I mean, what do you want to know? It's a green track, it's difficult to pass, it's behind another car – I mean, it's ridiculous!" As he has shown before, he knows the rules and blue flags play a big part.

His biggest meltdown though happened in the last few laps of the Mexican Grand Prix whilst racing Max Verstappen. Until then, things had been quite dull. Vettel was furious at Verstappen, who had cut the first corner. The Ferrari driver was adamant his rival had to let him past and the stewards eventually agreed with him, giving Verstappen a five-second penalty after the race. But before that the airways were certainly not for children's ears.

"Move, move for f***'s sake."

"He has been informed, he has to move," said the engineer.

"He is a BEEP. That's what he is. I mean, am I the only one or are you not seeing what I'm seeing? He's just backing me off into Ricciardo. He has to fight within, you have to fight within. Charlie? He cut the chicane."

This mostly one way rant had already lasted two laps. And there was a lot more but the line that made everyone sit up was his response to Charlie Whiting, the much respected, much loved and now much missed Race Director.

The engineer passed on the message that Charlie had told Verstappen that he has to give the position back but, up until that point, Verstappen had not.

Seb's reply: "Yeah? You know what? Here's a message to Charlie: f*** off. Honestly, f*** off."

By this point Vettel had lost control of his emotions. Team Principal Maurizio Arrivabene came onto the radio and told him to calm down. Vettel's outburst was both outrageous and disrespectful.

The odd thing was that he was very close to Charlie and at his funeral, he gave the most wonderful speech.

In the interview pen afterwards we talked about the race. He said he was sorry and had already apologised to Charlie. I pushed him on whether a four-time World Champion should act like that, should he not be a role model? He was really angry at my question and told me so after the interview – although unlike Charlie, I was spared the expletives.

Having mentioned emailing Lewis after the "Is it cause I'm Black?" interview, I decided to send my only other explanatory email to Vettel after "F*** off Charlie". Vettel likes to name his cars. I like to name my interviews.

Seb read it, and when we got to Brazil the following week, a polite smile and nod of the head from him showed it was dealt with. No discussion required.

Interviewing in the heat of the moment can be a precarious job. It is so important not to shy away from difficult questions, but there is also a way to ask a question to facilitate getting the best answer. In 2016 in Canada, I didn't do that or get any answer, really, but it did create one of the most memorable and "famous" exchanges – I'm not sure it deserves to be called an interview!

Vettel finished third. He arrived in the pen and made a remark to me that I should wear red to be like a Ferrari fan. I replied jokingly that I wasn't a Ferrari fan. He walked away and actually kept me waiting for about 15 minutes until every other interview was done. My boss was getting annoyed and telling me we really needed the Vettel interview. Eventually he came back and Channel 4 hit record. There were other interested broadcasters, so other microphones in the interview, which meant this shambles played out live. Thankfully, it went down a storm and has since been made into a strange animation.

I started with sensible questions, saying that in the race he did what he needed to do but did a poor strategy cost him the win? He was already smirking, but I did think he would just answer my very reasonable question.

"I'm mad at you. I'm mad at you. You said you're not a Ferrari fan. Everybody's a Ferrari fan. Even if they are not, they are a Ferrari fan. Even if you go to the Mercedes guys, even if they say, 'Oh yeah Mercedes is the greatest brand in the world,' they are Ferrari fans." He was smiling but also serious.

I explained, "I am a Ferrari fan. I was a Ferrari fan when I was little. I had two goldfish – Berger and Alesi."

"Call your dad. Let me ask your dad," he said.

I tried again. "Tell us about your race, you made that incredible start . . ."

He then went on about seagulls and eventually added, "I know that has nothing to do with your question but . . . I am still mad at you."

I then said, "I am going to lose my job if you don't give me one question." With my boss's raised tones in my ear, this felt like it was becoming a distinct possibility!

"You won't."

I then said loudly, "I will. Please answer," sounding embarrassingly like a teacher or parent.

"You know, if they make you lose your job after this, I will never answer a question to Channel 4 again."

The funniest bit for me in all of that madness was that he said it like it was Channel 4's fault! All he needed to do was answer my one question. If you haven't seen that 1 minute and 35 seconds of chaos, it is worth a look. And I am not sure if there ever was an answer!

Thankfully, 2017 was a better year for Vettel and his team. It was also a time of celebration: the seventieth anniversary of Scuderia Ferrari. The season got off to a great start with wins in

Australia and Bahrain before he followed it up with Monaco and Hungary. In fact, he led the championship right until after the Belgian Grand Prix. Twelve races down and eight to go. But as he used to do to others, Hamilton did to him: the Mercedes driver dominated the second half of the season. There were wins for Bottas and Verstappen but not for Vettel. In Mexico, Sebastian needed to outscore Lewis by sixteen points to keep the championship fight alive, but he finished fourth whilst Lewis won and took his fourth title. I remember how down Vettel was in the post-race interview in Mexico. Surely, he saw it coming, but his reaction was like he had lost it on the last day of the championship, not with two races to go.

The two had battled hard throughout but the moment that really stood out was in Azerbaijan and the streets of Baku. It is a race where you expect a safety car and that year there were several.

On lap 19, whilst still under safety car conditions, Hamilton slowed down to back up the pack. In doing so, Vettel ran into the back of the Mercedes, damaging his front wing and Hamilton's rear diffuser. Vettel came on team radio shouting, "He brake tested me. What the f*** is going on?"

He then drove alongside Hamilton and swerved into his car, gesticulating to reinforce his thoughts.

Lewis said, "Vettel literally just came alongside me, turned in and hit me."

Sebastian was given a penalty for dangerous driving but still finished the race a place ahead of Hamilton.

I remember the interview pen with Lewis speaking eloquently about life lessons and children watching and the precedent that sets. Sebastian, on the other hand, looked more like a naughty child and talked only of the "brake test" without ever addressing his actions, no matter how many times the question was asked.

The final year that Vettel properly challenged for a championship was 2018. Again he finished second with five victories: Australia, Bahrain, Canada, Britain and Belgium. The first half of the season was tight, with the championship lead flipping between the Ferrari driver and Hamilton, who by this time was also a four-time world champion. After his win in Canada, he led Hamilton by one point. Lewis led after France, Seb after the next race and, so it went on until Hungary. Even Vettel winning in Belgium wasn't enough to retake the lead of the championship, and from then on Hamilton won six of the eight remaining races.

If Sebastian felt frustration that year, then worse was still to come. In 2019 he had a new teammate in the young Monégasque driver Charles Leclerc. The two got on well but, as the season progressed, there was certainly a feeling that if Ferrari were looking for a new superstar, they had a strong contender in Leclerc. Charles got his first win in Formula One in Belgium and followed it up the next weekend in Italy, cementing his place in the hearts of the tifosi. Vettel only managed one victory that year in Singapore, but it was a much-needed win, over a year since his last.

The speculation about Vettel's future was coming from all angles. BBC's Andrew Benson wrote in his Singapore race report: "The German has continued a run of one major driving error every three races since June last year, and seen Leclerc, already a two-time winner in his first season at Ferrari, emerge as a serious threat to his position as number one in the team."

There was no doubt that Vettel was struggling, and it was not nice to watch. Ex-drivers in commentary and columns were tough and critical of the former champion. Some had even written him off.

To date, that win in Singapore in 2019 was the last victory Sebastian had in F1. In May 2020, during the global lockdown, when sport and lives were put on hold as the world tried to control the pandemic, Ferrari announced that they and Vettel would part ways at the end of the season. They spoke glowingly about the driver, who had won fourteen races for the team, even though the championship they both desired never materialised.

Vettel said in the statement, "The team and I have realised that there is no longer a common desire to stay together beyond the end of this season. Financial matters have played no part in this joint decision. That's not the way I think when it comes to making certain choices and it never will be.

"What's been happening in these past few months has led many of us to reflect on what are our real priorities in life. One needs to use one's imagination and to adopt a new approach to a situation that has changed. I myself will take the time I need to reflect on what really matters when it comes to my future.

"Scuderia Ferrari occupies a special place in Formula One and I hope it gets all the success it deserves. Finally, I want to thank the whole Ferrari family and above all its 'tifosi' all around the world, for the support they have given me over the years."

Formula One started back up again in the July of 2020 and Sebastian spent the summer weighing up his options. In September at the Tuscan Grand Prix in Mugello, he announced: "I'm extremely proud to say that I will become an Aston Martin driver in 2021.

"I believe we can build something very special together. I still have so much love for Formula One and my only motivation is to race at the front of the grid."

Some might cite money, but it is no surprise he was attracted to Aston Martin. It is a team of racers and one which has had many guises, from Jordan to Force India to Racing Point and many more in between, but the core of the mechanics and engineers are the same. Racing is in their DNA, just like it is for Vettel.

What the situation, change of teams and fortunes allowed is more time to be himself and spend on causes that are close to his heart. Conservation and sustainability are hugely important to Sebastian. At the Austrian Grand Prix in 2021 he handed out packets of seeds that would grow flowers to encourage bees. He also did a project with schools to create bee hotels in a meadow in Austria. At the British Grand Prix after the race, he went into the stands and picked up litter that fans had left lying around. And before the race he and I visited a school near Silverstone.

On the Thursday morning, Seb and I went to Nicholas Hawksmoor Primary School in Towcester to speak to the children about sustainability and the environment. Sebastian spoke to the children, told stories and answered questions. He addressed the fact that he could be seen as a hypocrite as the sport in which he competes is not exactly the most sustainable but hopes to help it change. He talked about trying to fix the calendar so we don't go to Australia for a standalone race, or Europe to Canada and then back to Europe. He covered the same topics a year later on *Question Time*, only to a slightly older and more critical audience.

The sport needs drivers like Lewis and Sebastian to speak out and show that they care about causes but also the future of the sport because the two go hand in hand when it comes to increasing the popularity of F1 and welcoming a younger audience.

One thing that Vettel values more than most drivers is the history of Formula One. By his own admission, he is a nerd, a "stato" who loves questions and quizzes about the history of the sport. When Formula One made a film asking the drivers to name as many F1 world champions as they could, Vettel was exceptional. He is not just a statesman of the sport but a scholar too, which is an incredibly valuable asset and shows the respect he has for Formula One and those who have driven in it.

And yet even knowing Sebastian as I do, it's hard to know how he really feels about his career and the success he experienced early on and, like many drivers, struggled to repeat.

The closest he came to talking about it was in 2019 in Monaco when I interviewed him. I asked if he looked back much and whether those early years felt special now.

"I don't think back that much because I'm still doing it and I always want to make sure I look forward.

"It would be quite sad if all that peak is behind me. Then what do you look forward to? Even if I had to stop now, I hope that I would still be looking forward to other things."

And that time to stop has sadly arrived. On the eve of the Hungarian Grand Prix in 2022, Sebastian announced that he would retire at the end of the year. He joined Instagram the same day, and in his four-minute recorded statement he talked about how he would dedicate his future to his family and helping make the world a better place for future generations. His mantra is now "There is still a race to win" as he turns his attention to sustainability and environmental issues, something he is passionate about. For the last few years, he has even driven to the European races rather than fly, as he tried to reduce his carbon emissions.

The retirement speech that he delivered was so impressive that many of the world's top athletes from all sports shared it to their social media profiles whilst drivers in the paddock posted pictures saying how much he would be missed. It was a universal outpouring of love and respect.

Hundreds of drivers have walked away from the sport, but few have made as big an impact as Vettel. Having Sebastian in Formula One for the last fifteen years has added a huge amount of value, entertainment and class to the paddock and sport. History will show that he is a four-time world champion, but real life shows that he is so much more.

4

MAX VERSTAPPEN

DRIVERS WITH "POTENTIAL", "BIG FUTURES", who "could be a world champion" come and go in Formula One. Most drivers get to the highest echelon of the sport because they won championships in the formulae below and have earned the right to take their seat, yet very few realise their dream of winning a race in F1, let alone a world championship. The pressure, the incredibly high standards, the mercurial performance of the cars; there are many reasons why some hugely talented drivers struggle to repeat their earlier success. But occasionally someone comes along who is more than just hype. Who manages to out-hype the hype.

Enter Max Verstappen.

Thursday, 21 August 2014 was the first time I met Max. It was a typically cool and damp day in the F1 paddock in Spa, Belgium, and just three days before, it had been announced Verstappen had signed for Toro Rosso. At just sixteen years old, he was preparing for his future in the sport and would make his racing debut at the Australian Grand Prix six months later. He had chosen Red Bull despite approaches and discussions with Mercedes. The Dutchman had opted for Austria over Germany, but really it was a race seat over what initially would have been a test driver role.

Before he had even reached the paddock, his arrival in F1 had been the hot topic in the drivers' press conference. That day the line-up consisted of Felipe Massa, Nico Rosberg, Daniel Ricciardo, Romain Grosjean, Jules Bianchi and Daniil Kvyat.

From the transcripts of the FIA press conference, he was much discussed.

Question to all: We had news this week that next season there will be a seventeen-year-old driver on the grid. Can I have your reaction from a driver's point of view? And maybe we'll start with Felipe.

Felipe Massa: "Definitely, he's a very quick driver. He shows talent in a go-kart, in Formula 3, winning many races; I think he's second in the championship. It's his opportunity. First of all, I think it's great that teams are still interested in the talent of the driver and not the money and I think that's really positive, it's good for the sport in general. I'm happy for that. Seventeen is a little bit young! For sure, we need to wait and see how he's going to perform in his first year. I think the most important thing is that he has the talent; I mean he's quick. I hope he can be clever as well, to learn everything from Formula One."

Nico Rosberg: "The same as Felipe said. All the journalists are always asking 'is it only with money that you can get to the sport?' and things like that. It's great to see that if you have the talent and you really deserve it [you can break into the sport]. Of course, it's very young but I think we'll be OK."

Daniel Ricciardo: "Not much more to add. It makes me feel a bit old! Obviously, the age is the question mark but the talent, as Felipe said, is there."

The other drivers echoed the sentiments but around the paddock there was definitely an air of "this kid is very young". Unlike most of the drivers in the paddock, he had not come up through the usual paths and been seen in the F1 paddock whilst competing in the support races, then known as GP2 and GP3. To many he was known as "Jos Verstappen's son". Twelve months later, Jos would be known as "Max Verstappen's dad".

I was waiting upstairs in the Red Bull hospitality unit, or the Red Bull Energy Station to give it its official name. I had been given an interview with Max for our live BBC programme that weekend. David Coulthard was waiting with me. He knew Max and we both knew Jos, with David having raced against him in F1 for years and me having interviewed him in A1GP when he was a driver for Team Netherlands. David is a very pragmatic person and, whilst others debated age versus talent and maturity, his take on the situation was very simple: "If he's quick enough, he's old enough." We would find out soon enough.

Up the staircase came an awkward, thin, rangy teenager in an oversized Red Bull hoodie almost hiding under a cap. David chatted to him for a little while and then introduced me. The intro was witty, funny and completely inappropriate – in other words, very DC. I took my usual stance and eye rolled and levelled something cheeky back to David, but poor Max went bright red, like any normal teenager would. But he wasn't a normal teenager and, just a few minutes later, I was interviewing him about his hopes and dreams of becoming a Formula One World Champion. What stuck out for me was how assured he was. He knew he was an incredible talent. Not because everyone was saying it or because Red Bull and Mercedes had been bidding for him, but because he genuinely believed it. There was no arrogance when he talked, just a calm clarity and unfaltering belief.

"Ever since I was seven years old, Formula One has been my career goal, so this opportunity is truly a dream come true," said Verstappen.

Do many seven-year-olds have a career goal? It all sounds very intense! Maybe that's what happens when you come from a family of racing drivers, especially if you have shown great skill early on.

His whole world was motorsport. His life always has been – his parents, his childhood and his friends lived and breathed cars and karts. The career of his father Jos is well known: 106 F1 races over a decade for six different teams made him a household name when it came to motor racing. The images of his car bursting into flames during a pit stop at the German Grand Prix in 1994 are some of the most iconic in the history of the sport. During his career, Jos stood on the podium twice.

Max's mother, Sophie Kumpen, was, as a teenager, one of the hottest racing talents out there. She was revered as a karter, beating many drivers who went on to F1 and race all over the world; from Giancarlo Fisichella, Jarno Trulli, Dario Franchitti to Jenson Button. During a podcast, Button said, "Sophie, Max's mum, was a fantastic driver. When I was racing in karts in 1995, she was my teammate, so I saw her drive. I knew how good she was."

Also a former competitor and rival of Sophie's was Red Bull Team Principal Christian Horner. The two raced against each other in the Junior World Kart Championship in 1989. Horner's evaluation: "She was in the top 10 in the world, for sure."

But her career path changed when she met Jos. Her dreams of making it to Formula One were put on hold for his and whilst he pursued his F1 dream, she brought up their two children, Max and Victoria. Both children were known as excellent talents in karting, but it was Max who eventually became the focus when it came to a full-time racing career.

When Jos stopped racing, he turned his attention to Max, becoming his manager. To get a sixteen-year-old an F1 contract and be ready to compete at that level was an incredible feat. For Jos, the first part had been achieved. He told me during an interview that, for him, the most difficult time was Formula 3.

"I was nervous last year. That's where he needed to impress. That's where he needed to win races. I was more nervous in F3 than I am now [in F1]. Of course *he* has to perform but it's easier for *me*." Jos was visibly emotional during that part of the conversation. You could really see how much he had dedicated his life to creating the best opportunity for his son. It felt that the first chapter was complete but there was still a big story to write. That responsibility would be on Max; for Jos, he had done the hard work and put his son in the best possible place.

When I filmed with Max in 2015, six months after his F1 debut, he wasn't able to drive to any of our filming locations. In fact, he didn't have a driving licence, being too young for public roads despite being one of the fastest people on the planet! Luckily, there were plenty of willing chauffeurs to take him wherever he needed.

The first few races of his F1 career were made up of highs and lows but he showed why he was held in such high regard. His talent had never been in doubt. He had already made global news when he became the youngest driver to compete in a Formula One race. Seventeen years and 166 days is unlikely to ever be beaten, especially now with tighter restrictions when it comes to gaining a super licence, which is needed to drive a Formula One car.

In his debut in Australia, Verstappen was in a points-scoring position for much of the Grand Prix before his engine failed. Sadly, the precarious reliability of the Renault power unit became a theme that season. In Malaysia, to the amazement of the paddock, he qualified in sixth and finished the race in the points in seventh. But there was still lots to learn, and Monaco saw him in the barriers after a high-speed crash when he clipped the back of Romain Grosjean's Renault. The stewards gave him a five-place grid penalty and two penalty points on his licence and Felipe Massa said the accident had been "dangerous".

Just before the summer break in Hungary, a great drive saw Verstappen get his highest position of his debut season so far, finishing an incredible fourth. Amazingly, he repeated the feat in Austin several months later, and by the end of 2015 Max Verstappen had made his mark on the sport. Great skill and speed, combined with unfaltering bravery, made him a potent package. He may have finished twelfth in the Drivers' Championship, but it was with more than double the points of his highly regarded teammate Carlos Sainz Jr. Max Verstappen had arrived.

Earlier in 2015 I was given some of the best and longest access that I have ever had with a driver. Whilst at the BBC, I had been trying to do a feature with Max at home, to see what he did in his personal life, get a flavour of him as a normal teenager. This of course he was not, and yet in many ways, he was. It was such a well-received film, not just in the UK but around Europe – and, actually, by all F1 fans who somehow managed to watch it despite geo-blocking and not being available in every country! To this day, I am constantly asked or reminded by race fans about this interview. It was one of the longest features that we broadcast on the BBC F1 coverage, so good was the access. The other bizarre thing was that there was no PR person there at all. No one to say we couldn't ask something, to tell us that our time was up, ask us not to film certain things. It was just me and the Verstappen family and their friends. It was very special, and I will be forever grateful to Max, Jos, Raymond Vermeulen (who manages Max now) and everyone who made us so welcome for the two days.

We spent a lot of time at the family home were Max lived at that time. It was just on the Belgian side of the border with the Netherlands. When I say on the border, it was only a field and dyke at the other side of the garden which separated Belgium from the Netherlands.

In those days, Max might have been an F1 driver, but he was still a very young man, as demonstrated by the lack of driving licence. His entire life was dedicated to racing. I am not saying that's not the case now, but he certainly has more capacity and appetite for a life away from the track. When he first started in F1 he raced at the weekend, came home and raced on a simulator, used the gym to get stronger and went karting with his friends. Eat, sleep, repeat. Off to the next Grand Prix!

He has always been a huge fan of sim racing and still competes in it. At that time, he was doing around four hours a day, but the funny thing was that his own Toro Rosso car wasn't on the game he played, so he had to use a Mercedes!

I remember being at an airport somewhere in the world and we were all going through the security checks. Max was in front in the queue. Sebastian Vettel and a couple of others were there. Max had a few bags and asked if anyone would carry a small, hard-shelled Peli case. I asked what it was. "It's my travel simulator, of course!" he replied incredulously, as if I should know. We all laughed and someone, probably Seb, asked why on earth would you bring a travel sim to an F1 race when you are an F1 driver? Max carried the case himself.

What stood out for me when I spent time with Jos and Max was how much they had done together as father and son. Almost every moment when Max wasn't at school, and plenty of moments when he should have been at school, they had spent at kart tracks or together in their own workshop.

The workshop where Max had spent time since he was four or five years old was every motorsport fan's dream. Every kart he'd won races in, his first ever kart, trophies and old photos lined the walls.

Jos reminisced: "I remember Max's first kart race. He was seven years old but so little. Then it was the race and he just drove away. He was gone and you can't do anything anymore." The memories and emotions for Jos that day were as clear as ever.

Max's memories are a little different: "He was so nervous. I could see it," he said, laughing at his dad.

The two of them, along with Max's two close friends, Stan and Jorrit Pex, spent hours in the workshop and on the tracks of Europe. The Pex brothers were and are still some of the best karters around, so the perfect people for Max to be friends and rivals with. They encouraged and brought out the best in each other, elevating the group to the highest levels.

We spent time at Genk kart track, where Max had spent so much of his childhood and formative driving years. Jos and both Pex brothers all said the same thing – the Max they see in F1 is "exactly" like the Max they have known from karting. The spotlight might be greater but the fundamentals are the same, and that is something that Max echoes. He puts everything down to those karting days. That level is so much more hands-on: changing tyres, adjusting parts of the car and, if you have a workshop like the Verstappens', putting engines on the dyno to help find every little gain.

After the first day of filming, around eight of us went for dinner. At the end of the meal, we got out our cards to pay; obviously we would pick up the tab to say thanks to Jos, Max and the family for their hospitality and kindness. Jos, though, had other plans and used the occasion as a life lesson for Max. "Put your cards away. You came from the UK to film with us. Max will pay." All of us looked at Jos, surprised – and that included Max! The teenager looked a little stunned and certainly less keen on the plan than his father did. Whilst we sat there awkwardly, Jos explained to Max that we were their guests, we had spent money on flights and accommodation and were spending two days to make what would become a lovely feature and that he should pay to say thank you. We were very happy to pay and even more grateful for the filming opportunity, but Max got out his credit card and paid for dinner. Basically, we had become a life lesson on Max's discovery of the peripheral parts of being an F1 driver. Either way, it was lovely company and a lovely meal, so thank you Max!

As I left the workshop the following day and was looking at all the karts hanging up on the wall, I asked Jos if there was anything they didn't have that they would like there.

"A winning F1 car. That's what we are planning now."

And it didn't take long!

In terms of driver line-up, for the Red Bull teams, 2016 started in the same vein that 2015 finished. Red Bull Racing had Daniel Ricciardo and Daniil Kvyat behind the wheel of the RB12. The Red Bull sister team, or junior team as it is, kept the faith in Carlos Sainz Jr and Max Verstappen.

In Australia, we not only saw a new car for the season, but an updated Verstappen. MV 2.0 was certainly punchier, which became evident when some of his communication with his engineer was played out on team radio. It was a race driven in frustration. He was unhappy with strategy, the pit stop and upset he wasn't allowed to overtake his teammate, describing it as "a joke". The radio being broadcast throughout the race was filled with expletives, moans and outbursts. He later apologised to the team, but it was an interesting new layer to the teenager and one that some at Red Bull would have applauded and certainly not discouraged.

For Verstappen, the next races went without drama, for him anyway. Around him on the grid and within Red Bull, things were imploding.

Daniil Kvyat had long been part of the Red Bull Academy and seen as a real talent. He was promoted from Toro Rosso at the end of 2014 to the senior team alongside Daniel Ricciardo. In his first year with Red Bull he outscored his teammate by ninety-five points to ninety-two. No mean feat.

Kvyat got his first F1 podium of the year in China, but it was not without drama. Sebastian Vettel, by then at Ferrari, blamed the Russian driver for causing an accident at the start of the race. In the drivers' room afterwards, whilst waiting for the podium, Kvyat turned and said to Vettel, "What happened at the start?"

Cue a Sebastian outburst. "You ask me what happened at the start? You came like a torpedo," Vettel said to Kvyat. The discussion continued and this would have certainly been seen and heard by those high up at Red Bull and, despite leaving the team, Vettel was still held in very high regard in those corridors.

For Kvyat, things only got worse at the next race, his home Grand Prix in Sochi. At the start, he caused a crash which created chaos and ruined the race for several drivers. It led to one of the best and biggest outbursts on team radio. Vettel was hit twice – and he was incandescent. The pressure really mounted on the Russian driver when his own teammate, Daniel Ricciardo, also demanded an apology, saying he'd been pushed by Kvyat into another car. The stewards came down on him with three penalty points on his licence. As it happened, that became the least of his worries! Red Bull announced that they would summon Kvyat to talks about the incident, calling their race a "disaster". Summoned he was, and, shockingly and quickly, Kvyat was demoted back to Toro Rosso. Taking his seat at Red Bull was Max Verstappen.

The press release from Red Bull Team Principal Christian Horner said the switch would allow Verstappen to showcase his "outstanding" talent, and also help Kvyat "regain his form".

"Max has proven to be an outstanding young talent. His performance at Toro Rosso has been impressive so far and we are pleased to give him the opportunity to drive for Red Bull Racing," Horner said.

The Thursday of the Spanish Grand Prix always has a slightly frenzied feel about it. There are more TV companies and journalists at that race, simply because it normally is the first European race of the season. The team hospitality units are back, which gives it a sense of "home", and everyone is generally happy to have got on a flight which took less than two hours! Yes, F1 is a global sport but it still has a European heart.

So Thursday, 12 May 2016 felt a little like the Thursday in Belgium when it had been announced that a sixteen-year-old had been signed for the following season. This time, the eighteen-year-old had been promoted!

The press conference was tense – mostly because the FIA had chosen to sit Carlos Sainz Jr, Daniil Kvyat and Max Verstappen alongside each other in the front row. It did seem a little unneces-sary and inflammatory. Sainz had been overlooked for the big job, Kvyat had been sacked and Verstappen given the chance of a life-time. You can just imagine the process: "I know, let's sit them next to each other whilst journalists grill them."

The questions came thick and fast, as did the answers. Kvyat's were raw. Verstappen's considered and respectful, but with his usual directness.

"To be honest I'm very happy with the chance they have given me. I'm racing for a top team now, so that was always the plan, what I wanted to do. And yeah, with the risk, to be honest I think it was a bigger risk to be so young in Formula One, but I've handled it pretty well. From now on it's just getting used to a new car, which is not easy in the season, but already with the things I've done in the factory, already they've given me a lot of confidence. Of course, a lot of procedures to learn again but it will come race by race and I'm definitely going to enjoy it."

As a sub-plot, Red Bull's Dr Helmut Marko had said that one of the reasons for the switch between Max and Daniil was that it solved the issue between Sainz and Verstappen. Everyone knew there had been some close calls on track and moans from Max on team radio, but was the relationship really that bad?

Sainz seemed as surprised as anyone that it was being touted as a reason. "I think the personal relationship Max and I have is not a big issue, honestly. I think we both always maintain the respect off the track, and I think we showed it at every moment. I think it's more a matter of a team perspective of how the team was working and that's where Franz Tost and Helmut Marko take the decision. But from Max and myself there was always respect, there was always good vibes with each other. Obviously, we were fighting a lot on track, we were always very, very close to each other and there were always some battles going on, but they stayed at the track and out there it was just a matter of engineering."

Either way, the issues within the Red Bull teams had been sorted in one way and yet not in another. Verstappen was happy but Ricciardo a little unsure about the promotion of the "darling" of Red Bull. Sainz was frustrated he had been overlooked and Kvyat was devastated he'd been demoted, "not dropped", as he was keen to point out to the media.

There was needle all around heading into the Grand Prix. Nico Rosberg had won the first four races of the season. Hamilton had struggled with engine issues and was generally unhappy. Despite that, he still took pole position for the race from Rosberg. The Red Bulls of Ricciardo and Verstappen locked out the second row. It was Max's best qualifying and would be the furthest forward that he had started a Grand Prix.

As the lights went out, Hamilton and Rosberg went into battle. As did Vettel on Verstappen. The Ferrari briefly got in front, but the

Dutch driver re-passed the four-time world champion to keep fourth place. It wasn't fourth place for long, though, as the two Mercedes drivers touched and took each other out. Safety cars and strategy played their part but when the chequered flag fell, it was Max Verstappen who saw it first. At eighteen years and 228 days he became the youngest ever F1 winner beating Sebastian Vettel's record by two and a half years. He was the first driver to be born in the nineties to win a Grand Prix and the first Dutch driver to win an F1 race. There were stats and records galore but, ultimately, it was the pure emotion that really stood out.

The entire place erupted. You didn't have to be Dutch to celebrate this. The Spanish celebrated like Alonso had won and as is the norm at any F1 race, there were thousands of Dutch spectators there too. The Orange Army were out in force, and they aren't shy of a celebration! In the pit lane, Jos was in floods of tears. For him, it was the realisation of a dream. The culmination of years of work.

A few days later I asked Max if he knew that his father would be so emotional. His answer surprised me: "Of course he was happy I won the race, but when he came into F1 there was also a lot of expectation and in the end the career didn't go to plan like he wanted. Then once he stopped in Formula One, he spent a lot of time with me trying to get me better than him and to see his son winning is a bit like he finished the job that he wanted to finish himself.

"It's a feeling for both of us that we managed to win a race finally and that's why I say *we* because without my dad, I wouldn't be in F1 that's for sure."

It was an answer of a few sentences but heavy with decades of frustration, perseverance, ambition and ultimately triumph. Twenty seconds to sum up twenty years of Jos's life.

After I finished my post-race interviews in Barcelona, I went and sat downstairs in the Red Bull hospitality. I say Red Bull but the Energy Station is split in half. As you walk in, Toro Rosso is on the left and Red Bull on the right.

I was just sitting myself on the Toro Rosso side. It was an especially hot day and I wasn't feeling that great, so I was rehydrating after being in the sun for four hours. Daniel Ricciardo was a few meters away from me doing the same, although his exertion had been a little more than mine. The Aussie had finished just off the podium in fourth and was frustrated with his strategy. Add in the fact he had just watched the new kid win a Grand Prix with his team at his first time of trying, it hadn't been a great Sunday for Daniel!

Just at that moment Daniil Kvyat walked in. They both looked at each other and sort of stunned, laughed and shook their heads. "What the f*** just happened?" Daniel said to Daniil. Similar name, identical thoughts. I'm sure they both realised at that moment that Red Bull, their careers, their status, *everything* had just changed. For me, to be there and see their reaction was a really strange moment. It was very personal; a window into a pivotal moment in their lives. Mark Webber talked about that moment when Sebastian Vettel turned up and won; it was a game changer. The priority had shifted, the focus altered and, despite what a team boss says, even if it is subconsciously, there is a number one driver.

In Monaco, I interviewed Max on the Red Bull roof terrace beside their swimming pool to look back on the win in Spain and to the weekend ahead. For those of you who don't know, the Energy Station in Monaco floats in the harbour. It's built in Italy and sailed round the coast to berth in one of the most famous harbours in the world.

Max's summary of Spain was "unbelievable", a sentiment shared by Jos, Christian Horner and three-time world champion Alain Prost. It was an unbelievable weekend and, for me, and all journalists, to be there for a moment like that is always special.

Remember that the year before in Monaco Verstappen crashed his Toro Rosso in the race, which resulted in the stewards giving him a five-place grid penalty for causing a crash. I asked him about it because his attitude after the race struck me as very different to what I had heard from many other drivers who had crashed out – and trust me, I have spoken to a lot of them!

He intimated to me straight after that crash that it was almost good that he had done it as now he knew where the limits were. A year on he said the same. "It was a big one but it didn't hold me back. Before, I was always holding back a little to get to the limit, but after that I went towards the limit." A refreshing, if unusual, answer; but one year on, he was still struggling to find the limit again and again and again.

In fact, what a difference a couple of weeks can make, from the highs of Spain to the lows of Monaco. It can be summed up as five on track sessions and three crashes, all at the business end of the weekend.

In FP3 on the Saturday morning, he clipped the wall on the run-up to Casino Square. In the short period of time between FP3 and qualifying, the car was repaired and checked and ready for the all-important session. There is no race where qualifying is as important as Monaco. What happens on the Saturday sets the tone for the race, as overtaking is so limited. Famously, Nelson Piquet said it was like "riding a bicycle around your living room". In Q1 Verstappen was the last to set a representative time, but as he was on his flying lap, he touched the guardrail at the swimming pool complex and crashed into the wall. Red flag and game over.

At Red Bull, the emotions on either side of the garage had been reversed from Spain. Verstappen would start twenty-first whilst his teammate Daniel Ricciardo had taken pole position.

It was a race of mixed conditions, wet and then drying but

incredibly, less than halfway through the Grand Prix, Max had worked his way into the top ten. And then came the crash. On lap 35 he locked up his tyres and went into the barriers. It was race over and a weekend to forget for the new star of Formula One.

But it didn't take long for Verstappen to get his mojo back and by the end of the season he had stood on the podium a further six times with four second places and two thirds. His season wasn't without controversy, though, and at times he certainly wasn't making many friends with his style of driving. During the Belgian Grand Prix, Verstappen collided with Kimi Räikkönen at the first corner, pushed Vettel, Räikkönen and Perez wide at Les Combes, and then blocked Räikkönen on the Kemmel straight.

With Max, you feel that reputation and achievement holds no weight when he is wheel to wheel racing, or even discussing what happened. It is not often a younger driver would take on world champions, but after the race I said to him, "Three into one doesn't work, tell us about it from your seat."

"No, it doesn't work, but it could work – but the others just turned in. I wasn't even locking a wheel, so it doesn't mean that I am overshooting the corner. I was just turning in and I could just see they are squeezing me more, especially Kimi in the beginning, and then Sebastian turned in on both of us."

I said that there were plenty more battles with those two and asked if it was all fair. He replied, "After the disappointment of turn 1, I defended even stronger to them. I think it's pretty logical."

Verstappen finished in second and was criticised for his driving, with Räikkönen saying that he "was going to cause a huge accident sooner or later".

Christian Horner said he felt that Max's driving was "on the edge", and that Verstappen will "look at it and learn for future races". After that weekend, F1 Race Director, the late Charlie

Whiting, called in Verstappen for a discussion, and gave him a "gentle warning". However, in October, drivers' concerns about Verstappen's defensive tactics led the FIA to make a wholesale law change to disallow moving under braking.

His driving style, to this day, divides opinion, but his talent rarely does – and his third place in Interlagos, at the Brazilian Grand Prix, is considered as one of the best wet-weather drives in the history of the sport. He had qualified in fourth but horrendous conditions during the race saw crashes, red flags and rain delays. With sixteen laps to go, the Dutch driver had dropped to sixteenth after a pit stop but his drive back up to third was phenomenal. His car control was sublime and was the perfect reminder of why he started the season at Toro Rosso and finished it at Red Bull and fifth in the championship. Even rival Team Boss Toto Wolff couldn't contain his excitement, describing the drive in Brazil as "The Verstappen Show" and saying it was "physics being redefined".

Although Max did add two wins to his CV in Malaysia and Mexico, 2017 was a frustrating year for him. In the first fourteen races he had seven non-finishes, including four mechanicals and three accidents in Spain, Austria and Singapore.

At the US GP in Austin, Verstappen qualified sixth but started sixteenth due to power unit penalties, and in the race, with just a few laps to go, he was sitting in fourth. On the final lap he made a bold move to pass the Ferrari of Kimi Räikkönen to move up to third. Celebrations ensued although there was discussion in commentary as to whether he had left the track – the rule states that all four wheels must be within the white lines. Track limits is constantly and increasingly a hot topic in Formula One for reasons exactly like this.

Whilst waiting to go on to the podium, in front of the cameras, Max was asked to leave and go to the stewards room. He was penalised and demoted to fourth with Räikkönen back up to third. It was an awkward moment as Verstappen was led away from the podium. By the time he made it to the interview pen, it was evident that the cool-off room had not served its purpose!

After the race Max said to me, "It's just one idiot steward up there who always makes the decisions against me. At the end of the day I had a great race and I'm still happy with fourth but the way they did it is unbelievable." It was the lack of consistency that frustrated Max and Red Bull. Christian Horner and others were outspoken about the decision.

By the end of the season, Max finished sixth in the Drivers' Championship.

As so often happens in sport, Max Verstappen was growing up in the public eye. For some, his outspoken ways and uncompromising approach on track were too much but no one could deny his speed and skill.

In 2018, he had another frustrating start to the season. In each of the first six races, the Dutch driver was involved in at least one incident – not all his fault, it must be said.

In China, though, Verstappen was deemed to be at fault and given a 10-second penalty for causing an avoidable accident as he shunted Vettel off the track. The Azerbaijan GP had much bigger consequences in every sense. The speeds on the streets of Baku are incredibly high and therefore a crash can be serious business. On lap 40, whilst Red Bull teammates Verstappen and Ricciardo were tearing down the straight, they touched. Both cars crashed out in dramatic style. Christian Horner was furious, calling the contact "unacceptable". Both drivers were told to apologise to all members of the Red Bull workforce for the incident and received an official reprimand from the FIA.

At the next race in Spain, he finished third, despite running into the back of Lance Stroll at the end of the Virtual Safety Car period. Monaco was another weekend in the principality to forget. A crash at the end of FP3 meant Verstappen wasn't able to qualify. But disappointment doesn't linger long for Max and you always feel that an "upset" is almost a catalyst. The belief is so high that he can reset after any eventuality, and that's exactly what happened in Austria. The crowds were mostly dressed in orange. They had travelled in force from the Netherlands, and it wasn't to be in vain. It was another win in the sport, one which not only delighted the crowd but Red Bull too, who got their first victory at their home Grand Prix. The other win, which felt something like retribution for the previous year, came in Mexico.

And there could have been another in Brazil, but it was a race that became more known for an altercation with Esteban Ocon.

Having overtaken Räikkönen, Vettel, Bottas and Hamilton, Verstappen looked set to get his third victory of the season. But towards the end of the race he was spun round by Esteban Ocon, who at the time was trying to unlap himself on a set of faster tyres. Hamilton won the race with the furious Red Bull driver in second place. Ocon was at fault and received a 10-second stop-and-go penalty for the clumsy incident. But what happened at the driver scales is what surprised us all. Ocon was waiting to weigh in when he and Verstappen got into a heated conversation in front of the TV cameras. Suddenly emotions spilled over and Verstappen pushed the Force India driver. Ocon put his hands out as if to say "what are you doing" whilst knowing that there were plenty of witnesses to the whole thing, especially as the pictures were being played out around the world. Verstappen was given two days of "public service" as a penalty by the FIA.

By the time the chequered flag had fallen in Abu Dhabi, he ended the season in fourth place in the championship with 249 points, claiming two wins, eleven podium finishes and two fastest laps. It was progress, too slow for Max's liking, but progress nonetheless!

At the start of 2019 it looked like Verstappen and Red Bull would have to settle for being also-rans, but by the end of the year, Max had notched up three wins and two pole positions. It was another win in Austria which opened the account, much to the pleasure of the Orange Army and his employers. There were plenty of nice stats around it too. The victory marked the first win for a Honda powered F1 car since Jenson Button won the first race of his career back in 2006. It was also the first race that season not to be won by a Mercedes driver.

The second victory of the year came in Germany in a race remembered for surreal conditions. Max started from second on the grid. Four safety cars and sixty-four slow laps later, he was the driver who somehow got to a soggy chequered flag first.

Brazil was a more straightforward affair. A strong pole on Saturday. A great race on Sunday with a lights-to-flag victory. At the end of 2019, Verstappen's better car and engine reliability, a constant drip feed of points and three race wins meant that he finished third in the championship with only the two Mercedes drivers ahead. Now, the only question was how to crack six years of the Silver Arrows domination!

But the question certainly wouldn't be answered in 2020. The season, like life, was marred by the constant threat of covid and the stress of the pandemic. Throughout the seventeen races on the rearranged calendar, Lewis Hamilton was sublime and yet the racing still managed to be hugely entertaining. Whilst the top spot might have gone Lewis's way more often than not, there were plenty of drivers in the mix to be on the podium. Naturally, Verstappen was one of them, and that kept his points adding up. He also managed to break the stranglehold on the top step of the podium. The first of his two wins came at Silverstone, where for the first time in the history of F1, they had decided to host a double header at the Northamptonshire track. It was all part of the plan that would ease travel issues during the global pandemic. The same format had taken place the month before in Austria with great success. The first race was the British Grand Prix and a week later we had the Seventieth Anniversary Grand Prix – a commemoration of the first championship Grand Prix, which took place at Silverstone in 1950.

It was an impressive win for Verstappen, who had finished second at the same track the week before. Mercedes struggled with tyre issues, but the Dutch driver took every opportunity presented, making the most of clean air when the Mercs pitted. When Valtteri Bottas came out in front of him, he made quick work of passing for the lead. It was a commanding win; 11 seconds ahead of Hamilton. It was in fact Red Bull's first win at the track since Mark Webber in 2012.

His other win that season came at the final race of the year and it couldn't have been simpler. Verstappen led every lap of the race from pole position to the chequered flag. Once again, it was third in the championship but with the benefit of hindsight, maybe the clues were already there for 2021. How much of a boost or insight did that Abu Dhabi win give the team and driver about what was to come?

Because what came in 2021 was as big a battle as we had seen on track for many years. The season will forever be famous, now infamous, overshadowed by what happened at the final race of the season. But we should never forget what an iconic season it was throughout. It could have been a season of a stalemate, an add-on, as the major set of rule changes which were due to be implemented at the start of 2021 were delayed to 2022 because of the pressures of the pandemic. What actually happened was that the few changes made were big enough to cause ripples, which became waves and, by the end of season, a full-on tsunami!

The budget had been cut to a maximum spend of $145 million. Despite the protests of some of the bigger teams, there is no need to feel too sorry about the reduction in budget with those eye-watering numbers. Despite holding off on the major rule changes, there were still some amendments to the regulations for the 2021 season and, without getting too bogged down in detail, it was all about the floor, which might not sound too exciting, mostly because it's the part that we don't see. The fancy design is all above water, as it were. But that's the point. Every time a stranded car returns to the pit lane and is being lowered off the back of a flatbed truck, the sole purpose of the assembled mechanics is, of course, to get the car back safely but also to try and stop cameras, photographers and ultimately other teams seeing the floor of the car. The changes brought in for 2021 were enough to cause sleepless nights for aerodynamicists and shake up the grid, thus creating one of the most exciting seasons we have had in years. No one had really wanted to revise a car for a final year when for so many the focus had already been turned to the next generation – the ones we have on track now.

Pre-season testing should always be taken with a pinch of salt, but in Bahrain, where the test was held, times suggested that Red Bull had closed the gap on Mercedes. The team's engine supplier, Honda, had announced that it would leave the sport at the end of the season and had brought forward the more compact and powerful engine, originally designed for 2022. This would provide one last blast before they said sayonara.

After testing, the teams and drivers stayed at the Sakhir circuit as the following week it would host the first race of the season. During the three practice sessions, Verstappen was quickest, and it proved to be the same story in qualifying. It was a refreshing, welcome start to the season although we had seen it all before. In recent years it had been Sebastian Vettel and Ferrari who threw down an early gauntlet, but it didn't take long for Mercedes and Hamilton to get into their stride, and by the end of the season it was hard to remember any early challenge. And by the time we reached Sunday night in Bahrain, it felt a little like normal service had been resumed. Hamilton had won the race, although he had been made to work for it.

At the next round in Imola, the tables were turned. In qualifying Hamilton was quickest and it was Verstappen's new teammate, Sergio Perez, who was second ahead of Max.

As the lights went out in the race, Max made an incredible start, passing the two cars in front. He went past Hamilton at turn 1 with a bold move that meant the Mercedes driver was forced wide over the kerbs on the outside of Tamburello, which damaged his front wing. From that moment on the win was Verstappen's.

Hamilton took the next two victories before heading to Monaco – a place where the British driver has an almost spiritual affinity but Verstappen has struggled over the years. But as Monaco Grand Prix weekends go, this one couldn't have been easier. In qualifying, Max put his Red Bull into second whilst pole sitter Charles Leclerc put his Ferrari into the wall. It meant the red flags came out and no one could improve their time. The Monégasque driver was still on pole but there was a lot of work and risk for the race.

Ferrari rebuilt the car and deemed the gearbox as being safe without needing to change it – had they done so, Leclerc would have taken a penalty and dropped down the grid. But on the way to the start, a fault was detected which meant Charles was unable to start the race. Pole position was left empty, so Verstappen in P2 became the de facto pole sitter. Max covered off any threat at the start of the Grand Prix, and after that it was all about keeping his car out of the barriers and waiting to see the chequered flag. After that win, for first time in his career, Max Verstappen was leading the Drivers' Championship, albeit with seventeen races to go! And it stayed that way until after Hungary after an incredible run of victories.

In fact, if it hadn't been for a tyre blow-out in Azerbaijan then Verstappen would have been set for five wins in a row. France, followed by two wins in the double-header in Austria, meant that we were all experiencing something very real. Championship rival Lewis Hamilton knew that this was no fluke and, for the first time in several years, he had a serious battle on his hands.

It was at the British Grand Prix where the season took a turn in a different direction. Heading into Silverstone, Verstappen was in great spirits, 32 points ahead in the Drivers' Championship. Leaving, he was in pain: his lead had been cut to eight points, he had hit the wall at 51G and spent that afternoon in the medical centre. The other car involved . . . Lewis Hamilton.

Though at that time it was a standalone incident, on both sides, there had been a shift in tension. Max was furious, for a couple of reasons. Firstly, the stewards ruled that he had been the innocent party and penalised Hamilton by 10 seconds, but the Brit was still able to win. What also really upset Verstappen and Red Bull Racing was the manner in which Lewis celebrated his win, out on track with the jubilant home fans. They described it as insensitive to behave like that whilst Max was still being checked in hospital.

The next race in Hungary didn't exactly appease the situation. The Mercs were quick and qualified in front of Verstappen, but come a wet race day, a mistake from Bottas caused chaos and took out both Red Bulls. Verstappen continued but the damage to his car hampered any chance to battle and progress. Esteban Ocon won the race with Hamilton second, which meant he and Mercedes left for the summer break leading their respective championships.

Thank goodness for the summer break! It had been such a frantic and loaded start to the season; it was tricky to see how things could play out any better in the second half. One thing was certain: for the team and drivers, the August shut-down would be the only chance to recharge the batteries before Christmas. Between now and then, either way, history would be made. There would either be the sport's first eight-time world champion or we would see the crowning of a new one.

The first race back was a total washout. For the first time in the history of the sport, there was no racing under green-flag conditions, but instead of calling it off completely, with only a couple of laps barely managed behind the safety car, half points were awarded. Overtaking obviously wasn't allowed, so the result was purely based on qualifying. It meant that Max won from George Russell in second and Lewis in third. It was the first of many FIA dramas in the second half of 2021, and the governing body and Race Director Michael Masi were criticised for the handling of the event.

Belgium was the first of a European triple header and the next stop was the much-hyped and long-awaited return to Zandvoort for the Dutch Grand Prix. No matter what series I have covered there, I have never made my Sunday night flight home due to gridlock getting out of the track, so popular is motor racing with the fans. Add in the MV33 element and it was an orange frenzy! If Max felt pressure, he certainly didn't show it and he buzzed with positive energy. The track suited the car very well, and by the end of the weekend it was another pole and another victory. He went into Monza with a three-point lead in the championship.

But the Italian Grand Prix proved to be the next pinch point of the season. The moment that threw fuel on top of the embers from Silverstone.

The race on Sunday saw two drivers on different strategies who quite simply shouldn't have been near each other on the track at the moment when things went wrong. Bizarrely, both Hamilton and Verstappen had poor pit stops, which meant circumstance had them on the same piece of racetrack at the same time. Hamilton was side-by-side with Verstappen on the pit exit and on the rundown to turn 1. Into turn 2, Verstappen bounced over a sausage kerb and went into Hamilton's left rear tyre, which launched his car over the top of the Mercedes. There is no doubt that the halo saved Hamilton's life that day and thankfully both drivers were uninjured. Underneath the wheels of the Red Bull, Lewis was pretty stuck but Verstappen jumped out and walked off. There was a lot of criticism saying that he should have checked to see if Hamilton was uninjured, but both Red Bull and Verstappen said that he knew he was okay. This time, the stewards ruled that Verstappen was at fault and awarded him a three-place grid penalty for the Russian Grand Prix plus two penalty points on his licence. Some former drivers saw it a racing incident, others like three-time world champion Sir Jackie Stewart were much tougher, saying Max was "taking longer than expected to mature".

Wins in the USA and Mexico meant it was championship advantage for Verstappen, but the threat from Hamilton was getting closer, though it wasn't until after the penultimate race of the season in Saudi Arabia where the two drew level on points.

Everyone talks about what happened in Abu Dhabi, but I feel that the tone was set in Saudi Arabia. It was a chaotic race, which might be expected at a track whose slogan is "The World's Fastest Street Circuit". After fifty laps, one safety car period, two red flags and four virtual safety cars, it was a relief just to finish the race with everyone unscathed.

After the first standing restart, Hamilton and Verstappen were involved in an incident where Max overtook Lewis off the track, shortly before a crash involving four cars resulted in a second red flag. This left the cars lined up with Verstappen first, the Alpine of Ocon second and Hamilton in third. Initially, the FIA Race Director Michael Masi offered to re-order the cars with Verstappen and Ocon switching places, but that was later amended to move Hamilton to second and Verstappen to third, which would mean the order would be Ocon, Hamilton, and Verstappen. This proposal and teams bartering with the Race Director took place instead of an investigation into Verstappen overtaking Hamilton at the first standing restart. It was unorthodox, that's for sure.

What really stood out in the race was the divide that was getting bigger between teams, if that was indeed possible. On lap 36 heading into turn 1, Hamilton tried to pass Verstappen but the Red Bull driver went straight on and cut the chicane. Verstappen ended up with a bigger advantage over Hamilton. On team radio, Max was told to give the place back to Lewis. In the middle of the track on the straight and with little warning, Max braked hard – 2.4G was the number mentioned after the race. It meant Hamilton had nowhere to go apart from into the back of the Red Bull, damaging the front wing of the Mercedes. Cue a furious Toto Wolff smashing his headset off the table. And yet despite that lasting image, by the time the chequered flag eventually fell, it was Wolff, Mercedes and Hamilton who left Saudi Arabia happiest with another race win – although not exactly happy with how everything had played out. Red Bull's Christian Horner said the bartering with the FIA during the race was "like being at the local market". Everyone was a little stunned with the relentless on-track drama, but there was no time to recover. Within 12 hours of the chequered flag falling, we had left Saudi and headed to Abu Dhabi. It had been a rollercoaster of a season, with some unbelievable moments and yet, incredibly, as we headed to the final race, somehow the championship rivals were level on points.

The number was 369.5. Everyone had a different theory about who had the edge at the Yas Marina circuit and, to add to the unknown, some changes to the layout of the track had been made to encourage overtaking.

The practice sessions saw Verstappen fastest in the first and then Hamilton quickest in the final two. As the sun set for qualifying it looked like Hamilton was marginally ahead but an incredible lap from Verstappen, using the slipstream from his teammate Sergio Perez, saw him take pole by almost four-tenths from Hamilton. For the showdown, the two championship contenders would be alongside each other on the front row of the grid. A fitting way for the final battle to get underway. There was certainly a nervousness in the Mercedes camp. Should neither Lewis nor Max finish the race then Verstappen would be world champion, by virtue that he had won more races throughout the season. That led to much speculation that the Dutch driver could afford to be more aggressive at the start. He didn't need to finish the Grand Prix, so long as Lewis didn't either. That theory was refuted by Red Bull, who said Max would never deliberately take someone out. Thankfully, of all the issues that came up, that wasn't one of them.

There are some days in sport where you know you are going to be watching history being made. This was one of them. This one day had transcended the sport, made global news around the world. It was one of the biggest sporting showdowns for many a year. The atmosphere in the paddock was electric. Everyone knew that if this season was anything to go by, then the extravagant firework display at the end of the Grand Prix would be overshadowed by the fireworks on track during the race. But in all the speculating, surmising and discussion about what might happen, at no point did anyone imagine the situation that led to Max Verstappen becoming world champion.

A strong start from Hamilton meant that he took the lead from

Verstappen off the line, and whilst there were dalliances on lap 1, the rest of the race was about Hamilton staying calm and Verstappen keeping in touch during the melee of pit stops and strategy.

It looked like Hamilton was cruising to his record-breaking eighth title until Nicholas Latifi put his Williams into the barriers, which brought out the safety car.

Hamilton stayed out whilst Verstappen came into the pits for a fresh set of soft tyres. He emerged in second but had five lapped cars between himself and Hamilton. As the debris from Latifi's crash was being cleared by the race marshals, the lapped drivers were initially informed that they would not be permitted to overtake. Then Horner came on team radio asking Masi why the lapped cars couldn't overtake. The decision was then reversed. Some cars were told to go through – but crucially and inexplicably not all, just the five between Hamilton and Verstappen. As Vettel, the fifth and final car, passed the safety car to join the lead lap, race control announced the safety car would enter the pits at the end of the lap to allow for one final lap of leave "nothing out there" green-flag racing. Toto Wolff was stunned, saying on team radio to the Race Director, "Michael, this isn't right." On the final lap, Verstappen used his fresh, faster soft tyres to pass Hamilton into turn 5. With no DRS available, Hamilton couldn't retake the lead despite several attempts. As the chequered flag fell, Verstappen's dream was realised. Yes, there were protests and investigations, but Max Verstappen was world champion. Everyone there, everyone watching around the world, was stunned.

It was a race which in many ways summed up the career of the new world champion. It was flawed but it was brave, skilful, audacious and precocious. Max had his father there, girlfriend and friends, including the Pex brothers, the best friends and karting rivals who were in the film that I made with him and had been there since the start with him.

Yes, he has famous friends and can live whatever life he chooses to live, but at heart he is very much a family person, his roots mean a lot to him and have made him who he is now. Before every Grand Prix weekend, his mother Sophie lights a candle in church whilst saying a prayer to keep him safe. She has watched her son grow up, get his first kart at the age of four, taken him to F1 paddocks to support his father. His family created and encouraged those dreams of becoming a racing driver, a Formula One driver and then a World Champion.

There are plenty of reasons to criticise what happened in the last race of the season and, especially the way that things were handled, but you can't argue that Max won ten races to Lewis's eight. He didn't luck into a championship as many distraught Lewis fans have suggested.

At the start of the 2022 season, Max was asked if after the way the championship was won, he felt he had a point to prove. He replied: "No. I proved that with the most wins, the most pole laps and the most laps led. People forget that. They only look at Abu Dhabi, apparently."

Jos created the ultimate competitive animal but one blessed with belief, skill and speed. "Even when Max was young, he was only focusing that he wanted to become an F1 driver. It's his life, F1."

And now it's his legacy. It's hard to imagine that Max Verstappen will leave Formula One with "just" a single world championship. Whenever he has achieved something, he sets his sights higher. At the moment, Max Verstappen has the world of Formula One at his feet.

5
FERNANDO ALONSO

ASK ANY FAN TO NAME THE BEST DRIVER on the grid and Fernando Alonso's name will come up time and time again. Ask any driver to say who is the best in terms of race craft or who can wring the best out of an under-performing car and Alonso's name will almost always be at the top.

Winning two Formula One World Championships still puts Fernando into a very exclusive club, but there is a sense that it should have been more. Fans and drivers know it. The Spaniard certainly knows it. In all the titles he narrowly missed out on, just eight points separate him from being a five-time world champion. Take nothing away, he is still seen as one of *the* great drivers. Controversial? Yes. Charismatic? Definitely. An asset to the sport? Absolutely. As an interviewee: one of my favourites!

In my experience, there is never an interview where Alonso turns up without being fully prepared. He is softly spoken, considered and often calculated. He has been around long enough to know what will be repeated, make headlines and play out on team radio. He makes mischief and even chaos for those around him, yet it rarely strikes you as being red-zone reactionary. It's pre-conceived and delivered at a moment of his choosing. That is really what separates Alonso from the others: the absolute control he can assert in a situation.

Straight after every race, Fernando is shown a piece of paper with the classification on it so he can better understand the bigger picture before he gives interviews. It's the same during a race on team radio. He always wants to know exactly what is going on, mostly because he has an incredible capacity to take it all in, which lets him read a race so well. Abu Dhabi 2021 was many things, but it was also the perfect example of Alonso making sense of the chaos whilst battling hard for valuable points. As well as a discussion with his Alpine race engineer about the safety car period in the last laps which will be debated until the end of time, Alonso wanted to know exactly why he had not been in position to beat the rival Alpha Tauri. He wanted the breakdown, to know which tyres the opposition were on and on what lap they pitted. He was then given the top-ten finishers and instantly replied with a monologue about how good 2022 was going to be for the team. It was impressive, informative and inspiring for those who worked tirelessly day in, day out at Alpine.

Alonso is a thinking driver – although some would say he thinks too much and that this is one of the reasons that his career has been far from plain sailing. For me, it's that spark and electric mind that makes him the competitor and person that he is.

In 2022 at the Azerbaijan Grand Prix, after twenty-one years, three months and a day, Fernando became the driver with the longest Formula One career. The two-time world champion has been a fixture in the paddock longer than some of his current competitors have been alive! He has retired and returned and been part of some of the biggest moments of recent years. Even on his record-breaking weekend in Baku, he managed to create carefully crafted overtakes and chaos in equal measure – things that have become something of a trademark of the Spaniard's career! And how does he deal with it? A clever answer, a shrug and a smile normally do the job.

Like so many drivers, his love of motorsport came from his father,

Luis, who was a keen karter; but it was just a hobby, and one which he hoped he could encourage his children to take part in. Luis built a beautiful kart, a replica McLaren-Honda in the same distinctive red and white Marlboro livery, but it wasn't made for Fernando, it was for his older sister, Lorena. As a female encouraging other women to get into motorsport, I love this. Mr Alonso was very ahead of his time. Alas, Lorena didn't want the kart and it went to Fernando. It now sits in pride of place alongside his world championship winning cars in the Fernando Alonso Museum in Asturias, the northern part of Spain where the family come from.

"My father put some extensions to the pedals and the engine he put the throttle just a little bit on, so my throttle didn't work. It was just the same speed all of the time and it was walking speed!" Alonso told me as I spent some time filming at the museum and kart track.

His father wasn't spoiling Fernando's fun without cause. You see he was just three years old and tiny! Beside the kart in the museum sits his first photo driving licence.

"It's funny as it says on the back of the licence that the holder knows perfectly the rules and knows the implications to be a racing driver. For sure, I didn't know anything about that."

There is no way the blond, cherubic three-year-old in the photo knew how to spell his name, let alone understand the rules of racing.

One thing he did know how to do was drive, and it wasn't long before Alonso was seen as the hottest young thing in karting. By the time he had reached his teenage years, Fernando already had an impressive trophy haul. He didn't come from the kind of wealth that could support a young driver to climb through the ranks, paying for the most competitive seats possible. He knew that to get the best opportunities he would have to earn them on track by winning the biggest races, which he did. At the same time, he was acting as mechanic for younger karters to earn extra money.

In his debut season in cars, he won the Euro Open by Nissan and a year later moved up to the F1 support race, now called F2, formerly called GP2 and then known as F3000. He drove for the well-known Astromega team which was connected to Minardi. As part of the prize for winning the Euro Open in 1999, he was given his first taste of Formula One machinery with a test drive for Minardi. What they saw was raw speed, potential and hunger whilst Alonso saw opportunity and the key to his future.

His foot was in the door of F1, if not regularly in the car, but after a season of being a test driver in the lowly but much-loved team, Alonso was given his chance of a race seat.

In 2001 he lined up on the grid and, in what became a trademark of his, outperformed the car which certainly had its limitations. But limitations are something that Fernando did not have, which was immediately spotted by Flavio Briatore and Renault. Still, they needed him to be patient. For 2002, he was on the sidelines, signed as a test driver in a role where he would learn from the team whilst studying the race drivers Giancarlo Fisichella and Jenson Button. It was the perfect schooling, and when he was eventually signed to replace Button, the Spaniard was up to speed with the team and ready to wow.

In just the second race of 2003 in Malaysia, and his first competitive season for Renault, he became the youngest driver ever to take pole position in F1.

Alonso finished third in the race but had demonstrated that, when it came to outright speed and skill, he had plenty of both. The 2003 season was all about bedding in, but after the early shock pole at Sepang, he sprung another surprise later in the year.

The Hungarian Grand Prix, held in mid-August, was the first on the revamped racetrack. Alonso took pole position on the Saturday and when it came to lights out on the Sunday he made a great start, another trademark of his career. It was a race filled with calamity and safety cars, but after seventy laps it was Fernando Alonso who crossed the line first to become the youngest race winner in Formula One, a record which had stood since 1957 with the legendary Bruce McLaren.

After the race he said, "It is a dream come true. I am twenty-two years old, and I have my first victory. I hope I have a long career with lots more victories."

Everyone appreciated that, so long as he had the car, victories would not be an issue. But the following year, Renault did not have a competitive challenger, so whilst he finished fourth in the championship, 2004 was a season with no race wins.

But then everything changed. Enter the R25.

The year 2005 was a season of change in every sense. There was a new team in town in Red Bull Racing and a big rewrite of the rules too. As had become the norm in that era, there was a continued tinkering with qualifying, although that season the new changes to the format didn't last long – just six races. A new edict meant that engines must be used for two races, dramatic then but nothing in comparison to the endurance that engines must have today. But it was the change in use of tyres that made the biggest difference. Only one set of tyres could be used for both Saturday qualifying and the entire race. It was also the era of two tyre suppliers in Michelin and Bridgestone. The question was, who could create the more robust rubber that was still fast enough to compete at the highest speeds?

It became evident early on that, despite dominating the previous five seasons, it wouldn't be another title for Ferrari and Michael Schumacher. The Renault was working and working very well. They won the first four races of the season, Giancarlo Fisichella taking the first in Australia and the following three going the way of Alonso. As the season went on, McLaren became increasingly quick, but their package was fragile.

Despite having won in Formula One and proven his worth, the race that many hold up as Alonso's "arrival" was in Imola as he held off a hard-charging Schumacher. It was seen as the master versus the apprentice. "It was an iconic race for my career, but you only realise that years later," he acknowledged.

Alonso secured the Drivers' Championship with a third-place finish in the Brazilian Grand Prix, making him, at the time, the youngest F1 World Champion in the history of the sport. Despite the Spaniard and McLaren's Räikkönen having six victories each, it was Alonso's earlier consistency racking up five seconds and three thirds that meant the title was his with two rounds to go. It wasn't until the final round of the season that Renault claimed their first ever Constructors' Championship.

In the press conference afterwards, Alonso was understandably very emotional, and he looked almost shell-shocked. What was clear was that, although F1 is a team sport, he saw himself as the "lone wolf", or at the very least an underdog who battled hard to get where he was.

"I came from a country with no tradition in Formula One and I fight alone as I've not had any help from anybody all my career. I arrived in Formula One thanks to the results in previous categories and my sponsors. Now I think it is the maximum I can achieve in my life and my career, and it is all thanks to three or four people. No more than that. We fight alone. Always."

It was quite haunting as he sat beside the huge, larger-than-life figures and shakily said these words. In a global sport, watched by tens of millions, it was a single person saying thank you to less than a handful of people. Many drivers come with an entourage, bring a large group of friends and family, but Fernando never has done and since the day he started, he still has the same people around him. His trainer is his brother-in-law; his physio, a friend. In recent years he has a PR person who is also a friend, and his manager Luis is always there. Behind the scenes he is still very close to Flavio Briatore, who masterminded his career from as soon as he arrived in the F1 paddock. Alonso keeps it close and is very private. In that respect he arrived as a lone wolf, and he still is one. Always running to a different beat.

Formula One in Spain was never very popular. When it came to motorsport, two wheels were much more appealing than anything with four. But thanks to Fernando, the whole sporting outlook changed.

In 2005, at the last race of season, he explained to Jim Rosenthal on ITV, "It's good to feel the support of the people. They enjoy the races. I am very proud of this because in Spain, three years ago, they had 200,000 people watching on TV. Now we have ten million, so I am really pleased."

What also stood out from that interview was the pride Alonso took from the fact that he had won in an inferior car to the McLaren, "I think to win the championship in the way we did with not the quickest car is even better for me and my championship because if you win it with the better car people start saying it's the car that won the championship. I am really pleased and happy that people talk about Kimi because my championship gets bigger and bigger."

He's absolutely right, of course, but it was interesting and unusual to hear. He was softly spoken and very calm, but it was delivered with a slightly unsettling, steely resolve. Another Alonso trademark.

What we didn't know at the time was that, as he was waiting to step onto the podium in Brazil after his third place, he and McLaren boss Ron Dennis, who was also waiting to go onto the podium as his two drivers had finished first and second, had a discussion. Depending on who you speak to, Alonso offered his services to McLaren, but the others say that Ron asked the Spaniard if he fancied driving for the team. Alonso did and we will get on to that shortly. But before he could join the Woking outfit, he had another year with Renault and another title to battle for.

And 2006 did bring another championship for both Alonso and Renault but it was tougher. Ferrari and Michael Schumacher were back to their imperious form. The seven-time world champion announced in September of that year that it would be his last and therefore another championship would be the perfect leaving present. An eighth was certainly in his sights.

It was a battle royale going down to the final race of the season. Once again Brazil and Interlagos would be the backdrop to a dramatic finale and an Alonso world title. En route to the victory was a rapturous first home win for Alonso, further cementing him as his country's biggest sports star.

It had been a season filled with controversial moments. In Monaco, Schumacher famously parked his car at Rascasse, meaning no other driver could improve their time and thus giving him pole position. In Italy, a penalty to Alonso for holding up Ferrari's Felipe Massa was met with incredulity by most in the paddock. Even the FIA boss Max Mosley said that he would not have handed out the same punishment. Then halfway through the season the FIA banned the "mass damper" system used by Renault. The FIA had apparently been consulted about the system during its development and authorised it but said it had now moved away from its intended use. It was outlawed on the ruling that it was a "moveable aerodynamic device". The effect of the ban was clear, but it also coincided with the resurgence of Ferrari and Schumacher, who, in the latter half of the season, won five of the last nine races, keeping the pressure on right until the very end. By the time the chequered flag fell at the final race of the season, both had won seven races and just thirteen points separated the two.

Whilst drivers enjoy getting things sown up as early as possible, for fans there is nothing better than a final race championship decider: the penalty shoot-out of Formula One. But whilst it went down to the last race in Brazil, it was always in favour of Alonso. He only needed one point to become back-to-back champion while Schumacher needed to win with the young gun not scoring a single point. Qualifying didn't put either driver on the front row. The German suffered a mechanical issue, meaning he started from tenth whilst the Spaniard could only manage fourth. In the race, Schumacher suffered an early puncture, so he had to work his way back through the field, eventually finishing his then final race in fourth, while Alonso took second and became the youngest back-to-back world champion. It was a great drive from Michael, show-casing his talents right until the end, but, if anything, it further highlighted the rising star of Alonso.

"I always said to become champion when Michael is still on the track has more value than when he has retired. I was extremely lucky to win the last two championships he raced in."

Nothing sums up Fernando more. Like his comments about winning against Kimi, he is not wrong, but so often he manages to give a compliment to someone which ends up flattering himself!

It is incredible to think that, after that win in 2006 at the age of twenty-five and with all the talent he possesses, Alonso has never won another Formula One World title. Years have passed, over a decade even. It beggars belief.

With those two titles and the sporting world at his feet, he left for McLaren. But ominously for Alonso, whilst he was securing his second World Championship, his new team had failed to win a single race during that season for the first time in ten years. In the end though, that would prove to be the least of his worries!

In 2007, resplendent in his white and red McLaren overalls,

Alonso walked into the F1 paddock in Australia as a two-time champion and the most decorated man on the grid. Alongside him in the team, a rookie in Lewis Hamilton – brimming with potential, yes, but proven at the top level? Certainly not.

It only took until turn 1 in the Australian Grand Prix for the form book to be ripped up as Hamilton swept past Alonso on the outside. Kimi Räikkönen won the race, leading every lap in his Ferrari but both McLaren drivers were on the podium, Alonso managing to finish ahead of Hamilton.

Whilst Alonso won the next race in Malaysia, there was no doubt his teammate was putting the pressure on, standing on the podium at the first nine races of the season. Alonso was not as consistent in terms of podiums, but he did have three wins to Hamilton's two by the time they reached the Hungarian Grand Prix – widely seen as when the bomb went off, even if the fuse had been lit in Monaco a few races earlier.

Some thirty-five years after Watergate and a year before "lie-gate" came "spy-gate"! We will get on to "crash-gate" later!

What happened in Hungary was extreme, heat of the battle madness between two drivers doing whatever they could to get an edge – and it was only Saturday! In qualifying, which was run in yet another guise to the one we have today due to refuelling, Alonso was meant to be allowed to pass Hamilton in the latter stages. Despite the team telling Lewis to let his teammate pass him, he didn't slow up to let Fernando through.

The Spaniard realised what was happening and decided to take matters into his own hands, as Lewis had done just minutes before. Alonso completely backed off, which meant he could get into the pits ahead of Hamilton. These were the days of burning off fuel, doing quick laps and refuelling to the same level for the start of the race.

McLaren got ready to stack the cars. Through some cunning,

Alonso would still be in first in the pits as he was meant to be in the original plan. Tyres were slotted on and he would head back out on track. But when the lollipop was lifted, Alonso didn't move. For ten seconds he was stationary; the mechanics around the car were unsure what was going on and glanced around them to see if there was an issue. Hamilton was forced to sit behind him, waiting and watching the clock tick down. On ITV's commentary, James Allen questioned what was going on and realised quicker than most that Alonso had been "tactical". Damon Hill described it as a "little bit naughty" but until there was proof or until Alonso explained himself, it was a big accusation to level, because Alonso had essentially destroyed Hamilton's qualifying and opportunity of keeping pole position.

Because of the delay, the Brit didn't have enough time to complete his lap and, *che sorpresa*, the Spaniard took pole position from his teammate. It was one of those moments where you know as a viewer and a fan that you've just witnessed a game changer!

McLaren boss Ron Dennis felt he had all the proof he needed. Whilst Alonso was still on track, he stormed up to his physio – why him is anyone's guess – but until he could get his hands on Fernando, Fabrizio Borra was the closest Alonso ally that Dennis could reach.

When Alonso did get out of the car and speak to the TV crews, he didn't exactly clear things up.

"We always stop. We wait for the countdown and we go. Sometimes it's forty-five seconds like the first stop of today, and sometimes it's ten or fifteen like the second, but I think the calculation was wrong because my teammate didn't complete the lap and I crossed the line with two or three seconds, so it was really, really tight and these things unfortunately happened today to us."

He did neglect to mention his part in the miscalculation!

Later that night, the team was summoned to the FIA, where the stewards gave him a five-place grid penalty and said McLaren wouldn't be allowed any constructor's points from the race. Hamilton started from pole and led every lap until the chequered flag was waved.

On track it might have looked like "normal service"; off-track, though, things had taken an irretrievable turn. Fernando felt strongly that Lewis not letting him through provoked his actions in delaying the pitstops. But after what was said in a dramatic meeting on the morning of the Hungarian GP between him and Ron Dennis, Alonso's time at the team was limited, if not immediately over.

In an article on the BBC Sport website by BBC F1 correspondent Andrew Benson, he writes:

> For some time he had been telling Dennis that he and Hamilton should not be racing each other. The pattern was obvious. They were taking points off each other, and the Ferrari drivers were still too close for comfort. If they were not careful, Alonso believed, they would end up losing a title they should win.
>
> Alonso decided to play his hand. With his manager Luis Garcia Abad also in attendance, he had a meeting with Dennis a few hours before the race.
>
> Alonso told Dennis he needed to right the wrong Hamilton had caused him the day before. Hamilton had double-crossed him on the fuel-burn laps, Alonso said, and now he had a penalty and was sixth on the grid. It was not right.
>
> The relationship was already broken after Monaco. But what Alonso said next ensured on the spot that he would have to leave the team at the end of the year. It is well known that Alonso threatened Dennis that if the team did not do what he wanted, he would reveal to the FIA emails he had that were relevant to the "spy-gate" case, in which McLaren had recently escaped censure

for one of their engineers possessing a document of confidential Ferrari technical information that ran to nearly 800 pages.

But what exactly he asked them to do has previously been known only by a handful of privileged insiders.

Alonso insisted that McLaren make Hamilton run out of fuel in the race.

Dennis asked Alonso to stop talking. He called in Martin Whitmarsh, his second-in-command, and asked Alonso to repeat what he had just said. He did. Dennis sent Alonso and Abad away, turned to Whitmarsh and asked what he thought they should do.

Dennis said he thought they should phone FIA president Max Mosley. Whitmarsh agreed. They also both agreed that they could not allow Alonso to race. They could not have a driver blackmailing the team.

Dennis phoned Mosley and told him what had happened. Mosley asked him what he was going to do, then advised Dennis not to take Alonso out of the car.

Andrew is a friend, colleague and one of the best and most respected and connected F1 writers out there. His insight and intel are fascinating.

The matter of "spy-gate" had already been known to the FIA, but another investigation by the governing body ensued which resulted in an eye-watering $100 million fine – the largest fine ever issued in the history of sport. McLaren would also lose all points from the Constructors' Championship, which would have been worth a colossal amount, in the tens of millions. The penalty was global news.

Somehow, the relationship between Alonso and McLaren continued in that he remained their driver and, in the final six races, he was on the podium for five, including a win in Monza. His teammate had two more podiums, including a win in Japan. Ultimately, Alonso and many people's concerns became reality. McLaren had not prioritised a driver and therefore they lost the championship to Ferrari's Kimi Räikkönen at the final race of the season by a single point: Räikkönen on 110 points and both McLaren drivers on 109. Would McLaren have celebrated had Alonso become world champion in 2007? We will never know but we certainly could never have imagined that, after that toxic season, the two would get back together less than a decade later!

Throughout the year, it became a matter of who Alonso would drive for the following season. No one believed he would see out the final two years of his McLaren deal. He had been connected to both Red Bull and Toyota, but it was a return to the familiarity of Renault and Flavio Briatore that eventually was confirmed mid-December.

The 2008 season started slowly for the Enstone outfit. Reliability, spins and slip-ups were largely the story for the pairing of Alonso and his teammate Nelson Piquet Jr. So far, the season had been dominated by McLaren and Ferrari. No surprise really, as that had been the tale of 2007, a year that Renault didn't manage to win a race. But things would change in September when at the first Singapore night race, Alonso took his debut win of the season and gave Renault their first win since he left the team.

Watching the race went a little like this: lap 12, Alonso is the first driver to pit. They bolt on a set of soft tyres, and he comes out at the back of the field. Two laps later, his teammate Piquet Jr crashes into the wall at turn 17, blaming a lack of grip from the hard tyres. Alonso went on to win the race, after which he said his success came down to the team's strategy and bit of luck. He said the team considered the lack of overtaking opportunities and concern over brake issues and chose a two-stop strategy.

"I'm extremely happy. I cannot believe it right now. I think I need a couple of days to realise that we won a race this year. It seems impossible," said Fernando in the FIA press conference after the chequered flag.

"The first safety car helped me a lot and I was able to win the race."

Nothing wrong with anything that he said. It was all true.

But what emerged the following year in 2009 was that the crash on lap 14 by Nelson Piquet had been premeditated. It was shocking to learn. Piquet had been sacked during the 2009 season after a string of poor results. He's not the first driver to lose his seat but, for him, the circumstances and what he had been asked to do were different. Nelson felt he had the ammunition and evidence to bring down some of the biggest names in the sport at the time.

The evidence revolved around the fact that turn 17, where the crash happened, was the only part of the circuit where there were no cranes in position to remove a stranded car – therefore, the crash took place in the only part of the track which required safety car deployment.

"It did not have any cranes that would allow a damaged car to be swiftly lifted off the track, nor did it have any side entrances to the track," said Nelson.

Piquet Jr's statement also said that in the presence of both Flavio Briatore and Pat Symonds, he had been asked if he would be willing to "sacrifice his race for the team by causing a safety car".

Data from Piquet's car showed an unusual throttle trace after the back of the car drifted out, "in the knowledge that this would lead to my car making heavy contact with the concrete wall."

Renault were found guilty of race-fixing, but both Briatore and Symonds denied that the conversation ever took place.

Max Mosley, the former FIA boss, announced there would be no fine for Renault and their punishment would be a suspended two-year sentence, which the team subsequently did not serve. But it did have big repercussions for both Briatore and Symonds – for a while.

Briatore was given a lifetime ban from FIA events, but his ban was reduced to five years and he can still be seen around the paddock, on the grid before a race and behind the scenes in Alonso's career.

Pat Symonds served a ban but now works as part of the management of F1. What remains unknown is how much knowledge Alonso had about the "crash-gate" affair. Fernando categorically denies knowing anything about it. Either way it was another season shrouded in drama.

Early in 2009, I went to Alonso's hometown of Oviedo in northern Spain, where he was doing a roadshow. Tens of thousands of people lined the streets to see the homecoming of their hero who drove a series of Renault road and race cars, including his Formula One car, through the city centre. I was lucky enough to spend a couple of days with Fernando around the event whilst filming behind the scenes for BBC.

In the interview that was broadcast I boldly said to him: "It seems a long time ago that you were a world champion, does it seem it to you?"

"To me as well, unfortunately. It is the third year that I will be not champion. Two years ago with McLaren I was fighting until the last race but it didn't happen in the end, so it will be three years with not the possibility to win the championship. It is not long if you imagine the Formula One career for a driver after fourteen or fifteen years and it only happened three years that I cannot win, but it seems long and hopefully next year we can change the situation.

"I am a very consistent driver, I think. I am not the quickest driver, maybe I am not the most talented driver, maybe I am not the most tough working driver, but I am very consistent. One day I can be second, one day fourth, one day third, whatever, but it will not happen two or three races that I am off the points. I will always be there, so at the end of the Championship it's good because you score points in basically all of the races, which puts me in a good position for the title.

"Every day when I wake up, I need to beat someone, even playing cards or whatever. I need to have some kind of competition, call a friend, play a match or whatever because I need the adrenaline to beat someone, so Formula One is still my life and for sure winning is my goal every day. When I am not winning, it's sad day."

He summed himself up perfectly: throughout his career he has always driven to his potential, regardless of the car beneath him. But those championships just didn't come again with Renault.

The decision to join a team with championship winning potential had already been taken by Alonso. He was impatient and wanted more success. The driver move merry-go-round had started spinning even earlier than normal that year and quotes from Alonso in just the second race of the season in Malaysia only added fuel to the fire.

He was quoted as saying, "I always try to be in the best car. I'm at Renault now because I wanted to go back to winning, like in 2005 and 2006. But I have an option to leave so I can still be in the best possible car, and it is clear that Ferrari's is one of the best."

Following the bizarre pattern of what so often happens in F1, the worst-kept secret was announced six months later. Fernando Alonso would be a Ferrari driver.

For all F1 fans, the excitement was through the roof. Hamilton in a McLaren v Alonso in a Ferrari. Game on. Or so we thought.

Throughout the Spaniard's five years at Maranello, it was a rollercoaster of joy and disappointment. Similar to his Renault days in

2005 and 2006, Alonso spent much of the time over-performing in an under-performing car. During his time at the Scuderia, the biggest barrier to his success was Red Bull, by far the superior car of that era.

It was a dream start for the marriage of Fernando and Ferrari winning on his debut. Yes, Sebastian Vettel took pole position, and his teammate Felipe Massa was second on the grid, but it was Alonso who took the victory. He passed his teammate with relative ease on lap 1, and when Vettel's car suffered a failure, it was he who was there to capitalise. Vettel eased the Red Bull home in fourth, but the headlines belonged to the prancing horse.

After the race, Alonso said he expected three other teams to push Ferrari throughout the season: Red Bull, Mercedes and McLaren.

In the interview pen after Bahrain, Alonso explained to me, "Now with the good car that we have, I think that we can enjoy races, we can enjoy the weekends and Australia is the next opportunity to show our potential. I am sure this will depend track to track, maybe Mercedes or McLaren are in front of us."

And he was right. Just seven days later, Vettel once again took pole, but reliability issues ended his chances, and it was the first win for the Jenson Button and McLaren pairing. It was a messy, rain-soaked race with ten cars not finishing.

From then on, the race wins were split between Button, Vettel, Hamilton and Webber. It took Alonso until race eleven in Germany before he got back on the top step of the podium, and in true Fernando style, it was one of the most controversial moments of the season.

"Fernando is faster than you!"

Who can forget the Yorkshire tones of Rob Smedley delivering that line to his driver Felipe Massa. Undoubtedly, they were team orders very loosely disguised as a bit of information. Ferrari received a $100,000 fine for the debacle. Rule 39.1 is, as Martin Brundle said at the time in commentary, "Very simple and very short. Team orders which interfere with a race result are prohibited."

The issue was that after the suggestion that Fernando was faster than Felipe, Smedley then said, "Good lad. Stick with him now. Sorry."

It was obviously deliberate and emotive because Smedley and Massa were a team within a team and Massa was set to win his first race of the season. Rob felt hurt by the situation, and he knew that Felipe would be too. Up and down the paddock, we knew what we had seen; team bosses, drivers, ex-drivers all came out against it, but Ferrari denied it all.

Massa actually said to me straight after the race, "We didn't have team orders in the race. I was struggling on the hard tyre."

I asked him if he had decided to let Alonso pass.

"Yes."

Alonso then said to me, "I was surprised when I saw Felipe having a problem. I thought it was a gear problem." He added, "We drive for Ferrari. Ferrari pay us at the end of the month and we try and score the most points for the team."

It was obvious that the Scuderia meant business when it came to winning the Championship and that business came in various guises! Former team owner and BBC pundit Eddie Jordan called it "theft".

What enraged the other drivers and teams was the fact that it really did matter when it came to the championship. The top four drivers only had twenty-one points separating them, less than a race win. The McLaren pairing of Hamilton and Button led the way, then came Red Bull's Webber and Vettel, who were tied on points in third and fourth. The latest race winner, Alonso, was fifth but in touch now and twenty-five points richer for that win.

The championship battle raged on with different drivers leading at various points. The next race after the German fiasco was Hungary, which was won by Mark Webber, and it was he who led the championship throughout the summer break.

Hamilton and Webber kept switching the lead, but things changed for Alonso in September. Monza is home of the tifosi and a victory there for Ferrari means more than any other Grand Prix. They hadn't seen a home victory since Michael Schumacher won in 2006.

It was a messy race with crashes and chaos, but whilst his rivals struggled or retired, coming through unscathed was Alonso. It meant that when it came to the championship, he moved up from fifth to third.

And things would only continue to get better for the Spaniard in Singapore. He dominated qualifying as the top five championship contenders lined up 1–5 on the grid. Alongside Alonso on the front row was Vettel, with Hamilton and Button on the second row, and Webber fifth.

During the race, Webber and Hamilton touched, causing damage to each other. Alonso and Vettel were running together at the front, something that, for all the rivalry between the two, we have rarely seen in their F1 careers. They traded fastest laps but Alonso was faultless and crossed the line first, less than three-tenths ahead of Vettel. It meant that Fernando was second in the championship and just eleven points behind Webber, who retained the lead despite a couple of tricky races. That victory for Alonso is regarded as one of his best. It was controlled, calm, and whilst it was a street track with few overtaking opportunities, the fact he kept the faster Red Bull behind him was a stroke of defensive genius.

The following race in Japan had such poor weather conditions that qualifying and the race were both run on the Sunday. Vettel won, from Webber and Alonso. We had known all along but the

2010 season really was shaping up to be a classic. Heading into Korea, with three races to go, Webber still had a strong lead – fourteen points ahead of both Alonso and Vettel, who were tied in second.

It was another race shaped by the rain. The Red Bulls locked out the front row of the grid at the Korean International Circuit, with Alonso in third and Hamilton alongside. Four drivers all with a chance of being world champion. The ensuing fifty-five laps were a collection of red flags, safety cars and missed opportunities. In short it was survival of the best. Webber spun out, the costliest moment of his entire F1 career. Vettel had an engine failure whilst leading, and ready to capitalise on the misfortune was who else but Fernando Alonso. As well as winning the race, it meant that for the first time that season Alonso led the championship and by a decent eleven points thanks to the retirements of his nearest rivals. The drama and length of that race meant that daylight had almost gone by the time it ended. I remember standing in the darkness and when the drivers got to the interview area, it was indeed night. Red Bull were desolate but in the gloom of nightfall, Ferrari were in full celebratory mode.

The penultimate race of the season in Brazil went the way of Vettel. Alonso still led the championship, Webber was eight points behind, Vettel was third and Hamilton fourth. Button was now mathematically out of contention.

It meant that, heading into the final race of the season, we had four drivers all with a chance of becoming world champion. The Red Bull drivers were looking for their first and the atmosphere within the team was uncomfortable to say the least. Hamilton had an outside chance, twenty-four points behind Alonso. But Fernando was very much the man at the top – eight points ahead of Webber and fifteen ahead of Vettel.

In qualifying, it was Vettel who had taken pole and had the advantage come Sunday. Hamilton was second with Alonso third. Webber was over his shoulder in fifth. The permutations are always a huge headache on days like these, not just for commentators but for the strategists too. Ferrari needed to cover off both Red Bulls and that is a difficult thing to do when it comes to pit stops. Add in a track where at that time overtaking was limited, and the task was almost impossible. To the shock of everyone, including Sebastian Vettel, it was the German who won his first title, leading the championship for the only time that season after the race!

Alonso ended up four points behind in second, but that is definitely not what he'd driven his heart out for all season.

The race was incredibly tense and, in the end, Alonso's biggest challenger was Vitaly Petrov in the Renault. After the chequered flag, Fernando slowed down alongside and gesticulated at the Russian driver.

I said to him in the post-race interview, "At the end of the race you looked quite upset with Petrov, is that how you feel? Did he get in your way?"

"I tried to overtake him once and he protected like the last lap in the last race of the championship, like we were both fighting for the championship. He was very aggressive but that's the way it is. He drove very well. No mistakes. Next year we try again.

"For me, coming back to winning races, fighting for the championship in the last race, I won five races. I overtook in victories Niki Lauda, Fangio, big names in Formula One, so for me it's something amazing and I'm sure with this team it is very possible to fight for championships in the near future, so I am very happy and very confident."

But the pictures don't lie, and they showed an upset and shocked Alonso being consoled by his Ferrari team after the race. Two hours before, he had led the championship. It had been his and Ferrari's to lose.

Fernando said to me several times in that post race interview, "Next year we try again." These interviews happen so quickly after a race that sometimes the emotion is too raw for the driver to process but Alonso knew exactly what had happened. The dream he harboured of being a three-time world champion had been lost. He had plenty of laps in the car to process it.

"Next year we try again."

But it wasn't to be in 2011. Sebastian Vettel wrapped up his second title at the Japanese Grand Prix with four races still to go. Alonso was fourth behind McLaren's Button and Red Bull's Webber. He only managed one race win that season as did Ferrari. It came at a typically rain-soaked British Grand Prix. Alonso had qualified third and, like in so many races, whilst other drivers and teams made mistakes, it was Fernando who was there to capitalise. He eventually finished sixteen seconds ahead of Vettel.

At the following race in Germany I had a sit-down interview in the Ferrari motorhome with Fernando. I always enjoyed these as over the years you get to know people, and whilst you're not always friends in the meeting-up sense, you are friendly and have shared big moments along the way. This interview was particularly fun, despite an honest and tough start, a bit like his season.

"Fernando, surely you didn't sign for a team which starts their season halfway through?" I asked.

"Of course, we want to fight for the championship every year we race, and we know that the first half of the season is a key part of the championship. It's something we will improve in the next couple of years, and I think in Ferrari sooner or later the success will come because it is a great team and they have huge potential to do well."

But the truth was that, apart from the early win in Bahrain in

2010, for the last two years, Ferrari had not been challenging consistently for race wins until halfway through the season. No one wins a title like that.

Fortunately, we moved on to more fun stuff. Fernando is a magician, not just in the car but outside of it too. He loves his card tricks, so I gave him a pack and told him to do his best. As he was preparing the cards he explained:

"On Sunday morning if I have a new trick or something, I go in the garage with the guys and I try and play a little bit to make a good atmosphere before the race."

He then produced three cards – two ten of hearts and an ace of hearts. I am not really a fan of magic and to this day I am still confused as to how he did it. He certainly had all the chat (as you will see if you look it up on YouTube).

"Be careful! You think I am playing with more than three cards. Look at the cards."

After a lot of talking and shuffling, he laid out an ace of hearts, a ten of hearts and then says to me, "I give you the last opportunity. Which card was the third one?"

I was certain. "The ten of hearts."

He smiled as he turned over the final card. "The joker!" he said.

It was perfect, fitting and funny!

Ferrari did heed the warnings from the previous two years and produced a strong car for the start of the 2012 season, but it was evident that Red Bull had too. It was an incredible beginning to the season, with seven different drivers winning the first seven races, and it wasn't until June at his home Grand Prix that Alonso became the first driver to win two races.

Race two in Malaysia was the first win of the year for Alonso. He had qualified in a lowly ninth and it was evident that qualifying wasn't to be Ferrari's strong point throughout the season.

© MATTEO BAZZI / EPA-EFE / Shutterstock

Monza 2021 and a crucial point in the season. Lewis is saved by the halo after Max's Red Bull mounts the Mercedes.

© REUTERS / Alamy

Abu Dhabi 2010. One title and four drivers all in contention. Left to Right: Vettel, Alonso, Hamilton and Webber.

Austria 2014. With my dad in his last season of F1.

Belgium 2004. Interviewing Arden owner Christian Horner in F3000 before he became Red Bull boss.

Co-driving in Wales Rally GB alongside Tony Jardine. I competed nationally and up to world championship level.

Bahrain Grand Prix chatting with Bernie Ecclestone and David Coulthard.

Impromptu photoshoot in Monza 2011 using the Renault F1 truck as a prop!

Above: Interviewing Seb after the British GP 2022.

Top Left: Switzerland 2013. After he retired, I went to interview Michael. The last one we did together.

Top Right: A wonderful day with Sir Stirling Moss and Lewis.

Right: Max in Abu Dhabi.

Fernando about to perform his card trick as mentioned!

Below Right: Jenson explaining some difficult times with McLaren.

Below: Felipe at the Spanish Grand Prix post-retirement.

Interviews aren't always as personal as they seem and there is often a scrum to speak to the driver.

2009 BBC launch in between the great Murray Walker and Ted Kravitz.

My F1 pass with my John Button pin badge on it – 'pink for papa' shirt!

Pit Lane. My office.

Saudi Arabia 2022.

'Working' with my friend Karun Chandhok. He takes the relaxed approach to TV!

Left: Day 1 for C4 Australian Grand Prix 2016 with Karun Chandhok and Steve Jones.

Middle: Great friends – Eddie Jordan, David Coulthard and Mark Webber.

Bottom: Abu Dhabi 2021 with the team.

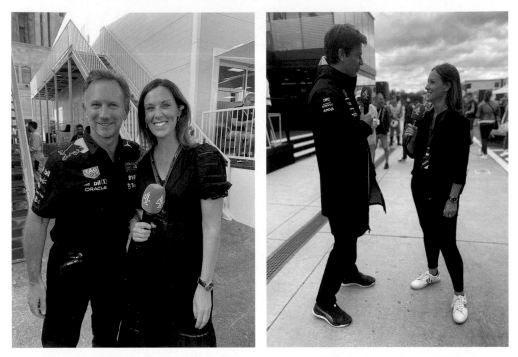

They might be rivals but I can be friends with both! Even as friends,
I love a tough interview with Christian and Toto. Never shy away
from what needs to be asked.

Nigel Mansell celebrates
30 years since he won the
World Championship in 1992.

At home with Sir Jackie Stewart,
a three-time World Champion
and F1 safety pioneer.

Presenting the Saudi Arabian
Grand Prix 2022.

The glamour of F1.

The real glamour of F1 – Monaco!

The Sunday was a rain-soaked affair with a fifty-minute delay, such was the deluge. After sitting behind the safety car, it was Alonso who emerged in the lead, a position which he held until the end despite the hard charging Sergio Perez in the Sauber, giving the Mexican his first podium in F1.

The next races went the way of Nico Rosberg, Vettel, Pastor Maldonado, Webber and Hamilton. It was obvious that consistency would be key this season and whilst race wins would be difficult to come by, podium places and a steady collection of points would make the difference over the twenty weekends and, by his own earlier admission, we know how good Alonso is at that.

It had been six years since Fernando Alonso won a race on home soil. The Spanish Grand Prix had been a shock result, won by Maldonado in a Williams, fittingly on Sir Frank's seventieth birthday. Alonso tried his best but had to settle for second.

When it came to the second of the Spanish races, the European Grand Prix at the Valencia street circuit, it looked like a victory was out of the question. It was another poor qualifying by Ferrari, Alonso was down in eleventh, far from ideal on a track with very limited overtaking opportunities. But the two-time world champion can always find a few places and is known for his lightning starts. Valencia was another example, and by the end of the first lap he had moved up from eleventh to eighth. He picked off Nico Hülkenberg for seventh and then put in a couple of blistering laps whilst his rivals had pitted. When it was his time to stop, he was soon back up to fourth and got to work. Hamilton had a pit stop issue which promoted the Spaniard to third. Second, he claimed from Romain Grosjean on the safety car restart and when Vettel's Red Bull broke down it was Alonso, like so often, who had put himself in the best position to take the opportunity and the win. He picked the field off in ruthless style. David Coulthard described it as a "world-class drive".

Gary Anderson, former F1 designer and at the time the BBC's expert analyst, summed up Alonso brilliantly: "One of the things that makes Alonso so good is that if he gets an opportunity to win, he will take it. That is exactly what happened in Valencia."

After the race in the FIA press conference, Alonso was humble and emotional. He reminisced on the win in Barcelona in 2006 but then said:

"Winning in Spain in this race is probably the best victory I ever felt in terms of emotion." And it was hugely emotional. The grandstands were a sea of red for Ferrari and splashes of yellow from the Spanish flags. Alonso collected one for his in-lap but then a problem with the car meant he stopped on track. Rather than a concern, it was a unique opportunity for the king to celebrate with his subjects. The crowd went wild and the scenes were amazing. Alonso left Valencia as race winner and a championship leader.

He didn't have to wait long for his next win either. Two races later in Germany he took a lights-to-flag victory. It certainly wasn't a relaxed race for him as he had to keep Vettel and then Button at bay, but he did so controlling it well and at the halfway point of the season, he had opened his lead to thirty-four points in the Drivers' Championship.

But sadly for him, that was to be his final race win of the year. Four consecutive victories for Sebastian Vettel saw him not only close the gap on Alonso but take the lead of the championship after the Korean GP with four races to go.

Heading into the showdown in Brazil, thirteen points separated Vettel and Alonso, in that order, but Fernando was no stranger to title shoot-outs in Interlagos. Just eight drivers had been crowned three-time world champions, and on Sunday, 25 November, it would become nine.

Neither of the title contenders qualified well, and whilst Vettel started in fourth, Alonso was in seventh. For most of the race it looked like Fernando Alonso would be the name on the trophy. A poor start saw Vettel in all sorts of trouble. He was then spun round and rejoined in second whilst Alonso was in fifth and working his way towards the front. Vettel had a lot of damage to his car but continued cutting his way through field. More chaos ensued for Vettel while Alonso kept his head down, continuing to plough away at the front. Massa moved out the way for his teammate; consequently, Alonso was up to second, and should any misfortune happen to the leader, Button, as we've seen so often, the Spaniard would be ready to gain.

Vettel was seventh behind Michael Schumacher and in what was his final Grand Prix, Michael let Sebastian through for sixth to make the final laps a little more comfortable for his countryman. I remember the debate at the time, would Michael support Ferrari for whom he was the poster boy for so many years, or would he support his good friend and protégé Sebastian. It was Vettel who won the battle for Michael's loyalty and also the championship. For what had been a spectacular season and race, it was a disappointing ending with the race finishing behind the safety car. Either way, the three-time World Champion was Vettel and not Alonso.

When you have just missed out on another championship, what you might not want to do is an interview on the podium; however, standing atop with a microphone was Nelson Piquet Sr.

A three-time world champion himself, he handled the interview well:

"I know what it feels like to lose a championship twice on the final day. I am sorry for you."

Alonso replied, "When you do something with your heart, when you do something with one hundred per cent, you have to be proud. I'm proud of my team and happy for them."

And then it came again . . . "We will try again next year."

The interview was as professional as you would expect. Almost emotionless, but the pictures of Alonso, helmet on, visor up, eyes hollow and staring ahead, were haunting. Three points. Just three points between him and Vettel and a third title.

It was a day of tears for various reasons. Vettel's were tears of joy after an exhausting race and the fact that he had become a three-time world champion. Hamilton was emotional as it was his last race for McLaren. Massa was in tears, as he so often was at the Brazilian Grand Prix. But in the interview pen, Alonso was quite cool. It wasn't until I was coming back through the paddock and he happened to be walking towards me that I saw him upset. What do you say to someone who has given his all and more, outperforming the car and coming so desperately close? I just gave a slight smile and shook my head. Surprisingly, Fernando stopped and hugged me. It hasn't happened since, and I doubt it will again, but it was one of those moments you don't forget. F1 is unique in our shared experiences of the highs and lows. No other sport is like it – the same people travelling together on the same flights, restaurants, lifestyle, celebrating wins and sharing the lows together. That was a moment in time that will stay with me forever.

"We will try again next year" had become something of a mantra for the two-time world champion. Yet again, in 2013 he finished second behind Vettel but there was no near miss in terms of the title this year. It was utter domination from the German and for Alonso finishing second, he was 155 points behind. He did win the Chinese Grand Prix and wowed the crowds in Spain once again with a great victory at the Circuit de Catalunya with an incredible drive. He started fifth, but a trademark lightning start saw him move up to third. He took Räikkönen and Hamilton round the outside before a clever pit-stop strategy meant that he undercut Vettel. He then picked off Nico Rosberg into turn 1, and after that it was another day in the sun for the home hero.

What stands out for me on that day was the joy, adulation and possibility for what was still to come. But sadly, as I write this, it was the last win for Alonso in Formula One. An unbelievable stat and one I struggle to make sense of. I hope that when you read this, things have changed!

In 2013 his Ferrari was widely regarded as the third best car and yet two wins, a further seven podiums and only failing to score points in two races shows how much he dragged out of the lame, rather than prancing horse.

What really riled Alonso during that time was that he really was outperforming the car, as he had done most of his career. There was an edge to him when Sebastian Vettel was mentioned. I'm not sure if I would go as far as calling it a lack of respect, but there was no doubt that he thought the Red Bull car and Adrian Newey were winning races and titles whilst Vettel was just the lucky pilot.

At the penultimate race of the season, at the US GP, I had another sit-down with Alonso. I wanted to push him on his thoughts about Vettel. Fernando is very clever and has seen it all, so sometimes you need to adopt different tactics to get a good answer. Vettel had just clinched his fourth title, putting him in a very exclusive club with Alain Prost on four, Fangio on five and Schumacher seven. Vettel had even more than the revered Ayrton Senna.

I had thought about it in advance, and I remember so clearly as I asked the question to Alonso:

"Sebastian Vettel has won his four consecutive titles before Alain had even won his first Grand Prix. But do you put Sebastian in the same category as Alain Prost and Ayrton Senna?"

"I don't know. Time will tell. When he will have a car like the others, when he wins, then he will be one of the legends in Formula One. When one day he has a car like the others and he is fourth, fifth, seventh, these four titles will be bad news for him because people will take these four titles in a worse manner than what they are doing now, so there are interesting times for Sebastian coming."

It sounds quite chilling, but maybe that is the benefit of hindsight. Because since then, like Alonso, Vettel has not won another title.

In 2014 things only got worse – in actual fact, neither Alonso nor Vettel won a Grand Prix. The Ferrari had serious limitations that even Alonso couldn't out-drive.

The Japanese Grand Prix had become somewhat tense. There were a lot of unhappy drivers, feeling they deserved more from their cars and teams. It goes both ways, and some teams were feeling that what they needed was a new driver!

It was well known that Alonso was getting impatient with Ferrari's lack of progress, and he wanted that third title. He was also speaking to McLaren, which, after everything that had gone before, seemed impossible.

On the Friday of Suzuka, the excellent Jonathan Noble reported in *Autosport*:

> Only a dramatic last-minute change of heart from either party will prevent their five-year relationship coming to an end.

He was, of course, talking about Alonso and Ferrari.
Jonathan went on to say:

> While it [Ferrari] is believed to have longer-term ambitions to sign Sebastian Vettel, the fact the German is under contract at Red Bull for next year means the Maranello outfit may need an

alternative in the shorter term. Its protégé Jules Bianchi is an option, but Nico Hülkenberg and Romain Grosjean have also emerged as more experienced contenders.

It makes for very sad reading knowing what happened to Jules that weekend – a crash which resulted in the loss of his life. One of the most devastating things I've been part of in my career.

That same Friday night, I was in the paddock, as I normally am, just walking around and seeing what was going on, finding people to chat to. Surprisingly, the eve of qualifying is a calm part of the weekend, most of the time.

As I described in the Vettel chapter (see page 77), I had been in Red Bull whilst many of the mechanics and team members were having their dinner. The atmosphere was terrible, although at that point I didn't quite know why. I did call my BBC colleague Andrew Benson to say that I thought something big was going on. Then Red Bull took the initiative and announced that Vettel had informed them that he was leaving the team – something that not only sent shockwaves through the paddock but the hospitality walls too.

The team buildings at Suzuka are temporary structures and the paddock is split into two halves. It is well known that the row between Alonso and Ferrari team boss Matteo Mattiacci was overheard by neighbouring teams, such was the volume and anger.

By the time we spoke to Alonso on Saturday post-qualifying, no one cared about his fifth place; the only question on every journalist's lips was where he would be driving next season and whether or not he had been sacked by Ferrari.

He is the absolute master in a moment like this. He doesn't get flustered, sticks to his story, even when it is totally implausible. His soundbites ranged from "I wish Sebastian well" to "I haven't decided on my future" and "I have a privileged position to more or less choose where I want to go, in the moment I want to go. I have gained that respect over the years" and even "Being the decision maker, some of the movements are a result of what I have decided."

So Fernando made the move the first and chose to leave Ferrari? Not the case, but he tried to own the rhetoric.

The fact that Alonso came so agonisingly close to winning the championships in 2010 and 2012, with the title battle going down to the last race, is testament to him and his ability. He finished runner-up in 2010, 2012 and 2013, but few remember that in a world of Vettel and Red Bull domination. It is seen as a lean period and the stats certainly don't give the full picture. At his museum, when I interviewed him in 2015, there is every Ferrari in which he competed. Surely one of the biggest Scuderia Ferrari F1 collections outside of Maranello.

He said to me, "For people who think Ferrari was a difficult five years and we didn't achieve a championship, I always show that." He pointed to a large wall dazzling with silver and gold. "Forty-six trophies in five years."

He had a point, but it was more titles, records and legacy that he craved. If you go on to the Ferrari website, you see that they don't have a roll call of drivers who have driven for them like other teams do. Apart from the yearly summary, there is no mention of Fernando Alonso or that honourable haul of silverware in an underperforming car. They do have a section called "Champions: the drivers who made history in Scuderia Ferrari". Obviously, Alonso doesn't feature.

Whilst Christian Horner announced at the Japanese Grand Prix that Vettel would join Ferrari, the Scuderia only confirmed the signing six weeks later. Two months after Japan, McLaren announced that Alonso would be returning to Woking. If this had been mentioned eight months earlier, you could have been forgiven for thinking that this was an April Fool's joke, but no; it was really happening! You have got to love Formula One!

In a McLaren statement the Spaniard said, "I am joining this project with enormous enthusiasm and determination, knowing that it may require some time to achieve the results we are aiming for, which is no problem for me.

"Over the past year I have received several offers, some of them really tempting, given the current performance of some of the teams that showed interest. But, more than a year ago, McLaren-Honda contacted me and asked me to take part, in a very active way, in the return of their partnership – a partnership that dominated the Formula One scene for so long."

Ron Dennis, who less than ten years earlier had been allegedly held to ransom by his new favourite person said in the *Mirror*:

> "The whole thing took on a momentum. It was a time when there was a very controversial environment for the sport as a whole.
>
> Everybody has moved on. I am mellower, Fernando is more mature. There were other people involved but everyone has moved on."

In the end, the line that stands out is Fernando's, "knowing that it may require some time to achieve the results we are aiming for, which is no problem for me."

It would be a problem. Of course it would. And it became a huge and embarrassing problem for all involved.

It wouldn't be the same if there wasn't drama, but this time it started earlier than normal. We all gathered in Barcelona for pre-season testing, but it went very wrong, very quickly for Alonso. It's a track that most drivers could drive in their sleep, even more so for him. He's had some of his greatest victories there and has done tens of thousands of laps throughout his career. When his McLaren hit the wall, you just knew something was wrong, especially after he didn't immediately get out of the car. He was eventually helped out before being airlifted to hospital, where he spent a couple of nights in intensive care.

I asked Ron Dennis the next day in the slightly chaotic press conference in the team hospitality if he had spoken to Alonso. He told me no, which seemed extraordinary. McLaren put out a statement saying:

"Our findings indicate that the accident was caused by the unpredictably gusty winds at that part of the circuit at that time ... We can categorically state that there is no evidence that indicates that Fernando's car suffered mechanical failure of any kind."

Alonso missed the first race in Australia, so it was a month or so later in Malaysia that we got the first chance to speak to him since the accident. In the press conference he totally dismissed the gust of wind theory.

"I don't know if you have seen the video but even a hurricane will not move the car at that speed! It was clear there was a problem in the car, but it was not found in the data," he said.

"There is not a clear answer. Definitely we had a steering problem in turn 3, and it locked to the right. I downshifted from fifth to third. Unfortunately, in the data we still miss some parts. The data is not there."

Alonso's headache might have gone away, but it was clear that for Ron Dennis and the McLaren communications team theirs was returning!

The 2015 season was one of reliability issues and, when it did work, the Honda engine was pointlessly uncompetitive. In the past, Alonso had struggled with the concept of not challenging for titles, let alone race wins. Now, McLaren struggled to get in the points and at the end of the season Button finished sixth in the Drivers' Championship with Alonso in seventh – hugely embarrassing for the two world-champion-winning drivers and the team.

The patience Alonso claimed he possessed ran out early. At Honda's home Grand Prix in Japan, the two-time world champion piled on the pressure, shouting on team radio, "This is embarrassing. Very embarrassing. GP2 engine. GP2. Aaargh."

Comparing an F1 engine to one from a lesser series was not going to help the situation, but frustration had boiled over. He had already said on team radio earlier in the year they were looking like "amateurs".

As well as stand-out team radio, Alonso's awareness of TV cameras and trying to lighten or heighten a situation made him social media fodder. The photo during qualifying at the Brazilian Grand Prix of him sitting in a deck chair whilst the other cars were battling it out on track went viral across social media with #PlacesAlonsoWouldRatherBe trending. As well as the original picture, which was funny enough, he was superimposed into thousands of different backdrops providing hours of scrolling fun!

Sadly for McLaren it was an image that summed up their season. His boss Ron Dennis was able to smile through the pain. He told F1.com:

"There's nothing wrong with a bit of humour. And Fernando is as hard-working as he is talented, be in no doubt of that. He's matured enormously since he last drove for us, eight years ago, and he's now one of the most complete drivers I've ever had the privilege of working with."

And still one of the most competitive. Though 2016 and 2017 were equally tough, 2016 started with a huge accident during the Australian Grand Prix.

Before the race, I sat down with Alonso and it was obvious that his legacy and future opportunity was on his mind.

"Do you think time is against you in your Formula One career to have another championship?" I asked.

"Yes, definitely, yes. But I cannot be unhappy or frustrated, not being a three-time World Champion. That's the thing. It seems I need to do it quickly or I have to retire without this third title – 'what sad news'. I don't see it in that way. I have been privileged to win two world championships, been privileged to be one hundred times on the podium. So many things that I never thought about when I became a Formula One driver in my debut here in Australia in 2001, so if I can do it yes, if I cannot do it, I will be so thankful to the sport and to my life."

But it was another violent start to the season and another bone-shuddering accident. The Spaniard ran into the back of Esteban Gutiérrez, which lifted his McLaren into the air at 300kph (190mph), smashing into the barriers before barrel rolling many times and finally landing upside down against the barrier. The G-force was reported to be 46G – forty-six times his body weight. Somehow, and testament to the increasing safety of these F1 cars, he walked away with minor injuries. Shaken but safe, thankfully.

That year, against the odds, he finished tenth in the championship – another case of flattering the machinery he had been given. His teammate Button finished fifteenth with less than half the number of points. Proof that Alonso was still motivated, if increasingly frustrated.

In 2017 Alonso decided to shake things up and give himself something to look forward to. He entered the Indy 500 in a McLaren–Andretti partnership. The race clashed with the Monaco Grand Prix, as it normally does but Alonso made a big statement by deciding to miss F1's jewel in the crown for the Brickyard.

F1 drivers used to drive all over the world in several different series but not for a while have calendars allowed that to happen. McLaren felt that the PR of Fernando in the US and not berating another poor F1 car, was worth the trade in. He became the first active F1 driver to take part in the Indy 500 since 1984. He made a brilliant start in testing, immediately getting to grips with not just the car, but oval racing. When it came to the notoriously stressful qualifying day, he outperformed some of the most experienced Indy drivers and oval specialists, making it into the top ten or, as they call it, Fast Nine.

When it came to the shoot-out for pole position, Alonso did it again, surprising everyone who thought, "Who does this F1 guy think he is, coming to the States to try and steal the biggest prize?", and there were many drivers and fans in the States who thought exactly that! He qualified an impressive fifth. It was an incredible performance for someone who had not driven an Indy car or experienced oval racing – apart from the ill-fated races in Indianapolis.

Some journalists, especially the Spanish, had decided to miss the Monaco GP and head west to Indy. To cater for those who were in Monte Carlo and for the team, McLaren decided to put on an all-American evening, so once we had finished our F1 duties, we could have a bit of a knees-up, beer, wine, hotdogs, burgers. Go full-American in support of Alonso's efforts. It was a great few hours, especially with Alonso leading twenty-seven laps of the race. It almost felt too good to be true, and in the end it was. In a cruel twist of familiarity, his McLaren was forced to retire. He left with no trophy but the accolade of "Rookie of the Year".

But the legend of Alonso had made it across the Pond, and he proved he was still one of the best drivers in the world. His Formula One season was sadly much less impressive, and at the end of the year McLaren announced they would switch to Renault power in a move to appease the two-time world champion, who of course won his titles with the French manufacturer.

But it was still desperate in F1 terms, so he found his solace and champagne in other series, this time entering the 24 Hours of Le Mans with the hugely competitive Toyota team. He won Le Mans sharing the car with Kazuki Nakajima and Sébastien Buemi, and also the 6 Hours of Spa, another competitive sports car race.

Alonso also announced that in 2019 he would make another bid for the Indy 500, although when it came to the time, they failed to qualify. There was no doubt that Alonso was having to find his joy elsewhere, so when he announced his retirement from F1, no one was hugely surprised. Disappointed it hadn't worked out differently, yes. Surprised, no.

After eighteen seasons, over three hundred Grand Prix, thirty-two wins and ninety-seven podiums, Alonso called it a day.

For the first time since 1986, McLaren ran a special livery for Alonso's last race in Abu Dhabi. It was an emotional weekend for all in the paddock. Eighteen years is a huge amount of time to be part of the sport.

During the weekend he talked about immersing himself in the moment. F1 is so fast-paced in every way, there is rarely time to appreciate what we are part of. Alonso was determined to live every second.

On the way to his car for the final race, he received a guard of honour from the hospitality to the garage. People from all teams came up to him on the grid, from Ferrari mechanics to drivers and team bosses.

After the race, after the doughnuts, David Coulthard spoke to him along with Sebastian Vettel and Lewis Hamilton. Both drivers spoke about his achievements, the tough times and how much he would be missed.

Lewis Hamilton put it very well: "I've been asked all weekend if I would miss him. Naturally, I don't really feel I'll miss another driver ever, but the sport will miss him, we will miss him and I definitely will miss him being in the sport."

During his "retirement" from F1, he won Le Mans twice and became World Endurance Car Champion as part of a very competitive Toyota team and finished thirteenth in the Dakar Rally. As gap years go, they were pretty impressive! But then, in true Fernando Alonso style, he announced his return to the sport that he had become so frustrated with.

Whilst the successes in other series were great and added to his CV, it wasn't enough for him. Alonso is the master of the backhanded compliment and whoever is on the receiving end of the compliment at that given moment just laps it up. From having a go at F1 about being too predictable, he then massaged his way back in. Whilst revelling in winning in sports cars, he then said the buzz there wasn't enough. To be returning to Formula One and particularly to Alpine, the current guise of Renault, was like "coming home".

Before he came back as a forty-year-old, he conceded that he is not the same man as when he started. His age means he has to train differently, stretch more, eat differently. Alonso is twice the age of some of his competitors.

The return was due to coincide with the huge raft of rule changes but because of the global coronavirus pandemic, those changes were delayed from 2021 to 2022. Building a car to new regulations is where a driver of Fernando Alonso's ability can really make a difference and help develop a car to reach its maximum potential.

But 2021, his first season back, proved not to be a lost cause despite the status quo with the cars. Alonso finished tenth in the championship, ahead of his teammate Esteban Ocon, who surprised and delighted the paddock when he won his first ever Grand Prix, in Hungary.

But as we have come to expect, it was the consistency of Alonso, the drip feed of points, that showed his worth. In Qatar, a great drive and brave one-stop strategy meant that for the first time since 2014, Alonso was back on the podium. It was the ninety-eighth of his career and celebrated by all.

He was overjoyed. "I've waited seven years for this. I hope this is the start of a new trend."

And wouldn't it be good if it was? Seeing Alonso back, whether it be for points, podiums or race wins is great for the sport. He is one of very few drivers who has made F1 dance to his tune instead of the other way round. Through circumstance he has been part of some of the biggest stories of recent years, and yet he is still there almost two decades later, with a smile on his face – okay, sometimes it's a grimace.

Engineers say that he can take on more information on team radio that any other driver they have ever worked with. No matter where he is in a race, when you speak to him afterwards, it's like he has watched it on TV as we have.

The chaotic Abu Dhabi Grand Prix at the end of 2021 was the perfect example. During the infamous safety car period, Alonso's Race Engineer Karel Loos came on the radio: "So, he [Michael Masi] is not going to allow us to unlap ourselves."

Alonso burst out laughing. "Okay, understood."

Shortly after, Loos came back on. "Okay, we've got Verstappen in P2. He's four cars behind you."

"Yep, and he should be two cars in front of me," said Alonso.

Then came the instruction: "Unlap."

Alonso's response: "This should have been done three laps ago."

I have not seen any other driver come into an interview

immediately after a race and know the entire breakdown of where other drivers finished and how the race played out. Normally, they only know about themselves and the battles they were involved in, which is understandable. Alonso has proved himself different. In every sense.

And he showed it again this year, just as we all started to relax on day one of the summer break. Out of the blue, Alonso announced that he would be joining Aston Martin in the seat vacated by his old rival, Sebastian Vettel! The forty-one-year-old signed a "multi-year deal" and, in the announcement, talked about his intention to win again. It was not only news to the F1 world but to Alpine as well, who thought they had retained Alonso!

His career might seem like shock and awe but regardless of which series he has competed in, Fernando Alonso has shown he is one of the greatest drivers in motorsport. The print in the record books might not tell the full story, but dig a little deeper and his journey is fascinating. Movies have been made with less drama! And somehow, and thankfully, the story continues.

6

FELIPE MASSA

F EW DRIVERS HAVE HAD SUCH DEFINING MOMENTS in their careers as Felipe Massa. It would seem harsh to suggest that fifteen seasons of driving in Formula One could be boiled down to two major incidents, but if you ask people about Massa they will mention one of two things – the 2008 world title that never was or the horrific crash one year later.

But there is so much more to the likeable Brazilian's story than just two moments – even though they are two of the biggest stories in recent times in motorsport, if not the history of Formula One.

Massa has been a huge part of the F1 landscape for almost two decades. He and his family have provided joy, smiles, energy and kindness, and not everyone will have that legacy. At one stage, it seemed the paddock would never be without him, and indeed when he did retire, he didn't actually leave! He wasn't one of those drivers who left and then came back having missed it terribly, pining for the competition that his life lacked. His departure from the sport didn't even last a full month! We were all part of a hugely emotional fare-well for Felipe at the end of 2016 but the shock retirement of Nico Rosberg had a knock-on effect throughout the paddock. Valtteri Bottas was promoted to Mercedes, so Williams needed to fill that seat and fill it with someone credible, who could help guide rookie Lance Stroll. Before Massa even handed back his Williams pass, he had been announced as "un-retiring", or more simply staying with the team. It is pretty hard to come out of retirement when you haven't quite entered it, although psychologically it had been hugely emotional for the whole family.

And family is what defines Massa more than any other driver I have seen. I am not talking about the motorsport dad or manager father. I am taking about the stereotypical Brazilian extended family which comprises parents, brothers, sisters, a wife and child, and many, many friends. Having worked with and having many Brazilian friends in motorsport myself, I have seen first-hand how they love to have "their people" around them. Entourage makes it sound egotistical, which it isn't. They just love to be surrounded by friends and family and their inner circle – even if the circle is the size of a ring road. It never fails to amaze me that you give a Brazilian driver three passes to something and they manage to bring in ten people. They are magicians as well as great friends to have!

Throughout Felipe's career, the Massa family would be there in the garage and hospitality; his father, Luis Antonio, his brother, Eduardo (or "Dudu" as he is known to everyone), and his wife, Raffaela. Towards the end of his career, his son Felipinho also joined him in the paddock. You tended to know when Felipinho was around: the first sign would be a flying football, closely followed by "mini Massa" on the chase. In the evenings or between sessions, Felipe would kick around with him too, as would other passing drivers. It was lovely to see and created a really different feel to the paddock. You just don't see kids in there very often, but for Massa, to be able to enjoy being in F1 and the time away from home it entails, he needed to share it with his family. The two coexisted very well and made it a much better and friendlier place, in my opinion.

I always looked forward to chatting to, interviewing and just spending time with Felipe. He is a gentleman, a statesman of the sport, and whilst giving everything to what was his dream job, he still had so much time for others.

Felipe was born in São Paulo and grew up on the outskirts of the sprawling city surrounded by countryside and not the concrete jungle that we associate with the place. Like so many young Brazilians, he was brought up on a diet of F1 and football.

"Brazil is a country with so many drivers, so many titles and victories. Senna was king," Massa said.

He got the bug and, being small and light, he was making his mark in the world of karting. In those days, Brazil had a wealth of motorsport talent. At the top of the hill at Interlagos – the neighbourhood and now commonly used name of the Autódromo José Carlos Pace, the hallowed reacetrack in São Paulo – lies a kart track where Massa and some of the greatest drivers learned their craft.

I went to that kart track with him when he was fully fledged in F1. The sky was a deep grey and it threatened to rain all day, which made it hugely atmospheric. There was a definite aura about the place.

"I raced on this track from the age of eight to seventeen, and now I race on the other side of the wall. The fence actually separates the kart track from the racetrack, so they talk about getting to the other side of the wall."

It's a funny thing; everyone, even to this day, strives to get to the other side of the Interlagos wall. That's when they know they have made it. And yet, when they have made it, they keep coming back to the smaller track that taught them everything.

"Here is a place that I love and I actually come back here to just drive and remember the old times."

Like all racing drivers who come from Brazil, Massa knew he would have to leave his home, family and everything he knew and move to Europe in order to follow his dreams of becoming a racing driver. His grandparents were originally from Italy, so Massa already felt an affinity with that country. After being successful in karts, the inevitable transition to cars needed to happen. At the age of seventeen he entered the Brazilian Formula Chevrolet Championship and one year later, in 1999, he took the title. That was the moment he knew he needed to dig out his suitcase and passport.

In 2000 he came to Europe to compete in Formula Renault 2.0. It was a hugely successful start to his overseas career, winning seven races to claim the Eurocup and Italian titles in his debut season.

The following year Massa went up a level again, this time to the competitive Euro Formula 3000 Series and again he made his mark. By the end, he had won six of the eight rounds. Unusually for a young driver with an eye on F1, he also took part in some European Touring Car Championship races, but it wasn't saloon cars that the Brazilian was looking to drive – it was the raw power of Formula One that had captured his imagination as a child and still held his dreams. He had already bagged some F1 experience by the end of 2000, having completed five days of testing at Mugello driving a Sauber. Nowadays, five days testing in a year is something that drivers dream of, but in those days, although testing was reduced, it was still much more plentiful than today.

Getting into the Formula One paddock isn't easy if you are not part of the circus, but bizarrely, Felipe Massa had been allowed in before his association with any team. In 1999 he was given a paddock pass in exchange for delivering food to the Benetton team. His former manager owned restaurants in São Paulo and provided catering to the team.

The Benetton chef at the time was Felice Guerini – who went on to work at Ferrari. Whilst at the Scuderia, Massa recalled, "The chef at Benetton was Felice, who is our chef now. I remember the story of saying to him: 'Maybe we will see each other in F1!' He looked at this guy bringing the food and said: 'Okay, okay, okay.'"

At the time, the chef was disbelieving – he would have heard these words from lots of young hopefuls but Massa wasn't just any young guy. He, of course, spent the majority of his F1 career driving for Ferrari.

Massa explained, "A few years later I said to him: 'Do you remember me?'

"He said no but I explained what had happened and we became good friends."

Between getting to Ferrari and delivering food, his F1 dream properly began in 2002. He was announced as a Sauber driver alongside Nick Heidfeld. If you were looking for a word to sum up the start of the Brazilian's Formula One career, "mercurial" would be a good one. Points and prangs were plentiful.

It was a season dominated by Michael Schumacher, who finished first or second in every race bar one. Massa, however, was showing his potential with some excellent point-scoring performances. In Spain he finished fifth, and he brought the Sauber home in sixth in Malaysia and at the European GP at Nürburgring. But interspersed through the excellence were plenty of rookie errors. Major errors. The worst of them was taking out Pedro de la Rosa at Monza, which resulted in a ten-place grid penalty. Peter Sauber was so frustrated by Massa and the penalty that he didn't even let him serve it. He was removed from the United States GP and replaced by Heinz-Harald Frentzen. It was a big statement, but for the team, big points and dollars had been lost. Sauber was aiming for fourth in the Constructors' Championship and every result mattered. By the end of his first season of F1, Massa finished thirteenth in the Drivers' Championship, three places behind his teammate but with eight DNFs and being made a spectator for a race. It had been a roller-coaster year!

Being replaced by Frentzen for the USGP proved costly to Massa as Sauber signed the German as a full-time driver for the following season, leaving the Brazilian rookie on the sidelines. But what a stroke of luck that proved to be. He spent the season as Ferrari's test driver learning from fellow countryman Rubens Barrichello and the great Michael Schumacher. It was the perfect finishing school, a year with the reigning champions. But it could have been very different. He almost got a seat at the Jordan F1 team, yet the season he spent on the sidelines with Ferrari was probably more beneficial in understanding the demands and requirements for a top-level driver and helped set him up for the rest of his career. He does always take great pleasure in thanking Eddie Jordan for not signing him. At the time, Massa thought he had the job at Jordan until he read the news that they had signed Ralph Firman. Why did Massa think he had the drive? Well, he had made a seat and been told that, subject to some sponsorship coming through, the job was his!

"Thanks for not signing me. You really helped my career," he would often shout at EJ when they passed each other, accompanied by much hugging and laughter!

After his year of schooling, it was a rejuvenated Massa who returned to Sauber in 2004. His more experienced teammate Giancarlo Fisichella finished eleventh in the championship, but Massa was right behind him and more than held his own. Again, he scored some impressive finishes at some of the toughest tracks on the calendar. Around the unforgiving streets of Monaco, he qualified sixteenth, but in the race, which saw his teammate's Sauber upside down, he brought his car back in fifth. He then finished fourth in Spa despite contact which saw him need a new wing at the end of lap 1. The season ended on a high at his home race in Brazil and his beloved Interlagos. Whilst it was Barrichello who delighted the crowd by taking pole position, Massa gained a whole new legion of fans with an incredible fourth fastest time. The entire season had been a much more complete performance from the Brazilian, so it was no surprise that Sauber retained his services for 2005.

A straight swap between Renault and Sauber saw Fisichella go to Renault and the 1997 World Champion Jacques Villeneuve come to Sauber. Despite being at opposite ends of their careers, measuring up against a former champion would be a great test for Massa. By the end of the season it was felt that, on the whole, he had outperformed his more experienced teammate. A great fourth in Canada matched his best F1 result so far and meant that he finished above Villeneuve in the championship and outqualified him 13–6.

But by that time, where he finished in the championship was all relative because during the summer break it had been announced that Felipe Massa would become a Ferrari driver. In 2006 he would take the seat of his countryman Rubens Barrichello and partner the seven-time World Champion Michael Schumacher. It was a huge step up and an even bigger boost when it came to the constant question of "How good really is Felipe Massa?" Ferrari thought he was very good indeed. So much so that they had kept an option on him since 2001, before he had even made it to Formula One.

Throughout his career, Massa was managed by Nicolas Todt, son of the then Ferrari boss and future FIA President Jean Todt. The Todt family fully believed in Massa, helped by the fact that in a test at Mugello in 2001 he posted faster times than Schumacher. Five years after the test, two years after being a Ferrari test driver, Massa's dream of being a Ferrari race driver would come true. In fact, it was a season where so many of his dreams came true. Until this year he had not started a Formula One race from pole. As well as ticking that off on three occasions, he stood on the podium five times, won two Grand Prix and finished third in the Drivers' Championship.

His first podium came at the European Grand Prix held at Nürburgring, a track on which he had performed well for Sauber. But it was Turkey that gave him his first pole position and F1 victory. It was a track that he had a real affinity with over the years, but ask Felipe about his favourite win and he will single out not his first ever victory but his second. The final race of that year still makes him emotional even to this day.

Interlagos. São Paulo. Home. It was the perfect finale. Whilst the world might have been watching to see if the retiring Michael Schumacher could prise the championship from the grasp of Fernando Alonso, Brazil only had eyes for one man.

Felipe Massa started from pole and became the first Brazilian to win his home Grand Prix since Ayrton Senna in 1993. He slowed his car, picked up a Brazilian flag from one of the marshals and did a lap with the crowd in full carnival mode. What also lives on in memory was the incredible reaction that Schumacher gave to Massa. It was meant to be Michael's last Grand Prix, but he focused everything on the achievement of his close friend who he had mentored.

After the race Massa said, "Today is another dream, the dream of my life has become a reality. The car was perfect, the Bridgestone tyres were perfect, I drove an impeccable race and all of this at my home Grand Prix!

"I want to dedicate this race to my family, to my friends, to all those who helped me in my career and to the Brazilian people, who, today, made me feel their warmth through all the fans in the grandstand . . . Over the last few laps, I was trying to maintain concentration, but I could not stop myself from watching all the fans celebrating in the grandstands!"

Massa's 2007 teammate was Kimi Räikkönen, who moved from McLaren to the Scuderia. It was a big signing but nothing that should have fazed Felipe, who was already established within the team. It took until just the first race of the season for the shockwaves to hit. In qualifying Massa didn't even make it into the top ten after suffering a gearbox problem which meant he would have to start the race from sixteenth. On the other side of the Ferrari garage, they were ecstatic. In his first outing Räikkönen had taken pole. To compound the frustration, Massa needed an engine change, which meant he would start from the back and would have to work his way through the field if he had any hope of coming away with points. Despite the difficulties, it was a strong race for Massa, eventually finishing the race a commendable sixth. But things were much smoother for his teammate. Kimi won the race and was totally in control throughout.

After such a promising year before, Massa started this one on the back foot, but he held his resolve; by the third race in Bahrain, Massa was back on the top step of the podium and he won the next one too in Spain. Canada was a blow as he was disqualified for leaving the pit lane on a red light at the pit exit following Robert Kubica's horrific crash. Räikkönen won in France and Silverstone as their nearest rivals McLaren went into meltdown, stitching themselves up on and off track.

Massa's only other win that year was once again in Turkey. He kept the points trickling through but so did his teammate and at the business end of the season with a championship on the line, it wasn't Massa who was in contention. The McLaren drivers tied on exactly the same points and finished second and third, but it was Ferrari's new boy Kimi Räikkönen who achieved his dream and became World Champion. That hurt Massa.

But a worse pain was to come the following year.

If you speak to Felipe Massa now, he'll tell you that he is at peace with how 2008 played out. He has to be, otherwise the what ifs and whys would take over his life in a detrimental way. On paper, 2008 would end up another season with just a single point splitting the champion and the runner-up, but it was so, so much more than that and for me, even with the 2021 finale, it is still the defining moment of "I was there" in my career to date.

Yes, it came down to the final race, but for Massa there were other key moments in the season where crucial points were lost. He started with two non-finishes. The first race in Australia was messy. Massa spun on lap 1, damaging his front wing, but he managed to continue. That was until he and David Coulthard got caught up with each other – they inevitably blamed each other after both had to retire.

In Malaysia, it looked like his season would start there after taking his tenth pole position but he spun out on the Sunday and beached his Ferrari in the gravel.

The Brazilian's confidence didn't dip, though, and he relied on tracks where he had enjoyed previous success. His first win of the year came in Bahrain and his next was in Turkey. At that stage of the championship, after five races, it was Räikkönen who was at the top, seven points ahead of Massa and Hamilton, who were tied on points. But amazingly, and although he didn't know at the time, just five races in, Räikkönen had done his winning for the year.

It wasn't just left to Massa and Hamilton, although they did win the majority of the races in 2008, but Robert Kubica, Heikki Kovalainen, Sebastian Vettel and Fernando Alonso all tasted victory. Yet the most consistent were the two who battled until the last seconds of the last race.

There are two moments which Massa says stand out for him as the moments where the title was lost, and they weren't at Interlagos. The Hungarian Grand Prix looked like a given for the Brazilian. He and Hamilton had battled from turn 1 on lap 1 until the McLaren driver got a puncture. Massa pulled away and was just three laps from victory and lead of the Drivers' Championship when his engine failed. That was a devastating blow and the loss of a huge points haul that would have made the difference.

The other moment that Massa highlights as a game changer in the Championship was Singapore. The first night race round the city and the famous crash-gate race. Massa had started from pole position, the perfect place for a street race into the unknown. After Nelson Piquet Jr's crash, Massa and all the leading contenders came into the pit lane. The green light came on to tell the driver that his Ferrari was ready to leave the pit box, but the car was not ready and Massa headed down the pit lane with the fuel hose still attached. To compound the drama, a member of his pit crew was knocked over as he attempted to head back out. He reached the end of the pit lane, where mechanics struggled to remove the hose before he was able to rejoin the race at the back of the field.

Massa eventually finished thirteenth and out of the points, but more frustrating was that Hamilton was third and created a seven-point gap at the top of the championship with three races remaining.

After the race Massa said to the media, "It is hard to deal with losing in this fashion. It was a race that was within our grasp with a car that was just the way I wanted."

When Massa returned to the garage, the mechanic who pushed the green button too early was in tears.

"At the pit stop one of our guys made a mistake, but we are only human. Each one of us always tries to do our best and these things can happen."

Japan wasn't great for either of the championship rivals and then Hamilton won in China, which meant he had another seven-point lead as F1 headed to Brazil and the final race of the championship.

Massa's love and formative years at Interlagos, on both sides of "the wall", were only going to be in his favour. A local driver with the possibility of winning a championship in front of his adoring fans – even as a fairy tale, it seemed farfetched. And what about his challenger; the man determined to spoil the Brazilian party and create his own place in history? Lewis Hamilton had been through plenty in his short F1 career. Could this really be his moment?

Both drivers were relieved on the Friday, when the talking could stop and the driving could start. Massa was quickest in FP1 and then on the Saturday he clinched his sixth pole of the season. Hamilton was fourth, and whilst it's a circuit where overtaking is certainly possible and even plentiful, there is always the danger of being caught up in others' chaos, particularly into turn 1. With a clear view in front of him, Massa had the upper hand.

Interlagos on the Sunday had a frenzied atmosphere. As a Brit, our focus was very much on Lewis Hamilton, but for the Brazilians, the Italians and many others, they were supporting Felipe. A Brazilian winning a world title in Brazil was what dreams and headlines were made of. I got into the track on Sunday and the rain was falling hard. The deluge was enough to delay the start of the race by ten minutes. By this point, the tension was becoming unbearable and we hadn't even had a single lap, with seventy-one to go!

The changeable conditions meant an anxious couple of hours for all; drivers, teams, strategists and fans. Even now, I remember that tension and excitement. Interlagos is a spiritual place and carries its own atmosphere. When it eventually got underway, Massa made a good start and kept the lead, but the heavy rain was intermittent throughout the race. A team and driver's nightmare. Whilst some drivers came in, others took the risk to stay out. The rain fell, the laps counted down and the crowd went wild as Felipe Massa crossed the line first – and in that moment, he thought he was world champion. He said later that whilst his engineer Rob Smedley never said on team radio that he was world champion, Massa and all of Ferrari, the whole of the world, bar one man, thought that the title was his.

But the battle behind was still raging. Vettel had passed Hamilton, which played into Massa's hands, and Timo Glock was eighteen seconds ahead of the Brit, although Glock was seriously struggling on his tyres. Hamilton kept going, kept hunting him down and in the last meters of the race, the last seconds of the season, he passed Glock for that all important fifth place – and with a one point difference, Massa's dream was over. Lewis Hamilton was World Champion.

As I was trying to make sense of everything that was happening in the pit lane, running between the Ferrari and McLaren garages, I was also watching on a little screen the same pictures that you might have seen. On ITV in Britain, the commentator James Allan was incredulous. "The Ferrari boys are celebrating. Both think they have won it. But Ferrari are wrong," said James, his voice getting higher. "They are absolutely wrong. Hamilton has finished fifth."

Then, as the camera moved to Felipe's father and brother, the celebration and tears of happiness turned to shock and sadness.

James added: "The father has just realised that he celebrated a little bit too early."

In the McLaren garage, there was shock but for different reasons. Hamilton's family and then girlfriend Nicole Scherzinger were ecstatic. Theirs were tears of joy. The celebrations in the pit lane and in the next-door garage to Ferrari were justly deserved. But no other moment has ever summed up the highs and lows of sport more to me than that one.

Massa's solace was and is to this day the fact that he could have done no more. He won the race. He did exactly what he needed to do, but some days that just isn't enough. What he did win, though, was a whole new legion of fans around the world. His tenacity, emotion and heartbreak had become global news. When Massa went into the press conference, every journalist was very emotional, regardless of nationality, and Massa was given a standing ovation.

Later in his career during an interview he said to me, "I think it was the most incredible end of the championship, maybe in history. I'm happy to be part of that. I didn't win but it was a big emotion and moment for everybody who likes and follows sport."

To have come that close to your dream; I still cannot quite fathom what that must be like and how you stop yourself questioning every result and decision that went before. The question for Felipe was how on earth he could come back from something like that and do it all again the following season. How much had it taken out of the likeable Brazilian?

But 2009 had its own challenges, and for Felipe Massa it can be remembered for only one thing – a life-changing accident. For Ferrari, the season had started with a handful of retirements and a car that struggled to get in the points. New boys Brawn were the talk of the town and Jenson Button won five of the first six races. Massa got his first podium of the year in Germany but it was at the following race in Hungary where his life would change.

It was Q2 in qualifying and towards the end of the session. As drivers were putting down their competitive times, the TV coverage showed a very odd crash for Massa as his Ferrari hit the barriers. At that time, we hadn't seen any cause for the accident and all we knew was that he had been following Rubens Barrichello's Brawn at the time. A minute later, onboard camera footage showed something from the Brawn car flying towards Massa. Brawn confirmed that it had been a spring from the rear suspension damper which had hit Massa's helmet whilst he was travelling at over 150mph (240kph). Also spotted by those around the car and seeing the data was that

Massa had his feet on both the accelerator and brake pedal at the same time and whilst the car was in the barrier the engine could still be heard revving on the limiter, suggesting his foot was on the accelerator and that he was unconscious.

A long delay ensued as the medical team carefully extracted Massa from the car. Photos emerged of him, bleeding and cut above his left eye. The helmet was badly damaged where the visor and protective area joined. His right eye was wide open and staring. The images were haunting.

Qualifying continued, but the atmosphere in the paddock was understandably bad. Everyone was in shock, waiting for news that was never going to be immediate. Many journalists decamped to the hospital where Massa was being looked after. That weekend his brother and two friends were enjoying Budapest with him, but as soon as the accident happened Ferrari had arranged to bring out his mother and father, his sister and his wife Rafaella, who was six months pregnant, from Brazil.

It's odd what you remember, but the hospital, or maybe Ferrari, had asked journalists not to congregate outside. So we at the BBC decided to wait at our hotel for any news. The problem was that the phone network provider O2 went down globally, which meant silence. Is no news good news? Ultimately yes, but at the time we were all shocked to hear that Massa had been sedated in a coma for forty-eight hours in order for his condition to improve.

Ferrari President Luca di Montezemolo and Rubens Barrichello visited him in hospital that evening.

The Sunday of the race was a quiet day. A statement had been released that Massa was expected to make a full recovery, but in an induced coma it didn't feel a cause to celebrate.

What is always even more strange in these situations is that when the chequered flag falls and the paddock finishes its work, we all go home. Massa and his family couldn't. You are leaving someone behind and that is a desperate feeling.

It transpired that all the bone above his left eye had shattered and an operation to remove the broken fragments above the eye socket was needed. An acrylic plate had been inserted to strengthen and replace the bone.

Incredibly, just days after his accident, Felipe was discharged and flew back to Brazil to recuperate at home. Before he left the military hospital in Budapest, he did an interview with Ferrari which was distributed to the media around the world:

"It is sort of a strange feeling. I know exactly what happened, that a spring came off Rubens' car and hit me on the helmet. I know that something happened to me, but I didn't feel anything when it happened. They told me that I lost consciousness at the moment of the spring's impact on my helmet and I ran into the barriers, then I woke up in hospital two days later.

"I don't remember anything and that's why what the doctors did had to be explained to me. When I saw Rob [Smedley, his race engineer], he asked me if I remembered Rubens, but the last thing I remembered was when I was behind him at the end of my fast lap in Q2, and then it's blank. It's difficult to explain. I'm feeling much better now and I want to recover as soon as possible to get back behind the wheel of a Ferrari."

Massa went straight into hospital in São Paulo for two days of tests but was released to recover at home. Time and patience was what he needed.

I went to Felipe's home in São Paulo to film with him before he retired, and as we chatted, I saw the helmet on a shelf in his living room. I was amazed that something associated with such an upsetting time of his life had such pride of place. He handed it to me to look at.

I held this broken and blood-stained lifesaving piece of engineering in my hands. It felt very personal, almost too much for me to handle it.

"This chills me," I said to Felipe. "In fact, you can hold it. It is an incredible thing to look at because it saved your life in many ways, but it is a reminder of how close things came."

He replied, "Many people said, 'Ah, you were really unlucky.' I was really lucky that this happened to me and I am still here."

I pointed out the blood on the helmet.

"Yes, it still has my blood around the helmet, inside. This always definitely stays here inside my house, but also inside my heart."

And that moment, standing with Felipe, holding something which undoubtedly saved his life and seeing the blood whilst he relived that story with me, is something that will stay inside my head and heart for the rest of my days.

Massa didn't race again in 2009, but he did return to the cockpit in October of that year at Ferrari's test track in Fiorano. He drove a two-year-old Ferrari to see how he felt and test himself behind the wheel again. The team were taking no chances and, even though he had been passed medically fit, Ferrari put him though some neurological tests in Paris a few days before.

After the test, Massa said he would be keen to race again that year and had no problems with vision but Ferrari said they would not rush him and that he would return in 2010. Massa would be returning to a new look Ferrari. Out was Räikkönen and in his place came double World Champion Fernando Alonso.

When the season got underway, it was a great return for Massa but it was a better start for his new teammate. Alonso won the Bahrain Grand Prix on his Ferrari debut, but if there had been any doubts about whether Massa had been affected by his accident, they were quickly dispelled. He qualified second and finished second. Of course he was disappointed to be beaten by his team-mate, but after everything he had been through, it was a wonderful and welcome start for the Brazilian.

The season was dominated by a championship battle that Massa was never really in. Whilst Alonso was never too far away, after that victory in Bahrain, he failed to win another race until the eleventh round of the season. Germany 2010 now simply remembered for "Fernando is faster than you".

Although it is discussed in the Alonso chapter (see page 145), here we can learn an awful lot more from Massa's perspective. You might remember that, at the time, Ferrari and their drivers denied any team orders. However, it was obvious to all that, whilst Felipe was leading, he had been given the instruction or "information" from his engineer Rob Smedley, "Fernando is faster than you." Alonso overtook Massa, who had let him through, and won the race. Afterwards teams, drivers and ex drivers were furious about the situation, which was illegal in the sport at that time. Ferrari were fined, but for Massa that situation was just a matter of time.

In just the third race of the season in Australia, Massa had been in front but Alonso was catching up. The team came on the radio and asked Felipe to let Fernando through. He didn't and finished ahead of Alonso on the podium; but from that point, he knew the writing was on the wall.

As Massa said in the official F1 podcast: "I couldn't accept in the third race of the season you need to give a position. If I had that in the third race, I knew every race it can happen."

Let's keep in mind that after the team orders race in Germany, Massa actually said to me, "We didn't have team orders in the race. I was struggling on the hard tyre."

"So you decided to let Alonso pass?" I asked.

"Yes," he replied.

Time passes and people feel they can speak more freely. Since that day and since his retirement he has spoken very differently, describing it as "one of the worst days of his life".

Massa further explained on the podcast, "That message was already discussed as we couldn't say let him by. It was clear these things could happen because of Fernando."

If Fernando was in front of Felipe, things for the Brazilian were almost easier. But when Felipe was in front, "I was worried," he said.

What also upset Massa about what happened at the German Grand Prix was that it was exactly one year to the day since his horrific accident.

His summary of Alonso is so interesting. I think all imagine this but we have never had a driver admit it. In the same podcast, Massa said:

"To beat Fernando, you need to be on your day. He has everything in the perfect way. But the way he is and the way he works, you have no idea how much power he has and he likes that. He likes to show his power.

"He's able to put everyone in his pocket. Everybody, even a Montezemolo, everybody. The only problem is that he is able to split the team because of that."

Massa had re-signed with Ferrari until the end of 2012, but he increasingly knew it would be in a supporting role.

It was an odd season, 2011. How often have we seen Lewis Hamilton getting involved in one-to-one scraps throughout a season? Recently with Max Verstappen, but even then it only happened a few times. You could say the same for Felipe Massa. These are great drivers who give space and have skills to get themselves out of trouble. Well, not that year, they didn't!

Massa and Hamilton in 2011 were like magnets, drawn to each

other on track, scrapping, crashing, hindering each other and in interviews publicly berating each other. Monaco, Silverstone, Singapore, Japan and India – a roll call of contact and crashes between the two.

It started in Monaco. Hamilton felt that Massa had held him up in qualifying on the Saturday – but in the race, things got a lot more heated. The two came together at the hairpin on the run down to the tunnel. Wheels locked, bodywork flew, but they untangled and continued. A few minutes later Hamilton emerged from the tunnel at speed and intact. Massa emerged battered and slower. He had been in the barriers. His Ferrari was still running but with huge damage to the left-hand side. Hamilton was penalised but the damage was done.

The next time the two came together was at Silverstone during a long battle for fourth place. Hamilton held off Massa, who was trying to pass round the outside, but they got too close for comfort. Former drivers felt Hamilton had the edge.

So far there were definitely grievances, but it was polite – until we got to Singapore! Saturday night in the top ten shoot-out of qualifying, the pair came so close to crashing into each other.

Massa told me after, "It was too much. He didn't use his mind, one more time."

But on the Sunday night, in the race, they did come together and Hamilton was given a drive-through penalty for the incident.

I was waiting to do the driver interviews in the media pen and Lewis was answering some questions when Massa grabbed his shoulder and sarcastically patted him. "Good job, uhh," ranted Massa.

"Don't touch me again, man," replied a shocked and angry Lewis. He then left the interview pen and didn't come back.

Massa stayed and was more than happy to talk about Hamilton

and his faults. He said to me, "My thoughts are that, again, he cannot use his mind – even in qualifying. He has done it to me so many times this year.

"Again, he could've caused a big accident. He's paying for it and he doesn't understand that. It's important the FIA study this and penalise him every time."

It is really unusual to get that sort of confrontation in front of the cameras and assembled media. I remember being really surprised with how it all played out, especially with two "senior" drivers. When I went on the Singapore Flyer, the big wheel, an hour later to film with Vettel and Webber for Red Bull, they were desperate to know what had happened!

The next race that year was Japan. I had an interview booked with Massa on the Thursday. Ferrari and Massa knew the main topic of conversation would be Lewis. They could easily have cancelled it and I often wonder why they let that interview happen, but they did and I am pleased they did. Normally, especially with Ferrari, you do an interview in a set position, no discussion, but they didn't really want anyone knowing we were doing the interview; so, bizarrely, I did it in Felipe's driver room. Normally it's a very private place that drivers like to keep to themselves. By this point I was thinking that he must be very keen to get something off his chest!

I asked him, "Do you regret speaking to Lewis in the drivers' pen in such a public fashion when there were lots of cameras there?"

"Well, I tried to speak to him without the media, but he didn't even turn his head. I called him twice so . . ." He shrugged his shoulders and let the sentence tail off before adding ". . . and then I saw him there so I had to say something, and for sure I was disappointed. Maybe what I did wasn't the right thing, but anyway I was disappointed and what he did was ten times worse."

I went on, "You seem to attract each other . . ." But before I could finish Felipe said, "Well, actually, I think he has something with me, because I never did anything to him, to be honest, and everything he did, he is paying for that – and not just me, with other drivers as well. He doesn't have two problems this championship, he has many."

I will admit, these are the interviews that make someone like me light up. Not very often do you get an interviewee away from a race so full of pent-up emotion and so keen to unload into a microphone.

I wondered if it was a subconscious hangover from the way 2008 finished, but Felipe was quick to dismiss that.

"No, nothing to do with that, otherwise I don't know what he is thinking. He just needs to learn, otherwise he will have a drive-through every race."

We played out over three minutes of this on the BBC before the Japanese Grand Prix. The race started and – well, you couldn't make it up! Going through the chicane, the two collided. Neither received a penalty, but afterwards Massa just said, "I think the footage speaks for itself", whilst Hamilton dispelled any conspiracies, saying there was no bad intention towards Felipe.

"I've got the utmost respect for him."

The final blows came in India on lap 24, and this time it was Massa who was given a penalty for causing an accident. It was such an odd time for both drivers but great theatre for all fans. Although, if it had been written as a script, you would have said eight incidents at five races? No way, that sounds too far-fetched!

It looked like 2012 would be Massa's last year at the Scuderia. Rumours were circulating early, not helped by a poor start to the season. He didn't make it into the top five of a Grand Prix until the ninth race of the season at Silverstone. But Ferrari extended his contract by a further year thanks to some better results in the middle part of the season. By the end of the year, Felipe had only managed to get on the podium twice and finished seventh in the championship. That wouldn't be too bad if his teammate's results had been similar, but Alonso finished second in the title race with three wins and a further ten podium finishes.

Thankfully, 2013 was better in terms of Massa's results; however, it was widely understood that he would be leaving Ferrari at the end of the year. There's a horrible time in F1 when rumours are circulating and everyone is talking about which drivers will be racing for which team. The knock-on effect means that someone will be ousted from their seat, and some from the sport completely. I had done so many interviews with Felipe throughout 2012 and 2013. It's really not nice, and I would always say beforehand or after that I was sorry but he knew I would have to address the contract situation. I always felt it was better for him to have his say and confirm or deny whether the rumours were true. Felipe understood that we are all in this weird world together and asking these kinds of questions was just part of my job. I always tried to make sure I did it with a bit of sympathy and understanding. I know I would be pretty pissed off if someone started asking me about my contract situation: "Oh hey Lee. I hear you are probably going to lose your job?" No, I wouldn't be happy!

As it happened, a couple of days after the Italian Grand Prix, Massa announced that he would be leaving Ferrari at the end of the year. The following day it was announced that former Ferrari driver Kimi Räikkönen would be returning to the Scuderia in place of the Brazilian. The team that had sacked the Finn and paid him a vast amount of money to buy him out of his Ferrari contract and replace him with Alonso was now re-hiring him for more vast amounts of money to partner him with the driver they replaced him with — Fernando Alonso. What a world!

In November it was confirmed that Felipe had signed for Williams for 2014 and would become the sixth Brazilian to drive for the historic British team. So, after eight years and a roller-coaster career with the Italian outfit, it all came to a close – and where else but Interlagos. The race didn't go well and Massa was given a drive-through penalty for cutting the white line on the entry to the pit lane. He was furious and it ruined what could have been a strong race for the outgoing Ferrari driver. Fernando Alonso even said afterwards he would have let his teammate past and sacrificed his own third position so that Felipe could stand on the podium in front of his home fans as a Ferrari driver for one final time.

As Massa crossed the line, team boss Stefano Domenicali came on team radio.

"We love you and you will always be in our hearts and don't forget an important thing . . . you are always a World Champion for us. Thank you, Feli. Thank you."

Massa replied back in Italian, "Thank you, guys. Thank you so much. Don't say such words because I could cry at the wheel."

In the interview pen afterwards, whilst talking to me, he was visibly emotional. He often was at Interlagos, but this was the end of an era, not of his own choice and soon the tears were flowing – for all of us.

But a new chapter was starting. Williams and Massa. It was a great fit. A family man driving for a family-run team. They embraced the fact that Felipe turned up with his wife and child, Raffaela and Felipinho, and often his father and brother. It was everything that Williams was about.

Massa and Valtteri Bottas were a great pairing too. Whilst at different stages of their careers, both were very talented drivers with the ability and understanding of how to push the team. Change was afoot in 2014 and saw the introduction of hybrid turbocharged power units, which created a new order on the grid. That season, Williams were ahead of the game, taking full advantage of Mercedes power before the rest put money behind the issues and ultimately overtook them in the following years. Mercedes was the form team, and playing catch-up was the previous dominant force in Red Bull. Amazingly, it was Williams who finished third in the championship ahead of Ferrari. By the end of the season, Massa had stood on the podium three times, had a fastest lap and taken a sensational pole position in Austria.

It was the first time F1 had raced in Austria since 2003, when Massa was the Ferrari test driver. However, he did take part for Sauber in the 2002 Grand Prix. And twelve years on, despite a season of Mercedes domination, that Saturday in Spielberg was all about Williams. Massa became the first driver other than Hamilton and Rosberg to take pole that season. Alongside him on the front row of the grid was his teammate, giving Williams their first front row lockout since Juan Pablo Montoya and Ralf Schumacher at the German Grand Prix in 2003.

In the race, the Mercedes cars proved too strong but Bottas was able to get on the podium in third. Massa finished in fourth.

We also remember 2014 for the desperate accident suffered by Jules Bianchi which ultimately claimed his life the following year. This was something that really shook everyone, but especially Felipe. He and Jules had been very close. They had the same manager and Felipe had known Jules when he was just driving go-karts and dreaming of getting to F1. Jules had been part of the Ferrari "family" and was widely tipped as a future driver. The accident in Japan when his Marussia car struck a recovery vehicle, in the torrential rain, shocked the entire paddock.

Massa said afterwards to the media, "I was already screaming on the radio five laps before that there was too much water on the track, but then they just took a little bit too long and it was dangerous."

By the time we reached Russia a week later, the severity of the situation was sinking in. Massa was shocked but spoke well in the Thursday press conference alongside other senior drivers.

"For me I think it was the worst race of my life. It's a really bad race, worse than the race of my accident – because I didn't remember. It was the worst race of my life. Yeah. It's so difficult to be 'everyday' because I can just be thinking about him, thinking about Jules. It's a very difficult weekend for all of us. Maybe tomorrow it will get a little bit better because at least you are working. Try to race and do the best we can for him, for his family. But anyway, it was the worst race of my life."

Let's not forget that Felipe had already gone through the devastation of his mentor and friend Michael Schumacher's accident less than a year before that. It had been such a tough time for the Brazilian. For him Michael had been what he was trying to be to Jules – a friend and mentor.

Felipe said about Michael, "He was my teacher. He was very nice to me all the time and he was very kind to me." This was exactly the approach that he had taken with Jules.

Jules died in July 2015. A week later in the press conference at the Hungarian Grand Prix, the drivers shared their memories of the Frenchman who had so much potential and personality. And there were serious things to discuss, including how to prevent anything like that ever happening again.

In the FIA press conference Massa said, "I really agree that Formula One has changed a lot, especially after Ayrton Senna's accident. I believe the car is very safe now. We always need to keep working to improve the safety, you know – not just the cars but the tracks and everything is very safe now – so what happened in Japan was a different situation. What happened in Japan is something that we cannot . . . I cannot accept, because a car crashed into a tractor."

And on the discussion of closing the cockpit or how to protect the vulnerable head area of the driver: "I'm not completely against it [open/closed cockpits]. I think it's something that needs to be . . . If it's better for everybody and it doesn't change the aspect of Formula One – maybe not closing the cockpit but doing something to improve the safety on that area – I'm not against it."

This was the start of the "halo" discussion. It was tested in 2016 and 2017 and became mandatory from 2018.

Massa continued for Williams in 2015 standing on the podium in Austria and Mexico. Brazil provided more drama when he was disqualified from the race classification after his tyre temperatures were discovered to have been too high before the start of the race. By the end of the season, Williams had once again finished third behind Mercedes, who won the Constructors' title, and Ferrari, who had unlocked an improvement in their performance. Red Bull were in fourth. Whilst in the Drivers' Championship, Massa was sixth. The idea that leaving Ferrari would mean a tough couple of years hadn't proved true. Williams were competitive, out-performing much bigger-budgeted teams and Felipe was still enjoying his racing.

But the following season in 2016 at the Italian Grand Prix, Felipe called time on his career.

"After twenty-seven years of my racing career, since I started karting and with fifteen years in F1, this will be my last season in F1."

The location of the announcement was no coincidence either.

"I choose this place because ten years ago Michael announced his retirement here. The only way for me to stay [at Ferrari for 2007] was for him to stop. He chose to give me this option to stay."

For Felipe, the decision had been incredibly difficult but the timing felt right.

A few days before what was meant to be his final Brazilian Grand Prix, I went to film at Felipe's house. Even though we were guests, Raffaela had put on a beautiful lunch for us. It is not often everyone is made so welcome or allowed to film in someone's private space. It was a really special experience and one that summed up the kindness of the Massa family. After we finished filming in the house, we got in his Range Rover to drive to Interlagos and visit the kart track where it all began. Inside, it was the car of any parent. There were toys all over the place; I had to move little plastic figurines from the seat including a tiny Superman, Felipinho's superhero of choice!

"I wonder how different it will feel for you this weekend?" I asked.

"It's very special. You know, I grew up here, so this is my garden – so when you get there and see the love from the people, it is very special."

We slowed down in the thick of the constant stream of traffic that weaves it way through one of the most populated cities in the world. Motorbikes screeched past at breakneck speed.

"Here you need to drive for you and for the bikes. If you don't leave the space for them to pass, they're complaining like . . . Vettel!" He laughed.

In amongst the laughter and humour, there was emotion and he knew that would be the hardest thing for him to control throughout the weekend. "This is really a special week for me. My last home Grand Prix in F1. It would be fantastic to have a fantastic race," he said to me.

But it is Felipe Massa, and a straightforward "fantastic race" at Interlagos would surely be too simple going on their history. On his "last" F1 weekend, he qualified in thirteenth and, come Sunday, it was another rain-soaked race day as the cars lined up on the grid.

The race was led almost as much by the safety car as by the eventual winner Lewis Hamilton. Crashes and rain delays shaped the Grand Prix. Massa had navigated most of the race – and then it happened.

Fifteen years of F1 came to an end with a crash.

As he climbed out of his damaged Williams in the wall at the entry to the pit lane, the place went into hysteria. At first the crowd were stunned; the pictures showed marshals and fans crying. Others went wild, cheering and waving Brazilian flags in support of Felipe. Massa was in floods of tears as he walked up the pitlane and then something that I have never seen before happened. Other teams started coming out of their garages and clapping, mechanics stood in a line almost the whole way up the pit lane cheering and applauding Felipe on his walk back to Williams. Engineers and team bosses on the pit wall opposite were celebrating him as well. Felipe and his family who had run down to meet him struggled to take it all in. Even now, it gives me goosebumps just thinking about it and watching back videos of it. Who would have thought that such a disappointing end to his race would mean the most incredible end to his time at Interlagos!

Abu Dhabi came with more emotion, but the eyes of the world were on the Rosberg–Hamilton showdown. In these situations, on such an incredible day, it's easy for people to leave the sport before you even realise they have. The chequered flag falls, the main story takes over and before you know it, drivers have slipped out of the paddock and their personal story and everything they dreamed of is over. Massa had really wanted his farewell to be Interlagos, so when he left the paddock in Abu Dhabi, he was at peace.

That was until a couple of weeks later, when new world champion Nico Rosberg announced his immediate retirement from the sport. It made headlines around the world and made shockwaves in the paddock. Mercedes had not been prepared or expecting to replace one of their drivers. Pretty quickly, Williams driver Valtteri Bottas was the target for Toto Wolff, who had been a shareholder in Williams and had also managed Bottas, but Williams were in a tricky position. They didn't want to block the progress of a talented young driver, but they did need an experienced driver in their team, and also one of legal drinking age to honour the Martini sponsorship deal. So as I mentioned at the start of Felipe's story, before the Christmas parties had even happened, Massa was back. I do wonder, if the Brazilian Grand Prix had gone better, whether he would have returned or if he felt there was still unfinished business at "home".

His extension year was trickier than previous years. His teammate was rookie Lance Stroll, and Massa was very much the experience guiding the team. But the Williams was struggling more so than seasons before. He didn't stand on the podium once, but it was never really about how high he finished in the championship or whether he would decide to stay in F1. It was a one-year bonus, and with everything building towards Interlagos, the Brazilian Grand Prix and redemption.

Whenever I film at someone's house or in their private time away from their work responsibilities, I have always brought a small thank you gift. However, 2016 felt more special, so as a thank you and retirement gift, I gave Felipe a nice bottle of whisky from Scotland. When I did his second retirement interview, I made clear my rule was only one retirement gift per person! We sat in the Williams hospitality in the paddock for the farewell chat.

"I really hope we can enjoy a lot, like last year. But I don't need that much in terms of emotion," he said, laughing. "The only change that I really hope we can do is that we have a much better result at the end of the race. It finished not in the way I wanted last year but in a way I never really expected to have, walking through the pits."

I said to him, "I remember interviewing you here when you left Ferrari and that was emotional. I interviewed you here last year and that was emotional. Do you think it will be the same on Sunday?"

He laughed. "Of course! Hopefully it will be another one. It is a hugely emotional place, Interlagos.

"The only thing I can say is thank you – for everything I passed through. The many people I met, many friends, the best drivers in the world that I raced against. So it's definitely been a big pleasure for me and I have no regrets."

Race day came and Massa's wishes were granted. He started from ninth on the grid and finished in seventh. Fernando Alonso was behind him in eighth, and his other adversary, Lewis Hamilton, in the sublime Mercedes, was just a few places ahead in fourth. The reaction from the crowd was as wild and jubilant as expected. Vettel might have won the race, but the hero of the day was Massa.

The unsung hero in everything that Felipe Massa did in Formula One was Rob Smedley. They were their own team within a team, regardless of whether they were in Ferrari red or Williams white. The Brazilian English/Yorkshire accent combination made team radio a thing of joy:

"I crashed, Rob," said Felipe in Monaco in 2011.

Rob replied, "Box now, box now."

"Rob, I crashed!"

And in Malaysia, 2009, a panicked Massa shouted, "I need a white visor, please come on, a white visor or I cannot see anything!"

"Felipe, baby, stay cool. We are bringing you the white visor. Stay cool. We are in a good position. We are bringing you the visor."

That one made everyone laugh.

And we've heard enough about, "Fernando is faster than you."

It was a duo that everyone loved. An unlikely pairing that seemed to bring the best out in each other. Massa's highs and lows were

Smedley's too, and Rob was as famous in Brazil as he was in his hometown.

Standing on the kart track on the original side of "the wall" talking to Felipe, I said to him, "You are a very humble person, but when you look back on your career, how proud are you of everything you have achieved? Because you are inspiring people on this side of the wall now."

He replied, almost shyly, "I'm really proud of my career. I have definitely, definitely achieved a lot more than what I expected. I've had an amazing career, an amazing everything. I am really, really proud for everything that has passed and I am ready to finish with my head up, like I started."

Interlagos and Felipe Massa – what a story. Coming back from adversity and Felipe Massa – a life lesson for us all.

7

JENSON BUTTON

J ENSON BUTTON IS PROBABLY THE MOST normal F1 driver, let alone world champion, that you could ever meet. Don't take that the wrong way. When I say normal, I don't mean it in a "nothing special" way, because he is very special. I mean it in the best way: relatable, genuine, unchanged. True to himself and to his roots.

If you watch the interview he gave after his first ever Formula One race in Australia in 2000, you will see the same person who is on TV now. Yes, he is a little more polished, a little older and a hell of a lot richer, but how he speaks, his mannerisms, his humour and composure are exactly the same. You get so used to seeing people change throughout their careers that it actually threw me when I saw it. Not very often does someone who's achieved, travelled and developed as much as Jenson remain so unchanged.

When people chat to me about F1, especially around the time he won his championship with Brawn, without a doubt someone would say, "Jenson Button seems like a good guy." Even at the pinnacle of his career, they could imagine having a pint with him in a pub, talking about cars and life. He's not flashy, he's not going to the swanky parties and when he does, he keeps it quiet. He's private yet comes across as accessible, and people love that.

I've been to parties with Jenson, dinners, family memorial services, visited schools, and in all the time I have spent with him, one thing that stands out is that he is exactly the same with everyone. There is no occasion where he takes on a different persona. He is as true to himself as anyone I have met.

But his childhood was a little different. By his own admission he had two lives when he was growing up: his school life and his racing life. At school he was reserved, shy and "not very cool" but on the racetrack he very quickly became unstoppable and a recognised name. Karting was his other world and an environment where he felt belief and confidence in himself. Motor racing was something that he not only enjoyed but lived for.

Those formative days in karting really did shape how he drove throughout his racing career, especially when he won his world championship. His father, John, who will almost be as much of a fixture in this tale as Jenson, didn't lavish money on things like wet weather tyres, he let Jenson feel his own way through the different conditions. Look back at some of Jenson's best races and biggest wins, many of them are rainy affairs. In fact, of the fifteen Grand Prix that he won, seven of them were in the wet. He has a feel for the car in the rain and variable conditions that very few drivers have.

Clay Pigeon Raceway is where Jenson started his karting career, more as a hobby than harbouring any dreams of becoming an F1 driver, but there was no doubt that he had a love for speed. Jenson had been riding 50cc motorbikes, but John was nervous and Jenson was never really that comfortable on two wheels. So if two wheels didn't suit, what about four? It was to be the perfect solution and everything changed on Christmas Day in 1987, when he got his first kart. Just two years later, the young driver was racing against the likes of Anthony Davidson, Dan Wheldon and Justin Wilson – drivers who went on to win at the highest levels around the world.

But it wasn't just Jenson who had a way with karts. His father sold the car dealerships he owned to start up Rocket Motorsports. He had such a way of tuning engines that for a while they came under scrutiny from organisers. But there was never any cheating, just expert preparation to a level that surpassed everyone else. John's engines soon became the power of choice and helped many young drivers to win races and championships, including Lewis Hamilton.

In 1994 Jenson started racing in Europe and in subsequent years his trophy haul around the world was impressive. But as for every driver, the decision to move to cars had to be made and Jenson's height and weight certainly played a factor in that. Even in F1, he was always one of the taller drivers and that was the same in his younger days too.

At what seems late these days, at the age of eighteen, Button moved up to single-seater racing. David Robertson, who went on to manage Kimi Räikkönen, found him the funding for an F3 test with the renowned Carlin team at the Pembrey circuit in Wales. In a decision which few would have had the nerve or humility to make, Button decided that he didn't want to do F3 at that stage, feeling it was too big a step. He opted for British Formula Ford and became champion with nine wins. He also finished runner-up in the European version with one victory from four races. Formula Ford always came to a crescendo at the end of the season with the Winter Series and Formula Ford Festival at Brands Hatch. In 1998, that too went to the rising star from Frome.

Speaking of stars, one of the quickest ways of getting the word out to the world about your talents as a young driver is to win the prestigious Autosport BRDC Award. During a star-studded night in London, at the end of his rookie season in cars, that is exactly what Button did. As well as all the plaudits, the main prize is a test in a Formula One car. The roll call of winners is a roll call of motorsport talent, and almost all have gone on to great things.

Whilst competing in the British F3 International Series, Button got his prize and drove the McLaren. It was the 1998 F1 Championship-winning car that gave Mika Häkkinen his first world title. Button's F3 season had gone well, and against a much more experienced field he banked three wins and finished as top rookie driver and third in the championship.

But now what? He was uncertain how to continue his career. Whilst he was very much on the up and not wanting to linger in F3, he had already tested the International F3000 cars and wasn't a fan of how they drove. He decided to bide his time before making his decision and went on holiday to Mexico with his then-girlfriend.

The couple had barely unpacked when Jenson got a phone call telling him to get on a plane to Barcelona. Alain Prost, his childhood hero, wanted him to test for his Prost Grand Prix F1 team. John met his son at the airport with his helmet and Formula Ford overalls, and they went to business. Seat fittings, meetings and discussions all took place whilst Jean Alesi, one of the biggest names in the sport, was testing the Prost F1 car around the Circuit de Catalunya.

Eventually it was Jenson's turn, and he revelled in it, instantly feeling at home in the car. He didn't know his lap times and had been told not to focus on them. His job was ideally not to crash and just to enjoy the experience. Sadly, when he was really getting into it, the engine seized and it was game over. He returned to the pits and was told that he had gone a second and a half quicker than Alesi and had surpassed Prost's expectations.

Shortly after, Jenson and John were en route to Paris for a meeting with Alain Prost. He recounts in his autobiography, *Life to the Limit*:

Alain made an offer. He wanted me to join the team as their Formula 3000 driver for two years, then one year as a test driver and then into Formula One. It wasn't appealing. Not because I'd expected to leap straight on to the frontline of their F1 operation;

I was happy to pay my dues and spending a couple more years honing my race craft was a good idea if – and here was where more doubt crept in – if they definitely offered me an F1 drive at the end of it. The problem was that they weren't prepared to commit to that bit of the contract. Effectively I could be throwing away three years of my career on what was little more than a promise.

The Buttons headed home for Christmas. It had been some year and a bit of a break to process it all was high on the agenda. But on Christmas Eve, whilst in his local pub, Jenson got a phone call that would change his life. Answering his phone, he thought he was on the receiving end of a wind-up. The caller claimed to be Frank Williams, but Jenson wasn't buying it, thinking it was a prank from either his dad or one of his friends.

But it is difficult to mistake Frank's voice, and when everything sank in, Jenson realised it really was the great man on the line. He relays the conversation, the panic, the emotion so well in his autobiography:

"I hope you don't mind me calling on Christmas Eve, but I wanted to make sure you don't think I'm not interested in your career, just because I haven't phoned you yet," he said.

"Do you think you're ready for a season in Formula One?" he asked.

And, of course, I said . . . "No, Frank. Truthfully, no. I don't think I'm ready." There was a pause.

"I see. Well, that's a shame. Perhaps we'll talk in the future, then. Merry Christmas, Jenson."

"Merry Christmas, Frank."

The call ended. Oh God. Why did I say that?

He spoke to his father and then hurriedly called Frank back, which resulted in a meeting at the factory between Christmas and New Year.

Frank made it clear that there was no seat available but that he would like to test Jenson alongside another driver who turned out to be the highly regarded Brazilian Bruno Junqueira. A few weeks later, they headed to Jerez but the test was blighted by engine issues so both drivers took part in another test a week later, this time in Barcelona. Jenson was fractionally quicker, two-tenths of a second, but quicker all the same. The two drivers, who were rapidly understanding that this was indeed a shoot-out for the seat vacated by Alex Zanardi, were then told to do a debrief with the engineers followed by a four-page-long written test!

Unbelievably, this was all going on the day before the team's official launch. Ralf Schumacher was confirmed, but who was going to be his teammate? In the micromanaged world of Formula One, it seems extraordinary that a team like Williams left things so late.

The day of the launch came and neither Button nor Junqueira knew whether they had done enough to get the seat, or in actual fact whether they were even in line for the seat. If this was happening now, it would sound like a reality TV show with a Formula One drive as the prize.

Jenson and Bruno were taken to Frank's office. Bruno went in first but was inscrutable when he came out. Then it was the turn of Jenson. I am not sure why I have images of *The Apprentice* in my head, but it sounds very similar! Button describes the moment when his whole life changed in his autobiography:

> I took a seat across from Frank, who looked at me, an unreadable smile on his face, knowing full well that for me time was standing still. And then he said, "We've decided to go with you."

This was when his dream came true. All the doubt, effort, sacrifice by the whole family had led to this one moment. Minutes later and the nineteen-year-old F3 driver was being ushered into the media room where the press were waiting, as the drivers had been, to find out who would be lining up on the grid for Williams in just a matter of weeks.

To get an F1 super licence nowadays is very tricky, but even then, a lot of red tape was in place to ensure that the driver reaching F1 had demonstrated his ability to be there. On reaching Australia, Button had only managed fifteen per cent of the miles required. The FIA decided to grant the licence, something which raised eyebrows around the paddock. Three-time world champion Sir Jackie Stewart was famously outspoken, saying, "I don't believe you can go straight from kindergarten to university." The other drivers who would be lining up alongside Button on the grid had also voiced their displeasure. It wasn't exactly the welcome that Button had been hoping for!

And what a debut race weekend it proved to be. There was just about everything thrown in apart from a fairy-tale result.

He had coped well with the media attention and hostility of some drivers, past and present. He did have the formidable Sir Frank Williams and Sir Patrick Head in his corner who were supportive and straight to the point when it came to advice.

Jenson came unstuck in the Saturday morning practice session with a heavy crash which meant that the team had some work to do to repair the car before he was able to head out for his first ever F1 qualifying session. The car was ready, but additional problems and the unfortunate timing of a red flag meant the best Button could do was twenty-first position and on the last row of the grid.

When it came to the race, though, he was able to show that he could mix it up with the big boys. Through retirements and pitstops, at one point he was running as high as sixth, but an engine problem meant that he became one of the twelve DNFs.

After the race ITV did a live interview with Jenson and his father. The presenters weren't onsite, so he was handed headphones and a microphone. This is the interview that I mentioned earlier. It surprised me how similar today's Jenson is to the twenty-year-old on camera with just one Grand Prix under his belt. He certainly didn't come across as a rookie:

"My first experience of F1 is better than I expected it to be. It's good to be here with all the best drivers and teams in the world. It's what I've dreamed about for many years and now it's reality," said Jenson.

John told how he watched from the grandstand surrounded by a passionate Aussie crowd enjoying themselves. He could have stayed in the paddock or in the garage and watched on monitors and listened on a headset, but as a racer and a fan, John wanted to be in amongst it.

The next race was Brazil. It was another unfamiliar racetrack, but in qualifying Button outqualified his more experienced team-mate, Ralf Schumacher. It was a great performance, putting the Williams driver into ninth at only his second race. Schumacher was just outside the top ten in eleventh place.

When it came to the race, though, Button narrowly missed out on points, coming home seventh. He had left the circuit when he heard the news that David Coulthard's McLaren had been disqualified for an illegal front wing end plate which meant that he moved up to sixth and became the youngest driver at that time to ever get a championship point.

When we think of the calendar that we are familiar with now, it was an odd pattern of races in 2000. That year, the British Grand Prix was in April as the fourth race of the season. There was a real buzz around it with Button, the new Brit, carrying the hopes of the home crowd along with David Coulthard, Eddie Irvine and Johnny Herbert. On the Saturday, Button qualified a superb sixth, and in the race he went one place better. It was a mature drive, bringing the Williams home in fifth and securing another two points in the championship. The race was won by a fellow Brit, and someone who took Jenson under his wing – David Coulthard.

It is easy to forget how tumultuous those early years were both on and off track for Button. Through no fault of his own, he left Williams at the end of his first year. A deal had already been in place to bring back Juan Pablo Montoya after his time racing in CART in the USA. Button was very aware of the situation and his one-year contract reflected that.

Fortunately, his skills had attracted the attention of other teams, and it was announced that he would be going to Benetton to partner Giancarlo Fisichella under the watchful eye of Flavio Briatore. For watchful eye, read critical. For a man who signed Button for two years, Briatore acted like he didn't really want him to be there. He spent much of the time being outspoken against his driver in press conferences and to the media.

He called Jenson a "lazy playboy" whilst giving quotes doubting his future and, in some cases, his talent as well. There was concern that Button might not even make the second year of his contract, but he did. Even at that, Briatore didn't sound convinced that it was a good move, even though it was within his power to change things.

Whilst speaking to Italian newspaper *La Stampa* before the start of the 2002 season, Briatore took an odd approach for a pre-season pep talk:

"This will be Button's make or break year. He started really well with Williams, but after that he let us down a bit. He can't afford to make mistakes now, because he risks losing his place. The same can be said of Trulli: he too must make the most of his chance of racing in a top team. You can't have pity for no one in this business."

Not what a sports psychologist would call a great pep-talk, and I can't imagine the drivers appreciated that build-up to the season.

Although he was only twenty-two, he had also spent a lot of time in the press for his perceived lavish lifestyle. They loved and loathed the fact that he lived in Monaco, had a yacht and model girlfriends. Some of it was true, of course, other parts fabricated to stoke the image of what a young F1 driver's life must be like. At the same time, Button had worked hard during the winter break, to assimilate himself with the team and tailor the car more to his liking, and it was a move that paid off.

Throughout the 2002 season Button was better, but so was the car. Much more so than the previous year. In the second race in Malaysia, it looked like he would get his first podium but, as he started the last lap, he suffered a rear suspension failure. Michael Schumacher, who had been six seconds behind, swept past him for third whilst Button was able to limp home in fourth place. It had been a much-improved season, so when Button took a phone call from Briatore in July, telling him that he would not be kept on for the following year, he was understandably shocked. Despite being ahead of Trulli in the championship, it was the Italian who would stay at the team and be partnered by test-driver Fernando Alonso, both of whom were talented drivers, both managed by Briatore.

Once again, Button was back on the market, but it wasn't long before he was snapped up. British American Racing, or BAR as they were known, had a big budget and big ideas. Jacques Villeneuve was already at the team, but in terms of new blood, as well as Button, there was a new team principal in Dave Richards.

Whilst he never had Briatore on side, Richards' and the entire team's attitude was a breath of fresh air. Well, everyone apart from his teammate. Villeneuve set his stall out early, saying to press at the launch that Button "brings to the sport what boy bands bring to music" and added that he would need to improve his performances to earn the former world champion's respect.

Turning up in F1 without the required licence, having been at three teams in four years, navigating a bumpy road with the press, given a tough time from an all-powerful team boss and now with a former world champion disrespecting him in public, it's fair to say Jenson Button had had his quota of tests – and he was still only twenty-four!

Monaco saw one of the biggest crashes of Button's career. In practice on the Saturday morning, he came out of the tunnel, bouncing off the walls like a pinball. He was taken to hospital and did not take part in the rest of the weekend. By the end of that season and even with sitting out a Grand Prix, Button had outperformed the outspoken Villeneuve. Respect earned? It seemed so. There was certainly a thaw in the relationship.

Not that it mattered as the Canadian was out and Takuma Sato was in. For the first time Button felt that he was in the main seat with a team that respected him. Big things were planned for 2004.

At the first race in Australia, Button's BAR showed promise in qualifying, and after starting the race from fourth, he finished in sixth place. Race one completed, chequered flag crossed, points in the bag and, although he finished further back than he started, things would just keep getting better.

In Malaysia, Button ticked off another thing from his bucket list: a podium in Formula One. He qualified in sixth but finished the race in third. Next on the calendar was the Middle East and the Kingdom of Bahrain for the very first time. Just fourteen days after his first podium, Button was up there again. Another third, no champagne but rose water on that occasion. Next up was the San Marino Grand Prix and another first – pole position. In qualifying, Button put in a superb lap. He said himself that as he came out of the final corner, he knew it was good enough for pole and it was. By his own admission, Jenson was a better racer than qualifier, but on that day, no one was faster. In the race he scored his highest ever finish in Formula One with second place to Michael Schumacher.

It was shaping up to be a great year, and by the end of 2004, it was his strongest season yet. There was still no win, but a constant drip feed of points and podium places meant that Button finished third in the Drivers' Championship behind the two Ferrari drivers, Schumacher and Barrichello.

One thing that stands out with some drivers is just how complex things become around them. In F1 terms, life had never been better for Jenson Button, yet during that year, he had taken the decision to leave BAR and return to Williams. Instantly, the situation got messy. BAR thought they had a contract with Button, as did Williams. Dave Richards referred the matter to the FIA contracts recognition board, which decided that the BAR contract took preference. It meant Button couldn't join Williams and he most probably spent 2005 getting dirty looks from mechanics who knew he would have preferred to be elsewhere!

In Formula One, 2005 was known for several bizarre events. After a podium for Button in Imola, it was discovered that his fuel tank was illegal. Very unusually, the team was banned for the next two races, so Button was back to being a spectator for the Spanish and Monaco Grand Prix. It was also the year of the Indianapolis debacle when the Michelin tyres were deemed not safe enough to race there. The cars went out as normal for the formation lap, but as they reached the pit lane entrance just before the controversial banking, all teams on Michelins returned to the pits, leaving just six cars from the three Bridgestone teams, Ferrari, Jordan and Minardi, to start the race.

In 2005 Williams were still using BMW engines but, due to the withdrawal of the German manufacturer, they changed to Cosworth for 2006. Depite the delay, Button was still planning on joining his old team, but the switch from BMW to Cosworth was not something he had signed up for or wanted to be part of. He paid himself out of the second year of the Williams contract and opted to stay at BAR, now renamed as Honda. This was much more than a name change, and there lay the appeal. Honda had the power and finances to get the right people in to build a great car and create a world-class engine.

The revolving door of F1 continued and as Sato went out, in came Rubens Barrichello. The Brazilian was also looking to prove himself, finishing second in the Drivers' Championship several times, but mostly living in the shadow of Michael Schumacher for years.

There is only one place and date that stands out for Button in 2006. Hungary on 6 August 2006 was an unusually damp Sunday in Budapest. Normally the temperatures are very high as the sun beats down, but on this day, rain in the morning had sent cars spinning off in GP2, the F1 support race. The rubber laid down over the last few days was washed away and the combination of high temperatures and rain created a slippery surface.

The track was still damp several hours later when F1 was getting ready to race. Kimi Räikkönen was on pole and, although Button had qualified in fourth, a ten-place penalty for an engine change meant he started from fourteenth. That day, it was a competitive place to be, with Alonso and Schumacher also starting further back than normal.

The spray made for tricky racing, whilst at the front Räikkönen pulled away in what was classified as the first wet Hungarian Grand Prix. The mixed conditions were ideal for Button, who worked his way through the field. The Bridgestone cars, such as the Ferrari of Schumacher, struggled whilst other cars tangled. Cutting a clear path through it all was Jenson Button.

As a boy, he had seen these conditions most weekends karting. He learned how to "feel" the car underneath him, to know where and when time and opportunity might be lost and gained. As others misread the situation, for Button there was total clarity. Seventy laps and 190 miles later, Jenson Button realised his dream and won his first ever Formula One Grand Prix.

The pictures after are well known – a wide-eyed Jenson, helmet still on, visor up, looking as shocked and excited as anyone ever has been to win a race. It was a victory for his father and whole family, as much as it was for him and Honda.

In the post-race interview Jenson was quick to thank the entire team, and especially the strategists describing them as a "thinking team" winning without the fastest car.

"I didn't want the race to end. Normally when you're in the lead it goes on forever, but I was loving it."

But there was to be no party – well, not for Jenson anyway. The rest of us went on the Red Bull Boat on the Danube and made a decent effort of a party. Jenson wasn't there. He had a host of countries to visit for PR commitments, starting with China and then on to Honda HQ in Japan, and that really sums up Formula One: fast racing and fast living. The sponsors pay big money and will get their return through driver appearances. For Honda, it was a huge result, and they too needed to see the winning driver up close.

The next couple of years, 2007 and 2008, were forgettable, with Button battling in an uncompetitive car and managing only six points in 2007 and three the following year. The only good thing in amongst this was the arrival of Ross Brawn, who had joined Honda with an eye on 2009.

But on Friday, 5 December 2008, the news broke that Honda were pulling out of Formula One with immediate effect. The global financial crisis was forcing even the biggest of companies to rethink their spending and for Honda, having a Formula One team was a step too far. Unless a buyer could be found, Button was out of a drive. There was interest from several parties and in December, Honda team principal Ross Brawn said that whoever bought the team would inherit a car "ahead of their rivals". He knew how good the car was looking. He should, as he and his team designed it.

But it was still a surprise, a very welcome surprise, when on Friday, 6 March 2009 it was announced that Ross had bought the team and would run it as Brawn GP. Button took to the track just a few days later at testing in Barcelona. By the end of the month, he had won the Australian Grand Prix.

It was the start of a fairy tale. A story which transcended Formula One. The new boys were beating the establishment. It was David v Goliath, but the reality was that the work to create this championship-winning car was done when the team and budget was still Honda. Now though, it was under the guidance and name of those who had done that work, who had used their brains and brawn. The clue was in the name all along.

But the previous few months and weeks had been stressful. The drivers had signed big money deals for Honda. Brawn didn't have that kind of money, so Jenson took a large pay cut to remain part of the team. Then there was the question of an engine. Honda couldn't really pull out of F1 and then continue to supply the power. For them it had to be a complete withdrawal from the sport. It was Mercedes-Benz who stepped up to the fray late in the day and powered Brawn, and later became the team that is on the grid now.

Button knew straight away in testing that the car was good. He described feeling as if the car was an extension of him. Barrichello had been retained by Brawn, and he also knew how impressive the car was. In testing, they were instantly much faster than their rivals, but testing is always an unknown, with plenty of subterfuge. Bizarrely, fast times don't always mean fast times, whilst slow times are often quick laps being hidden by various decoys, including heavy fuel loads.

The only moment to work out where the teams really are in terms of performance is when the circus hits town on the first weekend, and in 2009 the first race of the season was in Melbourne. As mentioned earlier, by his own admission, Button wasn't seen as being the quickest over one lap, but on that Saturday at Albert Park, he blasted away the competition. The closest driver was his teammate and at their first ever race, Brawn locked out the front row of the grid.

There was no doubt that the car was fast, but it was still unproven over a race distance. Twenty-four hours later, as Jenson Button took the chequered flag first, all those fears and worries came to nothing. Brawn were confirmed as the real deal.

What struck me after the race was the confidence that Jenson had in the interviews. He was revelling in it. Not bolshie in any way, but even if he had been, you would cut him some slack, as the team and drivers had been through so much and deserved all the rewards that were coming their way. Normally after the first race, you would get set answers about "taking each race as it comes" and "it's a long season ahead". We have all heard those!

Unusually, both Rubens and Jenson were brimming with confidence.

Jenson describes in his book how he had said to his team, "Come on guys, let's not throw this away. This is probably the best opportunity we'll ever have to win the championship." He continues,

You hear teams saying things like, "We didn't think about the championship until the end of the season, we just concentrated on race wins," but I call bullshit on that. Right after that first win, I was looking at the championship. I was thinking, this is my chance.

The double diffuser was being heralded as the point of difference. Toyota and Williams were also using double diffusers at the start of the season. For the rest of the field, whilst they moaned about it to the press and talked about its legality to the FIA, they were frantically trying to catch up, and by the middle of the season almost every car on the grid was using one.

Button dominated the start of the year, winning six out of the seven races. Malaysia was wet and, for the second race in a row, it was the safety car that crossed the line first. In terms of the man who would take maximum points, that was Button.

Whilst most people were enjoying the success of Brawn, it seemed that Flavio Briatore wasn't one of them. Although they were never on each other's Christmas card list, describing Jenson to the press as a *paracarro*, which translates as "kerbstone", was not only disrespectful but a little confusing too! Barrichello didn't escape either, although his slur at least made sense. He was described as "almost retired", which was true but the context in which it was meant was derogatory. His gripe was that the championship was being contested by a *paracarro* and "someone who was almost retired". Either way, by the end of the weekend in Shanghai, it was more points for Button, albeit third behind the Red Bulls of Vettel and Webber.

A couple of weeks later, a crucial period of domination started for Button with four wins on the bounce: Bahrain, Spain, Monaco and Turkey. After a straightforward win in the desert of Bahrain, things got a little testy in Spain.

Jenson started from pole position and was on a different strategy to his teammate, who made a great start and took the lead at turn 1 but during the race the strategies were switched. Button won with Barrichello in second. This upset Rubens and the fuse was now lit, but the explosion didn't happen until a few races later. In the meantime, Jenson headed into Monaco with a formidable forty-one points from a possible forty-five. Not bad at all for a man who a few months before had been searching for a job.

The Brit was certainly starting to dispel his own theory that he wasn't a good qualifier. He was dominating Saturdays and Sundays, and around the tricky streets of Monaco he got his fourth pole of the season. Come the race, whilst there were the usual thrills and spills, all the action was happening behind the leader, which meant for Button it was pretty straightforward.

That was, until after the chequered flag.

The norm is for cars to go to parc fermé, but nothing is normal at Monaco, and the winner should draw to a halt on the main straight with the other two podium finishers alongside. Button, having never been on the podium at Monaco, parked up in the wrong place, jumped out in celebration and then realised his mistake. He then had to run all the way back to the start/finish straight, where the podium is located and the royal party were waiting to greet him. The pictures were great as he ran waving to the crowd, finally reaching the podium and explaining his error whilst apologising for being late to HRH Prince Albert. Luckily HRH has a pretty good sense of humour.

Button went on to win the next race in Turkey, but there was disappointment in front of his home crowd at Silverstone. There, he could only manage sixth.

Rarely does a championship battle not get a little tricky between rivals, and for the Brawn drivers, it came to a head in Germany.

Button was twenty-three points ahead of Barrichello and, even though the Brazilian hadn't won a race that season, he was still ahead of Vettel, who had two victories. The Brawn car was reliable and dominant, and Barrichello had only managed to be one of the two. He knew that to close the gap and have a real chance at the title, he needed to start winning races.

Mid-July we headed to Nürburgring in Germany. Surrounded by the Eiffel mountains and forest, the track often has mixed weather, very much like Spa in Belgium. It was the same in 2009. On the Saturday, there were different conditions for each qualifying segment: dry, wet and drying. By the time it came to the shoot-out for pole position the track was dry again and, for the first time in his career, it was Mark Webber who took pole position. Barrichello was second and Button finished in third.

The Brazilian led the race on several occasions and looked set for a podium at the very least, whilst Button had never really featured at the front. Webber battled back hard after receiving a drive-through penalty for a clash with Barrichello in the opening laps. He re-took the lead and went on to win his first ever Grand Prix. It was one of those days in F1, which doesn't happen very often, when everyone was delighted for the winner. It had been such a long time for Webber to realise his dream and at last he had. He stood proudly on the podium with Vettel and Massa either side.

But where was Barrichello? Well, he was furious in the interview pen talking to me! Rubens felt the team had used strategy against him. Button had jumped his teammate in the second round of pitstops and the two finished less than a second apart in fifth and sixth.

"It was a good show from the team on how to lose a race today. For me, I am terribly upset with the way things went because I did all I had to do," Rubens said to me.

I asked him what he would do next. Would he speak to the team as something similar had happened in Spain?

"To be very honest with you, I wish I could go on the plane and go home right now. I don't want to talk to anybody in the team because there will be a lot of 'blah, blah, blah' and I don't want to hear that."

"Are you saying the team are favouring Jenson?"

"No, I am not saying that. I am saying it was a good show in how to lose a race today."

It was around this time that social media was really taking off, which certainly had its pros and cons. I remember after this race someone remixed my questions and Rubens' answers to the Kaiser Chiefs' song "Ruby" and added some of Rubens' "blah, blah, blah, blah, blah, blah" into the mix. It was funny, unless of course you were Rubens!

It had been a difficult Sunday and one which saw the Brazilian drop behind Vettel and Webber in the championship. Button was still top. Sadly for Barrichello, he couldn't jump on a plane and head home just yet, as there was one more race before the August break. And it wasn't a great weekend for Brawn either. The whole occasion was marred by the dreadful accident which happened in qualifying to Felipe Massa, after the spring from the Brawn car of Barrichello flew off and hit Massa's helmet. Both Brawns were stopped for in-depth safety checks. It meant Button and his teammate started eighth and twelfth respectively. The race didn't go as hoped and they closed off the first part of the season with frustration. Button was seventh but still in the lead of the championship, 18.5 points ahead of his nearest rival, who was now Mark Webber.

Rejuvenated and ready for an intense seven-race battle for life-changing honours, F1 regrouped in Valencia to kick-start the second half of the season. It's a good job that Jenson had made such a strong start to the year, because in the second half he wasn't dominant. In fact, after the Turkish Grand Prix, which took place at the start of June, Button didn't win another race that season whilst his championship rivals, Barrichello and Vettel, won two each.

On the streets of Valencia, Button finished seventh whilst his teammate took his first win of the year, which moved him back up to second in the championship, just eighteen points behind the Brit. The gap continued to close in Belgium after Button was taken out by Romain Grosjean and had to retire. Luckily for Button, Rubens could only finish seventh.

As a former Ferrari driver, Barrichello always got a lot of love at Monza, so he was very much in his element at the Italian Grand Prix. As we saw so often that season, it was difficult to separate the Brawn cars regardless of where they were on the grid. In qualifying they were alongside each other on the third row, but a great start saw them quickly move up at the start of the Grand Prix. Ultimately it was Rubens who won from Jenson in second.

Slowly but steadily, the gap in the championship was closing, and Barrichello was very much in contention. After the chequered flag had fallen, Jenson told me, "I've got a very tough teammate. He's very competitive and he's been able to show it this year, especially over the last few races. It's going to be tough for the rest of the year, I know that, but I'm up to the challenge and I'm very excited by it."

Unknowingly at the time, that victory for the Brazilian turned out to be his last in Formula One. Yet the title race would go to the end.

As F1 left Europe behind and headed to Singapore, Button was fourteen points ahead. Hamilton had now conceded the defence of his title, which meant that only the two Brawns and two Red Bulls were mathematically able to win the championship. And yet on the hot, dark and demanding streets of Singapore, things didn't go the way of any of the title challengers, and it was the first race of the year which didn't feature either a Brawn or Red Bull driver.

It was an odd run of results for the Brawn team, but especially for Button. In Singapore he qualified twelfth and finished fifth. In Japan he started tenth after a penalty for speeding under yellow flags but still crossed the line in eighth. And yet if he finished with enough points in Brazil, the penultimate race of the season, the championship would be his.

Brazil. Home of his rival and teammate Rubens Barrichello and home to Interlagos, a circuit that can throw anything and everything at you. Though the championship was Button's to lose, with a track like that, it was by no means a done deal.

By Saturday evening, it looked even less likely. The session was wet and a mix-up with tyre strategy saw Button qualifying a desperate fourteenth. He could take solace in the fact that one of the championship rivals, Sebastian Vettel, was even lower than him in sixteenth place. There was no comfort, though, in knowing that his teammate and main rival was on pole position and the crowd absolutely loved it.

By the time it got to race day, it was almost a relief. By his own admission the pressure was starting to get to Button, and with a jeering, partisan crowd and an unfavourable fourteenth on the grid, he was feeling the tension. The fourteen-point lead meant it was his to lose, and yet he knew he only needed to finish four points ahead of teammate Barrichello to seal the 2009 Drivers' title. Vettel needed to finish first or second to keep his hopes alive.

The start of any Brazilian Grand Prix is a game of risk, and for so many drivers that year, the risk was much bigger than the reward. Not for Button, though, who went from fourteenth to ninth as others crashed, spun and retired in the melee at the start. He kept working his way forward, and with eight laps to go, Barrichello and Hamilton got into each other's space. The Brawn got a puncture and had to pit.

Barrichello emerged in eighth. Vettel was fourth. If it stayed like this, Button's fifth would be enough to take the title. That is exactly how things finished in Brazil.

After 169 Formula One Grand Prix and twenty-five years of driving and dreaming, Jenson Button was the Formula One World Champion.

I was waiting at the interview pen, viewing it on a tiny screen and totally immersed in the pictures. Watching Webber, Kubica and Hamilton on the podium, I didn't think that Jenson would come straight to the interview area, but after seeing his mechanics and John he came running into the pen. The emotion was flowing, everyone clapped and cheered as he arrived. He came straight over to me as I normally interviewed him first, then hugged me. I was caught up in hugging him back and shouting (and squealing) "well done!" when I realised that BBC had already joined me live! It might not have been the most professional moment of my career, but a lot of people found it very amusing and even emotional. When we stopped shouting and celebrating, I extracted myself and started the interview, with my boss Mark Wilkin's voice booming through my earpiece to "get on with it".

I am pretty sure that Jenson has a hundred people that he would rather have seen first but there was no choice, it was me! To share that moment and be part of that never-to-be-repeated season was so special, and for it to happen to Jenson was just incredible. I appreciate there is a lot of luck when it comes to the nationality of the driver who wins. Had it been Rubens, then the Brazilians would have got an equally emotional interview and talked about how much Rubens deserved it after everything he did in his career – and they would have been right. But, on this day, in that moment in time, it was Jenson. On the Sunday night we left Jenson and his friends in Brazil to party, but as it happened the new world champion was so exhausted and overwhelmed that he just stayed in his room.

I, on the other hand, headed for the airport. As Team Button had opted not to fly home and stay in São Paulo, a couple of others and myself were bumped up to the free seats in business class. I was shattered and *so* excited about lying down for ten hours through the night to Heathrow. It certainly didn't work out that way! I hadn't factored in the presence of Mark Webber, winner of the Brazilian Grand Prix, and David Coulthard, thirteen-time race winner and fun magnet – both of whom are great friends and now my colleagues! Let's just say sleep was not on their list of priorities and therefore we were all awake – team bosses, engineers, commentators, the whole cabin in celebration. The highlight was when Webber started the dinner (or was it breakfast service?) somewhere over the Atlantic. It was a great flight back. Thanks, Jenson, for staying in São Paulo – he definitely partied less and slept better than the rest of us did!

So what happens next for a driver when they have realised their dreams and their team is up for sale? Retirement? Contentment? Not for Button. He was just getting started.

It might seem odd now knowing the dominance that Mercedes has enjoyed, but when Button was offered the seat to partner Nico Rosberg for the 2010 season, he wasn't convinced. Ross Brawn and Nick Fry explained that Brawn would now be known as Mercedes Grand Prix although Mercedes wouldn't actually be funding its return to the sport. Sponsors and money needed to be found. Jenson thought it sounded disjointed and he also fancied his chances at McLaren – or more truthfully, fancied proving himself against one of the very best, Lewis Hamilton. He called Martin Whitmarsh, then Team Principal of McLaren, and said he would be interested in joining the team. At first Whitmarsh was surprised that Jenson was looking to move teams, but he quickly got to work to sign the new world champion.

As Button and Hamilton lined up on the grid in Bahrain in 2010, it was the first time since Jim Clark and Graham Hill in 1968 that two British world champions were teammates. The British media were in a frenzy over the pairing. Even with the coveted number one on his car, Button would need time to bed into his new team. In Bahrain he started and finished behind his teammate, but at least the new chapter had begun and the McLaren wheels were turning.

Australia next time out was a very different story. In qualifying at Albert Park, surprisingly, Hamilton didn't make it into the top ten shoot-out whilst Button put the McLaren into fourth. He would have plenty of work to do if he hoped to win the race, but his first podium for the team was certainly within his grasp. The start of the race was wet. Button dropped to sixth and was then passed by Hamilton for that position. Jenson stopped for slicks before the rest of the grid, but such is his comfort in these conditions he felt he could go early. He slid off the track on the dry weather tyre but managed to keep going, eventually crossing the line first.

His move to McLaren was validated and after just two races, his skills, in the same machinery, had beaten Lewis Hamilton. That victory also meant that he joined an exclusive group of drivers who had won a Grand Prix for three different teams. He went on to win in the mixed weather conditions of China, holding his nerve on the slick tyres early on when many went to inters. By the end of his first year for McLaren, he had won two races and stood on the podium a further five times.

At the start of May I went to spend a day with Jenson as he returned to Frome, the town where he grew up. As well as visiting all three schools that he attended, he was given the freedom of the town and thousands came out to see the return of their hero.

It was a packed schedule. At 9.30 a.m. we started at Vallis First School. "It's quite emotional seeing all the kids in the same outfit as I used to wear here," said Jenson. They performed a specially written song about Jenson and McLaren, not the easiest rhyming words for lyrics! We moved on to Selwood Middle School by 10.30 a.m., where we chatted to his old teachers, some of whom were still there. At 11.30 a.m. we had made it to Frome Community College, where he met his old maths teacher and they brought out his exam results for all to see. A B-grade in French was his standout performance and his favourite subject – maybe he knew he'd spend much of his time in Monaco!

You could see how much Jenson was enjoying his trip down memory lane and it was funny to see that, no matter what you achieve, your teacher will always be your teacher and bring back those old feelings. "I can't believe it's still the same teachers and they look the same too. They still scare me to death."

A good job then that it was time to leave and move on to the Market Square, where thousands of people had come out to see Jenson being presented with the Freedom of Frome. The town crier was there to welcome us all.

I asked Jenson what the freedom of his town let him do exactly.

"I've heard that I can take sheep through the town centre," he replied!

"You've got a road named after you in Frome and a bridge, if you get a second world championship, what will you demand?" I asked.

"An area, a burgh with a castle," he said, laughing. "I'm not asking for much."

Sadly that second world championship never came, but more race wins did – and some pretty fine ones too.

Arguably, the biggest moment that season came off-track at the Brazilian Grand Prix. As I've mentioned, the racetrack is not in the safest neighbourhood, and teams, drivers and media always take precautions there. We never fix the car park pass onto the windscreen so we can remove it as soon as we leave the track and not draw attention to ourselves. People never travel in team kit, or with watches or jewellery on. Basically, we try not to stand out in any way. Even at the BBC and Channel 4 we would always have a security officer and get a car with bulletproof glass at the very least. Sometimes, though, that is not enough.

Around eight of us were in a restaurant having dinner when someone started thumping the glass beside where we were sitting. It was my father, who seemingly had big news, or else he was being chased by a mob! In actual fact, he had heard that Jenson had been "held at gunpoint" and another team had been too.

It was a long and late night trying to speak to the teams involved and work out what exactly had happened. By the time we got to the track the next morning I was already primed to be at the front of the media scrum to hear from Jenson.

He had been leaving the circuit in a car with his friends, driven by his security detail, when he saw a man with a baseball bat covered in nails beside the window. A couple of seconds later, four men were coming through the traffic towards them with handguns and machine guns. The driver smashed his way through the gap in the traffic to get away. It sounded terrifying. The team involved in the other incident had been Sauber. Again, gunmen had approached the vehicle of three engineers, and taken their bags before fleeing.

On arrival at the track, Jenson said he was fine but shaken.

"You hear about it happening over the years, but until you are actually involved you don't know how it feels," he said. "It's a pretty scary situation because initially you don't believe it's happening.

"I feel fine now. There's a lot of attention because it's the first time it's been a driver that's been held up, but hopefully it will show the dangers that are down there and we'll take more care."

Thankfully, whilst it was terrifying for those involved, everyone was safe.

One of the attractions of joining McLaren was to pitch himself against Hamilton and, regardless of what position they were battling for, Button was thriving having one of the very best drivers alongside him. That certainly showed in 2011. He revelled in the challenge and by the end of the season had secured three wins, nine further podiums and a hugely impressive second in the World Drivers' Championship.

The most famous of his wins, possibly of his career, came in Canada at what turned out to be the longest race in Formula One history. If this race was written into a movie you would say, "No way, it's too far-fetched." And yet it happened.

The race started behind the safety car after some heavy downpours that morning. Button was seventh but within a couple of laps all bets were off. In real-time, it would take almost five hours to describe this race, so here is a much-abridged version. On lap 5, Hamilton and Webber made contact after the safety car went in. Button ran wide and then lost places to Schumacher and Hamilton. After much slip-ping and sliding, on lap 8, Hamilton found himself behind Button again and tried to make a move on the start-finish straight, which resulted in Hamilton hitting the pit wall and careering across the track whilst Jenson shouted on team radio, "What was he doing?"

Before the safety car came out again for Hamilton's stricken McLaren, Button had changed to intermediate tyres. It looked like it was another sound strategy call, and it was, but then he was given a drive-through penalty for speeding behind the safety car, drop-ping him back to fifteenth position.

A few laps later, a huge storm hit the track. Six laps were run behind the safety car before it was deemed too dangerous and the race was red-flagged for two hours.

Two hours is a terrifying amount of time to fill and yet we stayed on BBC One. It started to feel like I was covering an endurance race. Somehow, Martin Brundle, David Coulthard, Ted Kravitz, Jake Humphrey and I talked and interviewed our way through the 120-minute delay. Not all of it was award-winning and I seem to remember Martin and DC spending some time spotting Canadian birds – of which I mean the feathered variety!

The race eventually restarted seven laps behind the safety car, and then it was time to go racing; well, for a few laps at least. Button came across Alonso and contact between the two sent the Ferrari driver towards the wall, beached with no way to continue. Button came off badly with a puncture and needed a new front wing.

"It's Jenson's second contact of the afternoon. It's four pit stops and a drive-through for Button," said Martin Brundle in BBC TV commentary.

He came back out in twenty-first and last. But those mixed and drying conditions were Button's secret weapon and he rapidly made his way through the field. By the time he got to the last lap, there was still only one dry line around the track. He already had risked his car and himself to overtake his way up to second – could he do it one more time? On the final lap, with just a few corners to go, he was pressing down on the race leader, Vettel. The German ran wide and just managed to catch the Red Bull from spinning, but that mistake was enough for Jenson to take the lead, and with just metres to go.

After five pitstops, a drive-through penalty, being last twice and some 4 hours and 4 minutes later, Button crossed the line, bringing an end to the madness and bringing the chequered flag down on a sublime victory. Lewis Hamilton and the whole of the McLaren garage applauded at the magic of what they had just seen. It was one of those races that you will just never forget.

A while later, Mark Webber said to Jenson, "In mixed conditions, you were an absolute freak. I don't know how you did it so often. I'd say, 'Whatever JB is doing, let's do what he does.'"

Button had several milestones in his career and fittingly won his 200th Grand Prix in Hungary, the venue of his long awaited first win.

Such was Jenson's enjoyment at being part of McLaren, he signed a three-year extension with the team. It was announced in the build-up to the Japanese Grand Prix, another race that was special to him and that he went on to win. That weekend, Vettel claimed his second championship. By the end of the season, Button finished behind him, second in the drivers' standings and ahead of Hamilton. It was in fact the first time that Hamilton had been beaten by a teammate in F1. This is exactly what Button had come to McLaren to do.

In 2012, it felt that things at McLaren were getting a little fractious. The difference between Button and Hamilton's approach to an entire race weekend were huge. Walk into the McLaren motorhome and Team Button would be there, John, Jenson's friends and then-girlfriend Jessica Michibata. It was always great chatting to them, and between his driving and meetings, Jenson would be there relaxing too. It felt easy and most British journalists were comfortable approaching the group. This was very different to Lewis, who didn't sit out in hospitality, nor travelled with a posse. He was much more of a "sole trader". Let's not forget that McLaren had been "his" team, but by then and with the presence of Team Button, it was as if a not very hostile takeover had happened. It was a pretty friendly one to be honest!

On track, it was tougher for McLaren. Red Bull and Vettel were even more dominant, although by the end of the year, Button still had three wins to his name. He got off to a great start winning in

Australia for the third time. This was the season of seven different winners in the first seven races. Still incredible when you think about it.

Button's next win came in Belgium, but what a weekend that turned out to be, overshadowed by the battle and behaviour of his teammate. Jenson had the upper hand throughout the weekend and took pole position whilst Lewis could only manage eighth. Lewis had told me after qualifying that he had opted to use the old wing whilst Jenson had used the new Spa-spec wing. Lewis tweeted similar information but also mentioned the difference in speed that it created. It was odd behaviour from a world champion and such a hugely respected driver. He has never been someone who needs to validate his skill or talent – it is evident for all to see. But it got worse when later, on the Saturday night, Hamilton tweeted pictures of his and Jenson's telemetry. The telemetry sheet showed traces of the McLaren drivers' laps, where the two lost and gained on each other, and also secret information about the car's settings. Jenson subsequently said it was from the sim but, at that time, we didn't know that was the case.

When I spoke to Jenson about it that weekend, he described it as "disappointing". It certainly didn't affect him as he went on to win the race by thirteen seconds from Vettel whilst Hamilton, and many others, were wiped out by Romain Grosjean at the start of the race. The Frenchman was subsequently fined €50,000 and given a one-race ban.

Button's third victory of the season came in Brazil. Lewis, in his last race for McLaren, had been leading until a collision with Nico Hülkenberg on lap 54. The German was given a drive through penalty and Hamilton was out. It meant that Button took the lead and won for McLaren but with Hamilton leaving the team, the celebrations were more subdued than normal.

Things took a turn at McLaren in 2013, and not for the better. Sergio Perez was the new kid in town, but neither he nor Jenson were given the tools or opportunity to have a good season. The car was a compromise of 2012 and 2013 after the 2013 challenger was shown to have, well, little challenge at all.

Still Jenson kept a smile on his face and his family and friends certainly helped with that. The Hungarian Grand Prix was John's seventieth birthday and, in the build-up, the whole paddock had been involved in a video as a birthday surprise for him. We (BBC) filmed it for him, so between interviews and cars on track we were running around getting messages from drivers, team bosses and journalists. John was a friend to so many and the birthday made for a fun weekend for the Button family, most of whom had turned up in Budapest.

After the Korean Grand Prix, I went to Tokyo to film with Jenson. Normally, after the Japanese GP, most of the paddock heads to Tokyo for a night out. Sometimes, I have gone to Kyoto or other parts of Japan to sightsee, but Tokyo really is the go-to, and especially for the drivers who have it as one of their big nights out of the year. There is a bar where F1 drivers and sports car drivers all meet up. Often the big race at Fuji is the following weekend, so the Sunday night is the natural meeting point for all. This time the booze-up happened a week earlier, after a mass exodus from Korea. The drivers were straight out to Tokyo, where there was ample fun to be had.

I was filming on the Tuesday evening with Jenson, starting at a McLaren showroom in a suburb of Tokyo. I had somehow been drafted in to speak on stage at the event as well as present the feature for BBC. When I got there, Jenson had a bandage on his hand. We were told we couldn't film him wearing it – not ideal for a behind-the-scenes, fly-on-the-wall style feature. He was wearing it as a deterrent to stop the many well-wishers shaking his hand. He didn't want to be rude, so he wore the bandage and tried to get his greeting in first with a respectful bow. The problem with keeping the bandage on is that we were following him all night for the BBC. Of course, we agreed and we didn't show him wearing it, as requested. The question was, how had he injured it?

It was purely a social injury. In the bar that the drivers had frequented, in order to get drinks, there was a drum that you had to strike with a drumstick. Jenson hadn't been able to locate the stick so had struck it with his fist. Felipe Massa was hugely amused by this and insisted that he do it again. Jenson obliged, only this time his hand bounced back a slightly different shape to what it should be.

You have to worry when David Coulthard is the most responsible adult, but he instantly saw that Jenson's hand was not in a good way and most likely had some broken parts, so he got an ice bucket and stuck Jenson's hand in it to reduce the swelling. Well done, Dr DC. At that moment, sense kicked in and Jenson chose to go home whilst the drivers, concerned about his health, of course, went to a club! The next day, in a lot of pain, he decided he needed medical assistance.

Jenson elaborates in more detail in his book:

> "You've broken your knuckle," said a doctor the next day, looking at an X-ray. "You'll have to put it in a cast for two weeks."
>
> "Not sure I can manage that," I told him. "I'm driving a Formula One car in the Grand Prix in four days' time."

All things considered, our filming went well. Jenson spoke on stage, then drove me through Tokyo in the McLaren P1 to the next venue, which was an awards ceremony. I figured I would rather be driven by a one-handed world champion than your average Joe. I left the filming that night with several secrets and a couple of life lessons – never punch a drum with your hand and *never* take advice on a night out from Felipe Massa!

I should say I am writing about this now as Jenson has written about it in his book, otherwise the secrets would have stayed just that. Several others also knew and I am not sure how discreet some of the other drivers were. I was in the paddock talking to Jenson when Felipe came up laughing, "Man, how is the hand?" he asked, not quite overwhelming anyone with sympathy! Driving at Suzuka is tough enough without having a broken knuckle, so McLaren obviously had to be told. They had a reserve driver at the ready in Kevin Magnussen, but Jenson drove all weekend and come race day even managed to get a couple of points in ninth.

By the close of the season, ninth was where Jenson finished in the championship, having spent the year fighting for minor points.

Although he didn't realise it then, worse was to come in every sense. It was January and the off-season; I was away skiing in Austria when I heard the news that John Button had died. It was a shock, of course, but instantly you think of those left – in this case Jenson and his sisters.

A few weeks after, a group of us had been invited to Goodwood House for a memorial day and drinks and to share memories of John. It was lovely to see so many drivers from so many series, team members and friends who all knew John. He was a truly beloved face in the paddock and his presence and pink shirts were and still are missed.

It was something that naturally affected Jenson. It wasn't as if he could go to work as an escape as John had been such a big part of that too. There was really no escape from the void.

Whilst 2014 had started with desperate circumstances and nothing could be as bad as the previous event, it was another tough season on track. Kevin Magnussen was the latest driver on the McLaren merry-go-round, and he and Jenson spent most of the year trying to get decent points. Despite a few fourths and picking up a third when Daniel Ricciardo was disqualified hours after the Australian GP, there was no standing on the podium.

It was a season of Mercedes domination and the start of the Silver Arrows era. Seemingly against the odds, the rumours of Alonso returning to McLaren were circulating. No one knew if it was Button who would be leaving, but in December of that year it was announced that McLaren would once again have two world champions in Button and Alonso.

Yet the champions deserved better than the tools they were given. The only saving grace was that both struggled and could share their woes. They both knew they were great drivers, so in many ways they were in the clear.

It was during another torrid season in 2016 when Jenson decided that he had served his time and was ready to move on from Formula One. Without his dad by his side, things just weren't the same, and without a decent car underneath him, it wasn't as fun anymore.

He told Ron Dennis in Spa that he was retiring, but Ron in turn convinced Jenson to become an "ambassador" for the team. So when it was announced in Monza that Jenson would not be racing next year but still be part of the team, we didn't really know if it was a sabbatical or what exactly. Jenson probably knew, but the team were keen for him to not say "retiring".

Mark Webber interviewed Jenson for us on Channel 4 and held no punches: "As a fan of yours, I'm frustrated with this sabbatical of yours. I don't like it. I don't like it, mate."

Jenson laughed.

Mark went on, "I'm just nervous that after Abu Dhabi we won't see you."

"And there's a good chance you won't," said Button.

But that year, there was still more racing and milestones to reach, and in Sepang, Malaysia we got together in the hospitality unit to celebrate Jenson's 300th Grand Prix. Whilst they struggled to make a decent car, there is no better team when it comes to a celebration than McLaren. JB biscuits, "300 races" iced cakes, champagne; it was a lovely occasion.

Jenson saw the chequered flag at the next five races and then it was Abu Dhabi and the last race of the season, widely understood to be his last race in Formula One.

On race day, a guard of honour formed in the paddock from the McLaren hospitality to the back of the garage. Team Button had evolved and reduced over the years, but they were either there in person or in spirit that weekend.

Not every career gets a fairy-tale ending, and on lap 12 of the Grand Prix, a suspension failure saw Jenson retire. I remember having done all my interviews and walking down the paddock, seeing Team Button come towards me and then leave for the final time.

But that's the thing about being an "ambassador": the team can call on your services whenever they need. And in 2017 for the Monaco Grand Prix, they were in need. Alonso was chasing the American dream at the Indy 500 and back in the hot, almost wet seat, was Button.

Fernando popped up on team radio live from Indianapolis as the car was heading down the pit lane:

"Jenson, my friend, I am sure you wanted to hear my voice before the start of the race." Alonso wished him luck and told him to take care of his car.

"I'm going to pee in your seat," replied Jenson.

Lovely! Some things never change . . .

Jenson had qualified ninth on the grid but took a fifteen-place grid penalty for additional power-unit elements and then had to start from pit lane as the car had been modified in parc fermé. It wasn't exactly going to plan! He did make it deep into the Grand Prix, much farther than his last "final" race. Then at Portier, on lap 57, he put his McLaren between the wheels of Pascal Wehrlein's car. The Sauber was tipped onto its side and pressed up against the armco barrier. Wehrlein was fine, if a little stuck, and Jenson had to retire his damaged McLaren. That was the last time Jenson raced in Formula One.

Since retiring, Jenson has got married to Brittny and the couple have two children. It's lovely to be able to catch up in the paddock as he is one of Sky Sports' experts.

Jenson was always so good to the British media. Despite his earlier years when he was in the press for his lifestyle, he understood the game, and the fact that those who write showbiz and gossip stories aren't the ones turning up week in, week out at every Grand Prix. Each year in Brazil, he would take around forty British journalists to Fogo de Chao as a thank you and a bit of a knees-up for us. It was an evening of endless food and drink and an unhelpful hangover on the Thursday. It was a lovely gesture and something we hugely appreciated.

As a driver and a person, Jenson oozes class. Much of that comes from his parents and upbringing. I started this chapter by describing him as normal, but in fact there is nothing normal about 306 Formula One starts, fifteen victories and becoming a world champion. That's what makes it so special. A seemingly ordinary guy who has an extraordinary story.

ACKNOWLEDGEMENTS

THANK YOU . . .

It's been a labour love writing this but one thing I realised as I went back through the years, stories and memories is the huge amount of time I have spent with some of these drivers, often whether they liked it or not. I want to say a huge thanks to them – and to all people I have bothered with my questions over the years – drivers, rugby players and athletes across all sports. I appreciate no one started driving, kicking a ball or picking up a tennis racket with the hope of being interviewed by me, but media is a vital part of the job now. Done in the right way, it shouldn't be a chore, and I hope I have achieved more fun and pleasurable interviews than the reverse! Also a big thanks must go to the teams and PRs who are there throughout the highs and lows.

I wouldn't have considered this job had my father not taken me to sports events around the world as a kid. In fact, I had been to more F1, rugby, athletics, Wimbledon and sporting events as a child than most sports fans get to in their entire lives. Thank you, Dad/ Bob for letting me be the annoying child who turned up at every press box in sport sitting beside Murray Walker, Bill McLaren and some of the other greats in TV and newspapers!

To my mum, who is my biggest supporter – she is not a massive sports fan but, through my work, has come with me on holiday detours to rugby, F3, super bikes and random events all around the world. She does enjoy the fact I can take her to horse racing and equestrian events and the occasional trip to Monaco. A huge thanks to my brother, Grant, for keeping me grounded and for being present whilst I seem to be continuously absent.

My good friend Ben Edwards was good enough to read this book at various stages of its creation, and I firmly believe that if you ever need something fact-checked, find a commentator! Ben is one of the best in any sport and it has been a pleasure to work with him in various series over the years – nearly twenty years! Speaking of commentators, the wonderful Andrew Cotter encouraged me to write this and helped me choose Black & White Publishing.

To all my friends in the paddock over the years, who are too many to mention, but a few who keep me sane on the road include Karun Chandhok, Ted Kravitz and Mervi Kallio and all the girls and guys at the interview pen and paddock.

Huge thanks to David Coulthard for his friendship and support on and off track over the years and for writing the foreword to this book. We have a great Scuderia Ecosse from Sir Jackie (thanks for the lovely words) and also the entire Stewart clan, Allan McNish, the Franchittis – we are a close-knit group and support each other a lot. Mark Webber is certainly an honorary member.

I only told my mum and Grant and a few others, including my great friends Rebecca Banks and Grace Barber, that I was even writing a book, so a huge thanks to them for their encouragement.

Thank you to the BBC for so much, including giving me a chance. *Inside F1* was a programme I used to present on the BBC News channel, so thank you to Ben Gallop, who let me use the title for this book. Channel 4 and Whisper have been wonderful supporters since 2016 and I love working for them.

A big thanks to all at Black & White Publishing and Bonnier

ACKNOWLEDGEMENTS

Books UK, especially Campbell Brown, who was having zoom meetings with me at F1 races in order to get this book published, and to Ali McBride, who has the patience of a saint, as tested by me, and to Thomas, Rachel and Clem.

The photo on the front was taken by one the great F1 photographers and indeed characters of the paddock, Mark Thompson, who kindly snapped the picture of me between F1 practice sessions (and a missile strike on an oil field) in Saudi Arabia and donated his fee to charity.

Finally, thank *you* so much for reading *Inside F1* and for watching over the years.

Formula One. What a wonderful world!

BIBLIOGRAPHY

Vettel

Benson, Andrew. "Singapore GP: Sebastian Vettel beats team-mate Charles Leclerc." BBC, 22 September 2019, https://www.bbc.co.uk/sport/formula1/49787607

Alonso

Formula 1. "Fernando Alonso Re-Watches His Epic Battle With Michael Schumacher!" YouTube, 16 April 2021, https://youtu.be/vUMYzXiSgH0

Formula 1. "Interview Alonso 2005 Brazil" Youtube, 14 November 2020 https://youtu.be/dJfgOKcA7m8

Formula 1. "Brazilian GP 2006 - Alonso talks about Schumacher" 5 April 2009, https://youtu.be/4r55u6mDk1o

Benson, Andrew. "Fernando Alonso: Lewis Hamilton, McLaern, 'spy-gate' & threats & demands to Ron Dennis." BBC Sport, 19 November 2018, https://www.bbc.co.uk/sport/formula1/46226823

Briatore, Flavio. "Nelson Piquet's Crash in Singapore: What Really Happened?" *The Guardian*, 16 September 2019, https://www.theguardian.com/sport/2009/sep/16/nelson-piquet-singapore-flavio-briatore-inquiry

Tremayne, David. "Alonso linked with move to Ferrari for 2009." *The Independent*, 26 March 2008, https://www.independent. co.uk/sport/motor-racing/alonso-linked-with-move-to-ferrari-for-2009-800467.html

Noble, Jonathan. "Fernando Alonso and Ferrari F1 team heading for split after 2014." Autosport, 3 October 2014, https://www. autosport.com/f1/news/fernando-alonso-and-ferrari-f1-team-heading-for-split-after-2014-5046549/5046549/

Young, Byron. "McLaren supremo Ron Dennis: Spygate controversy is behind me and Fernando Alonso." Mirror, 2 February 2015, https://www.mirror.co.uk/sport/formula-1/mclaren-supremo-ron-dennis-spygate-5093732

2015 Malaysian Grand Prix - Thursday Press Conference, Federation Internationale de l'Automobile, https://www.fia.com/news/2015 -malaysian-grand-prix-thursday-press-conference

Lewis, Niamh. "Singapore Grand Prix: Still in F1 10 years after 'crash-gate'." BBC Sport, 12 September 2018. https://www.bbc.co.uk/ sport/formula1/45459334

Massa

Formula 1. "Felipe Massa on Championship Agony and Injury Recovery." (See pages 203-204). Beyond the Grid podcast. 22 May 2019, https://www.youtube.com/watch?v=eF5XKuDWq0s

Autosport. "Brazil Sunday quotes: Ferrari." 22 October 2016, https:// www.autosport.com/f1/news/brazil-sunday-quotes-ferrari-4406785/4406785/

Noble, Jonathan. "Grapevine: Massa clarifies food delivery past." 28 October 2008, https://www.autosport.com/f1/news/grapevine -massa-clarifies-food-delivery-past-4425424/4425424/

BIBLIOGRAPHY

Tremayne, David. "Jules Bianchi crash: Felipe Massa – 'I was screaming into the radio that it was too dangerous'" *The Independent*, 6 October 2014, https://www.independent.co.uk/sport/motor-racing/jules-bianchi-formula-1-crash-felipe-massa-i-was-screaming-into-the-radio-that-it-was-too-dangerous-9775787.html

Ferrari press office. "Massa's first interview since his crash." 3 August 2009, https://www.autosport.com/f1/news/massas-first-interview-since-his-crash-4432262/4432262/

Benson, Andrew. "European GP: Fernando Alonso savours emotional victory." BBC Sport, 24 June 2012, https://www.bbc.co.uk/sport/formula1/18573279

Button

Button, Jenson. *Life to the Limit: My Autobiography*, Blink Publishing, 2017.

Atlas F1. "Briatore Sends Warning to Button and Trulli." 16 November 2001, https://www.autosport.com/f1/news/briatore-sends-warning-to-button-and-trulli-5058520/5058520/